STOCKHOLM SERIES: 5

CITY IN THE WORLD

STOCKHOLM SERIES: 5

CITY IN THE WORLD

A novel
by
Per Anders Fogelström

Translated from Swedish
by
Jennifer Brown Bäverstam

The Stockholm Series:
City of My Dreams
Children of Their City
Remember the City
In a City Transformed
City in the World

Swedish copyright © 1966 Per Anders Fogelström
The fifth volume was originally published
in Swedish as "Stad i världen."
English translation copyright © 2015 Jennifer Brown Bäverstam
and Penfield Books, Iowa City, Iowa, aka Penfield Press
Library of Congress Control Number: 2015956491
ISBN-13: 978-1-57216-114-6

Penfield Books
215 Brown Street
Iowa City, IA 52245
www.penfieldbooks.com

Edited by Melinda Bradnan, Deb Schense, and
Joan Liffring-Zug Bourret
Cover design by M. A. Cook Design
Cover photograph and back cover photo by
Jennifer Brown Bäverstam

TABLE OF CONTENTS

THE AUTHOR

PER ANDERS FOGELSTRÖM is one of the most widely read authors in Sweden today. *City of My Dreams,* the first book in his five-volume *Stockholm Series,* broke the record for bestsellers. A compelling storyteller known for his narrative sweep, his acute characterization and the poetic qualities of his prose, Fogelström was highly acclaimed even before he wrote the *Stockholm Series.* Ingmar Bergman made one of Fogelström's earlier novels, *Summer with Monika,* into a film that is now a Bergman classic.

Born in 1917, Fogelström grew up in Stockholm and lived there his entire life. He was a vast resource on Stockholm's history, with enormous archives on the subject, and published much non-fiction about the city. He spent his early career as a journalist and, in the 1940s, he co-founded a literary magazine. His own prolific writing resulted in more than fifty books.

Fogelström's *Stockholm Series* has remained a favorite in Swedish literature among readers of all ages, and he continues to be greatly loved and respected as a chronicler of his people. Fogelström died on Midsummer Day, June 20, 1998, two days before the unveiling of a statue of him at the entrance to the hall where the Nobel Prizes are awarded in Stockholm.

THE TRANSLATOR

Jennifer Brown Bäverstam has traveled and studied languages all her life. She has translated several books and articles from Swedish and French. She holds a degree in French and economics from Georgetown University and has studied translation at the University of Geneva. She lives in Boston, Massachusetts.

Translator's Note

Swedish place names are generally one compound word with the proper name at the beginning and the kind of place at the end.

Because most of the place names in the book have not been translated, the following terms explain endings for names of streets, hills, bridges, etc.:

backen: hill
berget, bergen: hill, hills
bro, bron: bridge
gatan: street

gränd: alley
holm, holmen: island
torg, torget: square
viken: estuary

I

CITY
IN THE WORLD

You, city where our children will one day live and our ancestors sleep in the graveyards beyond the old tollgates. You, city of stone, mirrored in the water, warmed by the living warmth of the people who have made their dens out of stone. Illuminated by countless small lights whose reflection is visible for many miles distant, like a Milky Way across the sky.

The as yet unborn, the living, and the dead's city. With the footprints of the past and foreshadowing of the future entwined with each other in the collage of the present.

At one time he might have thought the city was the world, or at least his world. What lay beyond had not seemed real, had been more make-believe and pretense than life. The country one traveled through during a quickly vanishing vacation week—a theater set seen through a train window. And the countries one read about: the war, the misery, the concentration camps, meetings of statesmen. Everything so far away, so unreal.

The world had been closed, had closed just when he had reached the age when he could have begun to explore it. Almost all the news that had reached them from the locked outer world had born the marks of the war and war propaganda, as if someone had filtered out everything human, everything comprehensible. And when distant events became unreachable and unreal, his attention was focused on events close by and possible to cover. Or was it only that someone who was young was naturally caught up in tracking down the closest news, the most recently captured?

He didn't know. But as a result of peace, a new door had opened up and he had suddenly been able to see that there was a world outside the one he knew, beyond the city. Maybe he had been awakened by the violent thundering of the bombs over Hiroshima and Nagasaki. The roar from there proclaimed that there no longer were any closed and protected countries and cities.

As if he had discovered the world for the first time, at that moment he had become conscious, he realized it could be destroyed.

Out of the war and the dead, something with new life had sprouted forth, a newly wakened consciousness. The city was not the world. It was only one small part of the world that he had under his feet. Maybe a springboard, the small amount of firm ground needed to make the leap. Or the safe harbor during his travels, his home in the world.

Home. It felt that way now that the city was approaching—a sudden, unbearable longing to be home again.

The city was waiting for him. In an instant it was suddenly there. The train rolled out onto Årsta Bridge, and he saw the lights shining from all the windows of Söder Hospital and from the tall apartment buildings at Bergsund and lining Hornsgatan. Next came the dark groves of Tantolunden with its trees bare, lights glinting in between them from community garden cottages and warehouses. Södra Station slid past; the tunnel's darkness striped with light enveloped the train. And then he was in the middle of the city, the lights of the cars shining along Slussen and Kornhamn, the church towers soaring upward toward a sky faintly inflamed with light. The crowns on City Hall lit up and neon fireworks sparkled on the facades around Tegelbacken and Vasagatan. But the park along the railway lay dark and dug up, and among the doomed trees the statue of Nils Ericson waited to be removed to make way for a new era's traffic machines.

Henning picked up his suitcases and hurried out to the large waiting hall. His assignment was over for now; it had only been a short trip to cover a story from the magazine's point of view. He went to the phone booth to let them know he was home and to ask if he had to come in to see the editor before early the next morning.

The headlines on the evening papers said that the Social Democrats had elected Per Albin Hansson's successor as prime minister. Who was Tage Erlander? Wasn't he that fairly new minister of culture? If it hadn't been him people had expected it to be Gustav Möller or Torsten Nilsson...

Yet more proof that everything old was disappearing, no matter how unfamiliar everything new might be. Per Albin had been an institution. Branting's successor, seemingly with roots all the way back to the childhood of the work-ers' movement. He appeared as immortal as the king. The king, the prime minister—they were each one person, never changing. But late Saturday night, Per Albin Hansson had stepped off the streetcar out at Ålsten, taken a few steps toward home—and fallen down dead. Now it was Wednesday and his successor had been chosen.

What happened here, happened out in the world as well. More and more of the big names from the war years were swept away. Roosevelt was dead; Churchill had been replaced by Atlee. Mussolini and Hitler were gone, and the rest of the Nazi leadership with Göring at the fore sat in prison awaiting execution; the death sentences had been meted out in Nürnberg. The leaf had been turned over, and there were not many of the old prominent men who had succeeded in getting across to the new unwritten page.

People streamed past Henning Nilsson where he stood outside the phone booth that October afternoon of 1946.

So many, all unknown. He only had to be gone for a week to feel a little of an outsider.

A new era, he thought. A new world. What opportunities would present themselves? He was young, ready. At the magazine they had said that he would get to go abroad and travel, maybe in the spring. He had years to regain, the war years of death and confinement.

PROTECTED

Each time Henning came home after being away for a several days, he felt the same combination of well-being and unease. Of course, it was good to come home, he felt welcome. He had his cozy room, his books. And both his mother and John showed their happiness to have him home again in every way.

But this very caring and kindness scared him a little. He felt so protected and cosseted, so looked after. Like living in a padded cell.

Maybe he had had it all too good. Maybe he had succeeded all too easily? Could someone who had never been tested be able to withstand unexpected trials?

Sometimes he missed difficulties, the necessity to get by on his own. Not suffering and privation, just to fight with the will to fight. He did not even have to fight at the magazine; it was as if everything there, too, had been smoothed out for him. Adapting was easy for him, writing was easy. Perhaps too easy at times.

Had it always been like this? In school, among his friends. He had seldom come into conflict, seldom made enemies.

Still, he had not grown up completely without worry. They had been quite poor early on. He had been the son of an unmarried mother. Though to say it that way was an exaggeration. His mother and father had lived together for many years and the fact that they had never married had been due to his father's political views. He had been very radical when young. This year he had made it to the city council, elected by the Social Democrats.

They had never been very well off. Though his father had let Henning complete his high school degree and attend college for a while. Henning had emerged into life just when there was plenty of work again; he had escaped experiencing the years of unemployment. His father had even arranged the job at the magazine for him.

He felt like they had given him crutches, that they supported him every step he took. Sometimes he grew touchy and irritable at all the kindness. He wanted get away quite often. But then he would miss home again, after only a few days away.

Despite all the closeness and kindness he felt lonely. During his years as a student he had grown away from his old pals, made new friends. But the new ones never grew as close as the old ones had once been.

He should get married, he'd think. Have a life of his own, with his own responsibilities, too. He did not want to move away from home without getting married, for his mother's sake. Then she would just blame herself, perhaps imagine that she should have refrained from marrying John. That wasn't why at all. But he did not dare believe that his mother would understand this.

Amid the irritation and unease was also the knowledge that he had lost something. Lost something—even if he had relinquished it of his own free will. One spring, not the last one but the one before, he had been together with a girl he had liked a lot. But she was so young, he had thought. Just turned seventeen then. Somehow something had stood in the way: like seducing a child, the sister of a friend in fact. He had kissed her once and nothing more had happened.

Then he had met other girls, though no one he had liked as much. Once later on he had seen Barbro with a boy. She had her own life now. It was certainly impossible to forget her; the image of her smile remained with him and sparkled again and again.

Among all the successes there was something, there was a failure, and it took away most of the pleasure of the achievements. When he thought of how he had lost her, the longing felt so strong that he almost felt sick.

Just a little tired from traveling he assured his mother who opened the door and looked at him anxiously.

"The coffee is ready," she said. "And John has bought a cake since you were coming."

He took a walk after coffee, maybe mostly to get away, to avoid seeing them cheerful and happy, to avoid the questions that might arise.

Some young people were coming along the same sidewalk, in his direction. At first he meant to step aside and let them pass. But then there was someone who called his name and he stopped. He recognized most of them, some from the old gang.

Of course, they were going to get a cup of coffee now, and talk a while before they split up for the evening. And even though Henning felt like he still had the coffee and cake from home in his throat, he went with them. They appeared to be enthralled in a discussion, too, with the retorts flying between them like ping-pong balls flung hard.

"People have to be enlightened!"

"Though people are treated as if they were unenlightened!"

"It's your own fault—you admit that."

"What can you do?"

"Protest!"

"When no one is listening?"

"Then shout louder!"

"No one listens to anyone who is young."

"Have we really tried to make them listen?"

"Which 'them,' do you mean?"

"Society, our parents, the old guys in charge."

"What would you say if they woke up?"

"That they have to become aware."

Awareness. It kept coming back. It was the key word. People were divided into either aware or unaware. Everyone in an older generation seemed to be grouped as unaware. It did not really seem as if his friends knew what they meant by awareness.

Henning mostly listened.

At first it was just to be reminded of something old, of the time when he had sat there just as eager and bursting to talk. But soon he also felt something new, a new and fresh tone of voice, a stronger and more heated urge to participate, to be with them. And even though he himself was a few years older than most of those present, he, too, was in the same situation. Newly awakened, newly aware, unsure but also filled with ideas and speculations.

They could create some sort of a club…

No, not a club. But something, maybe—just a group. A few people. Those who were here now and maybe a few more, the kinds who wanted to discuss. Then they could take problem after problem and try to figure out what they really thought. About religion, politics, war, architecture, sports—everything. Invite guest speakers, people who believed so much in one thing that they were involved in it.

By the time they broke up the coffee meeting, they had decided to build a discussion group. It would not have any name, no board, no dues. They would just meet and discuss.

Henning did not really feel like going home. They were probably sitting there drinking tea now and would be hurt if he didn't sit down with them and have an evening sandwich.

He followed along with one of the boys, Julle, who lived down in the direction of the tollgate. They strolled slowly down Folkungagatan. They looked up Erstagatan when they passed by it. Mormor and Emelie's windows were lit up.

The street widened, down near Tegelviken and the harbor. On the other side of the dark water some small ferries left Djurgården, glided side by side a little way, then apart, one toward Slussen and the other toward Tegelviken. Up on Åsöberget the lights shone from the windows of the tumbledown houses.

Julle lived in one of the apartment buildings beside the candle factory; his father worked there. His father's parents had also done the same. From the beginning they had been one of the seasonal people from Dalarna who came down every fall from their farms and found work there. But Julle worked in a machine repair shop.

Behind the row of apartment buildings a few years earlier they had constructed a new highway to Danviksbron and now the cars rushed past beneath Julle's kitchen window on what had once been the quiet side with a yard. But the bridge was still just as narrow and the traffic going to the country had to squeeze through the barely sufficient space.

They stood on the corner by the telephone booth and talked. Behind the community garden cottages and the warehouse alongside dark Tegelgatan, the night sky was painted light by the countless bright light bulbs in the Luma factory's testing room.

A solitary figure came wandering over from the direction of the bridge, a fellow their age, in a rumpled suit and unbuttoned shirt. He gave a lurch when he saw them, then he changed course and walked up to them, suddenly giving a piercing wolfish smile.

"If it isn't Henning," he said. "You've got to help me for God's sake … and your buddy, too. You guys can surely cough up a couple of kronor."

"No way," said Julle, and shook his head.

"You can't just let me wander around out here all damn night."

Henning pulled out a few kronor but the other fellow would not give up until he had gotten a fiver.

"We should blow up this whole goddam town. Just peasant thieves all of them."

He smiled his wolfish grin again, waved with the five-kronor bill and wandered off.

"Did you know him?" Julle asked.

It wasn't until he denied it that Henning realized Per was actually his cousin. But they had met so seldom and he had never felt related to Per. It was different story with Per's siblings; he had met them every week once upon a time, at Mormor and Emelie's home. He still saw Allan now and then. Gun more seldom, she was married now. And Stig was dead, of course.

Per had actually never been there. A number of years ago he had committed a burglary and gone to prison. Now he was apparently out, in any case as long as it lasted. And did he want revenge? For what they had deprived him of? For some succeeding and others not?

Saturday after Saturday the explosions occurred. The first time was next to the Concert Hall, then in the courtyard of Klara Police Station. And it only continued. One Saturday evening an enormous explosion shook the southern arrival hall down at Central Station and it caused serious injuries. Walls split, sidewalks and motorways were paved with glass shards; as far away as Söder Mälarstrand in the other side of the inlet of Riddarfjärden, buildings shook from the shock wave. The next day, since it was Sunday, tens of thousands of people came to see the devastation. Many of them had traveled a long distance.

Rewards were offered for anyone who could apprehend the "Sabbath Saboteur." Large domestic and labor security forces patrolled the streets every Saturday evening, and made their way through the crowds that had come out in search of new excitement. But apparently the attackers had been scared off by all the attention; the series of explosions ceased.

Many of the young people in the discussion group were excited by what had happened, exhilarated. One of the boys went out every Saturday evening with a long empty cardboard cylinder under his arm and hoped he would be picked up as a suspect. Even Henning felt some of the need to draw attention and protest, the desire to oppose. Why, he did not exactly know, he had nothing to complain about.

The group had gotten organized, they met once a week. Their conversations felt like some kind of salvation, a safety valve. By throwing oneself into what was happening, one could become aware. And only the enlightened protests could bring about change. Bomb blasts were blind and meaningless protests. Whatever motives the saboteur might have, his work was still only entertainment for some, and a nuisance and danger for others.

Per had talked about blowing things up. Was he the one? Though it did not seem very likely since the attacks did not seem to be combined with anything profitable. Despite his talk Per was probably too old to satisfy himself with some bangs and a fuss. And in any case Henning knew nothing.

Even though he could talk himself into feeling detached from the explosions, Henning walked around town on Saturday nights waiting for a bomb to go off, almost wishing it would. As if he imagined that the blast would wake him up and the world around him, as if it would drive forward the process that he felt was going on inside and outside himself. The questions were so numerous, the answers so few; he would grow impatient and long for the moment when he would see how the whole design grew clear and life's mysteries revealed.

DISAPPEARED, LOST

While Emelie sat home alone, her thoughts would often drift back to what had disappeared and been lost. It was there that her life was, when she had had responsibility and could mean something to others. Now she was just left over and could not be of much use anymore. It was possible she could help Jenny a little—but Jenny was in any case the only one.

Emelie and Jenny had lived together since the turn of the century when Jenny had started keeping company with Emelie's youngest brother, Olof. Jenny and Olof had never had a home of their own. He had been seriously ill already at the time of their meeting, and Olof had never had a chance to see their daughter, Maj, before he died. After that Jenny had one more daughter, Elisabet, with a singer by the name of Julius Törnberg, but never moved in together with him. She had stayed at Emelie's.

Even Törnberg was dead now. But Jenny still seemed almost young. No one could believe that she had turned sixty-five in the spring. And she had full-time work; now she was in the middle of rehearsals for a radio play. Since Jenny worked Emelie had sole responsibility for that evening's gathering. Once upon a time their "closest kin" had come every week; now it happened less often. But since it couldn't happen so often, there would usually be a large number instead; everyone who could make it did.

Emelie was eleven years older than Jenny and did not have as easy a time of it any longer. But she was stubborn and would not hear of needing any help. On the other hand she tried to warn Jenny sometimes, remind her of what had happened to Emelie's brother August. As people grew older they had to take it easy. But it didn't help to say that to Jenny. She thought in any case that August had had a good death; he had avoided suffering and being in the hospital, was productive to the end.

Jenny could even seem younger at times than her own daughters. She laughed more often, was full of pranks and ideas, ran up the stairs, exercised every morning. It must have been the fear of growing old that propelled her; it sat there like an irritating thorn and caused her to jump around faster and faster.

August. He often returned to Emelie's thoughts, in fact it was as if it were he who drew her thoughts back to the past. His wife, Ida, was also dead now, and with her practically all contact with their children. They got in touch from time to time—but very seldom.

The old people disappeared, all of Emelie's contemporaries. Mikael, whom she had known since they were children, was in the hospital now. Of Emelie's siblings only Gertrud was left, far away in America. So far away that sometimes it felt as if Gertrud were dead.

But could it be possible that despite everything she might see Gertrud once again in her lifetime? She had never dared believe it. She pulled out the letter from America that had arrived the other day and tried to decipher it again. Gertrud wrote so strangely now, used so many American words that Emelie usually asked Henning for help reading them. She would do that this evening, try to make sure she understood it. But it did indeed seem as if Gertrud was saying that she and one of her daughters were hoping to be able to travel back to the old country.

It would be incredible if that happened. Like getting someone back from the dead.

Emelie sat there for a while at the kitchen table, with the letter in her hand. She thought of all those who had once existed, all those who were dead now. Disappeared, lost. Parents and siblings, friends, work-mates and bosses.

Of the old ones there was actually only Jenny left within reach, Jenny who was still so much younger. And those whom Emelie had once viewed as children were beginning to grow middle-aged now: Jenny's daughters, Bärta's children.

Bärta was someone she had also shared a home with at one time. They had never grown very close to each other—but Bärta's children and grandchildren and great-grandchildren still came to see her.

How strange things could turn out. And yet so natural; Bärta's children had grown up at Emelie's. They were among the "closest kin."

The clock struck in the other room and she gave a start. She did not have time to sit here and fantasize. She had to go out and shop, would surely have to go out a couple of times to bring home everything that was needed. They would offer coffee first and then sandwiches, so there was a lot that would have to be carried home.

When Emelie was going to buy a little more than usual she always went to the shop on Folkungagatan where she used to work. The manager had been in training at that time, her apprentice. He would joke that she pulled his ear when he did not perform up to her standards. It wasn't true. And she would not have needed to either; he had been an exemplary apprentice.

At this stage she could see the store again without feeling loss or bitterness. She no longer felt swept aside or superfluous. Now she had accepted, realized that she would not have the strength to stand there from morning till evening. The forced, and at first so hateful, free time had become normal, in fact something to be thankful for.

I have it so good, she would think. Unbelievably good.

She thought this again when she walked down the street and as always looked over at the cluster of old houses on Åsöberget. The street of her childhood and her parents; there they lived out on the furthest edge of the hill. So different everything had been—streets and houses and living conditions. So poor and miserable. Unbelievable … that it had been the same city, that she had been there herself. Did people truly understand how good they had it? Oughtn't they be happy and satisfied? Often they looked dissatisfied.

I have it so good. Unbelievably good.

Yet she still felt like something was missing. That a lot was missing, almost everything that had disappeared. As a matter of fact she had never thought that she had it so bad and full of cares while it was going on. It wasn't until afterward—when people compared it to the present—that it seemed so.

Before, people had not been able to go out and shop like this. They had to scrimp for every penny, they had so little to shop with.

It wasn't completely easy to go and shop now either. They had believed that the rationing would go away when the war ended, but still they had to bring along bread and meat coupons. The harvest had been poor and Sweden, which had been spared, could not go and import large amounts of grain when other lands had such a hard time after the war.

They all got together, filling the little apartment.

As a child Henning had been here so often, practically every day. He had gone with Mormor to the Downhill Park on Folkungagatan or up into the White Hills, and was fetched here later by his mother when she came home from work. The apartment was so closely associated with his childhood that he almost felt like a child when he came back here. To some extent they treated him that way, too, as if Mormor and Emelie did not really want to admit that he was an adult now.

His childhood memories were reinforced by seeing his cousins. Allan, still a little boyishly clumsy in his movements, speech and manner. And Gun, the first girl he had fooled around with and dared to embrace. Though now he would have barely dared to do it; she had become a prim little housewife who talked about rationing and prices. And besides, she had her husband Olle with her. And was expecting. Allan's wife Daggan was at home with their two children.

So Allan would become something of an irresponsible boy again, bragging about the construction site and his workmates, laughing with his enormous braying that made Gun clap her hands over he ears. He offered Henning a Boy cigarette, lit the cigarettes, blowing smoke out toward the kitchen light and leaning back so that the kitchen chair creaked. But when Emelie asked how children were, he became transformed, his voice grew low and he became almost tender in his gestures. He told what his three-year-old daughter said and did, speaking almost as if he were speaking about a miracle.

This getting married and moving away from home seemed almost the only way to be accepted as an adult. The only way to be happy?

It might seem that way when he heard Allan talk about his children, when he saw the transformation. Also, Gun seemed more harmonious than before, had matured, mellowed.

But then he saw Elisabet, too; she said some words he couldn't make out to Lennart, and Lennart seemed to shrink away, duck. Maybe it was only that he put a photo back that he had been looking at—but there was a something anxious, evasive in his face.

Marriage was not a universal means to happiness.

Elisabet was Henning's aunt, though he had never called her aunt, of course. She had been just a girl during the time he had seen her here practically every day. A little over a year ago she had become a mother. Before the child had been born, Elisabet had been so sure that it would be a boy. They had brought their daughter with them.

Yet Elisabet was strangely unknown to him, something of a mystery. Sometimes he had felt a little scared of her, her temperament was so volatile and she was angry so often or at least dissatisfied. Most things irritated her. And Henning knew that she could never stand his father; that came out now, too.

The photo Lennart was looking at was really only a newspaper clipping that showed some of the newly elected city councilors. In the very center of them stood Erik smiling that slightly superior and sneering smile that he usually had when he was being photographed.

Henning knew it well—from the mirror. He looked like that sometimes when he was insecure and wanted to hide it.

Elisabet gave a sniff, she didn't have to put into words what she was thinking: a phony, a joker! Lennart wanted to calm her down and soothe her and this maybe irritated her even more.

Lennart was kind, careful, quiet. One hardly noticed him, he kept a low profile. He had always been like that at every level. He still worked at the same printer's where he had been since the middle of the thirties, without trying to get a promotion or changing jobs for something better. No one could guess that he read complicated technical books in several languages.

He was no genius, simply a person who read a lot and knew a lot—and who never made a show of it or even made use of his knowledge. If anyone wanted to know something they had to coax it out of him.

Lennart was a victim of the depression years. As John was, but in a different way. They were people who had had dreams and ideas but had never been able to realize them. They had suffered a loss; somewhere in the past their dreams had been buried and they still stood sorrowing, as if at the graveside.

Henning was the privileged one among those gathered here, the first one to continue his studies, the only one who would never go unemployed. The ideal society that previous generations had worked to create had been ready for occupancy just about when it was his turn. At least ready enough so that there was room for him and much of his generation.

And still he was not content.

He looked at his father's siblings. They were all here, all those that were alive.

Gunnar, the eldest. As a little boy bullied and beaten by his stepfather, saved by Emelie. He had finally received help from his real father, August Bodin, and been able to start his own company. Now, with a few years left till sixty, a capable, small business owner who had willingly refrained from opportunities to speculate and become one of the big shots, secure and safe within his limits.

And Bengt. Unemployed for several years, poor and hungry, still scarred. Now working on the streetcars since many years back, he was one of the crew who was going to do the electric work in the subway construction that had already begun. Quiet, hard working, kind. One of the many who were building the new society but were hardly seen or noticed.

And then Beda who had speech difficulties as a child, who had been considered backward and hopeless by teachers and friends. But who, through some miracle, had been transformed into a completely normal person, a talented seamstress.

They were here. But not Erik, his father. That hadn't happened since his parents had divorced.

Everyone except for Tyra was alive. And all of them had been moderately successful, at least become decent small cogs in the big machinery. Except for Tyra. Who had married an idle loafer and joker like David Berg; he was probably still consigned to the institution for alcoholics. Yet two of her children were here, were among the ones who had been rescued by Emelie. Allan and Gun. But Stig had died, of consumption as they used to say. And Per, of course, was in jail most of the time.

It was Emelie that they mainly gathered around, everyone who had come. Even if Jenny was seen and heard the most and was always in the center. It was Jenny they had fun with and laughed at. But it was Emelie who was the impetus, who had made room for them all.

Although it had been tight, there had been room for everybody. Even though it had been meager, everyone had enough to eat.

But Emelie herself kept to the side. She still persisted in considering the main room Jenny's and the kitchen their common space. She slept in the kitchen, and lived there. She didn't even sit in the other room when Jenny was out.

That did not mean that she was totally self-effacing. She certainly had a will of her own, a desire to organize and manage. It was not only goodness that was behind everything she had accomplished; there was also a wish to take charge of things, at times even a pure distrust of others' capabilities. And the responsibility she had once had to take on from her mother, the task of raising her siblings, to be the big sister. She could talk about it sometimes. It had happened an eternity ago, long ago in the past. And still she could feel the weight of her duty and feel the anxiety of not having enough strength left. Even though her siblings were gone.

Now she came in with the letter from Gertrud and asked Henning to decipher the words that were difficult to make out.

That made everyone talk about Gertrud and her family, and about the days gone by. And Henning would recall that evening as a visit to the past and a dream of regaining something of what was lost.

And he wondered if this clinging to something that was gone was a sign of unawareness. Or perhaps on the contrary, something necessary for the person who wanted to be aware and in the present.

He had his camera with him and had bought some magnesium flashbulbs. They exploded with their blinding glare when he took some pictures.

IN THE
DECEMBER MIST

The traffic rumbled across Kungsbron; it was as if the pillars of the bridge
sagged with the heavy trolley buses. A freight train traveled northward
and puffed giant rings of smoke that combined with the smoke from the
countless smokestacks on the other side of Torsgatan. A few sunbeams
had found a chink in the morning mist and sparkled on the windows of
the gasworks. The sheen produced burning reflections, long shimmering
pins that dipped into Klara Lake's lilac blue water.

Three wild ducks flew up and left light streaks behind them in the
dark water that still lay open despite a red sign warning of thin ice.
Down the hill from the cream Separator Company on the
Kungsholmen side of the waters, lumberyards and storage sheds were
sprawled on a hillside resembling a garbage dump. Inside the fence by
the railroad, rows of railway cars stood filled with wood, and horses
waited in front of their wagons next to a red shed where the drivers sat
inside drinking beer.

Per strode across the gangway from Noah's Ark. The barge was
used as a shelter; he had slept there a few nights. It cost one krona per
night. Though now that was over. There was not enough space and
others had been promised lodging. In the beginning they had only
accepted the unemployed, but now there were more and more who
had work but nowhere to live. When there was plenty of work it was
hard to be unemployed.

"Get a job," they would say to him—the people he was begging
from, social workers, probation officers. All these stewards and orderly
people, all these people who worked themselves and felt so indescrib-
ably proud of doing so.

Per preferred not to work. Of course, he tried to at times, but the attempts seldom lasted long. If he didn't get fired he would quit on his own.

Though he was afraid of landing in jail again and so had declined when old buddies wanted him along for "risk-free jobs."

The years in jail had changed him, maybe broken him. Before, he had also believed in the risk-free job. Now he was too afraid, even though he tried to look self-assured. When he could not frighten others he grew frightened.

He had avoided his relatives for a long time, despised them, felt like he had no need for them. He hadn't even been there for his mother's funeral. On the other hand, he had stayed living at his father's home as long as it was there, and he had been allowed to live there for free. After that ended he had not looked up his father either.

That's the way things had been when he felt secure, when he was doing his break-ins and when he was in charge of Rutan. While he had been in prison a more effective pimp had taken her in hand. There was no chance of getting her back.

He loafed languidly along the shoreline. Down the hill on the other side of the water a half-sunken barge lay at the edge of the shore; beneath the bridge, Sankt Eriksbron, an old man was kayaking. Before him he could see the city hall through a light mist that tinted the treetops along the water a lilac color.

He felt the urge to smoke and dug with his hands in his pockets even though he knew he would find neither money nor cigarettes. He looked around, in hopes of finding at least one person to beg from. A guy came along who apparently had also slept on the barge, but he just shook his head when Per asked him.

If it had been the old days, Per would have punched him in the jaw. Now he just ambled on, up the hill to Kungsgatan, in the direction of the rumbling traffic and the crowds of people.

They were in such a hurry, rushing along in a world that was not his and that barely had anything to do with him. They had so much to talk about and brood about; he could hear snatches of words and phrases passing by on the breeze, but did not understand much of it.

Nothing of what they said had any meaning to him, nothing of what happened either. When he walked his rounds through the city, he could see the big headlines of the papers. Words like "Sweden to the U.N., Danielson and Red Tape Sweden, Trade Agreements with the Soviets, Sales Tax Disappears." He barely read them and of the little he saw he comprehended nothing. Actually, when he saw that bit about "Red Tape Sweden," he gave a cackle. That concerned him. One big tangle of red tape, that's what it all was.

Right now the important thing was a cigarette and then some change so he could sit in some café.

He tried to reach out his hand into their, the other people's world, catch their attention, get the little he wished for out of them. That was the only reason they existed, he thought, once he had gotten what he asked for they could as easily be obliterated from the face of the earth.

They pretended not to see him or else they avoided him, moving out toward the curb when they passed by. Finally there was someone who pulled a pack of cigarettes out of his pocket and gave Per a Carmencita.

He lit it, inhaled the acrid smoke into his lungs and coughed violently. A little shock—but good. He spat out a clump of yellow phlegm and smiled when he saw how the girl who was walking by jumped and picked up speed. Putting on airs a bit, probably an office worker.

Now it was time for the change. He tried a few times without succeeding. Then he noticed a policeman at some distance. Maybe it was best to disappear. He continued on, down toward Vasagatan, wondering if he should head over into the Klara neighborhood, but decided to try in the other direction, toward the square at Norra bantorget. Salesmen with their office in their pockets carried out car sales beside the enormous stacks of wood that filled a large part of the square. They made good money on old wrecks that had seen better days since there was a dearth of cars; it was especially hard to get hold of car tires. But there was plenty of gasoline now, and basically all of the coal gas-powered vehicles had disappeared.

He got lucky, found an old fellow inmate from Långholmen Prison among the car dealers, one who had just made a sale on top of it. He still had to whine for a little while, of course, but that earned him a whole fiver. And then he could go find a café and take it easy for the next hour or so.

Accordion and clarinet it will be, hullabaloo and nothing else,
Leaping high and nimble we will be, hullabaloo and nothing else.

The gramophone played and Per hid in the quietest corner, drank his morning coffee and lit a new cigarette; he had bought a few loose Robin Hoods now that he had money.

Hullabaloo … the day had begun well; he felt some of the assurance of days gone by. Of course, he tried to hold on to the cheeky style he had had, intimidate as long as it worked. But he was always prepared to beg and cry, too, if it was necessary.

Before, he would threaten to punch people in jaw. If he threatened anything now it was usually that he was going to commit suicide.

"Go to hell!" the hardened ones said. "So jump now, dammit!" said one who had paid for a trip up the Katarina Elevator but would not loan him even one krona.

But Per would never jump. He would cry and plead until they threw him out or gave him a few kronor to get rid of him. A couple of days later he might come back, play the same scene all over again. It might make an impression on those who had not seen it before.

Now he was beginning to look up his siblings again, Allan and Gun. Allan was especially fitting to work on; he had a hard time defending himself. He felt some responsibility for his younger brother and tried to help him as best he could.

But the more help Per received the more importunate he became. His assurance returned when he felt he had the other in his grip. In truth, Per despised the giver. But if the one who had once helped him did not want to continue doing so, Per also saw that as a betrayal that should be punished, he would become morally indignant.

Allan had given him more than he could afford. And only gotten invectives and threats as thanks.

Now when Per was planning his day he also took up Allan among the possibilities. It would have been easier if Allan had stayed at home during the daytime. Since he was a construction worker and worked mainly on short-term small house construction it was hard to keep track of where he would be found. This irritated Per, seemed to him that Allan was trying to evade him.

Although, even if Allan wasn't at home, his old lady would be. Per couldn't remember what her name was and barely remembered what she looked like. Ordinary and quite fat was his impression.

The old lady would have household money. She couldn't justly deny her brother-in-law a few kronor. It would be no use her trying to either.

They lived a good ways out, Hammarbyhöjden. He would have to take a bus, though he did not like sitting closed in, stared at.

It took time to get out there and when he finally arrived no one was home. He stood and pounded on the door a while since no one answered when he rang the doorbell.

He did not want to imagine that he had traveled that whole way in vain just because Allan's damned old lady was out gadding about.

For that reason he tried ringing the nearest doorbells. Most people were seemingly out, probably working. An old woman finally opened. He introduced himself as the brother of Mr. Berg in the same vestibule and told her how there apparently had been some misunderstanding. His sister-in-law had promised to be at home to leave him ten kronor that he had spent for her. But now she had gone out and would surely be very sorry if she learned that he had come out there for nothing. Could the good lady possibly think to advance it to him—and do a favor for her neighbor?

That she could not.

"Cursed unhelpful bitch!" he screamed. She closed the door quickly and would not open it when he rang the doorbell again.

Finally, he got three kronor at the tobacconist in the same building, after doing his weeping song and dance. And against the promise that his brother would come in that very evening and pay.

He continued on to see Gun. She had recently had a baby and should be staying at home. But Gun was actually more difficult than Allan and it was her guy's fault.

The first time he had visited them at home he had received a few kronor. Then Olle had said stop.

Neither threats nor prayers made an impression on Olle, no weeping would touch him. He had gone through way too much, grown up during the years of unemployment in a home with many siblings.

"And still we made something of ourselves," Olle said. It was a judgment on all those such as Per. Olle viewed them all without any sense of forgiveness. Tougher punishment, forced labor, maybe beatings, too—those were the means he recommended for dealing with them. They had themselves to blame, they could not have had it harder than he himself had had. Not one öre of his hard-earned wages would be wasted by idle loafers, at least not one more öre than he was obliged to pay in taxes. He would prefer to see the whole social welfare system dismantled. Well, they should help the old, of course. And the sick—if they really were sick and not just faking it. The rest should be taught to work. He himself toiled hard, every coin he earned cost him effort and exertion, a little of his life and a little of his joy. And then his money was taken and given to some drunkards and shirkers. Society was rotten and favored the rotten ones, bred rottenness instead of pruning it away.

And Olle influenced Gun. But Olle wasn't home in the daytime and Gun couldn't very well let her brother go and kill himself.

Gun lived on Söder, near Skanstull. With a view over the greenhouses and sheds in the old city gardens.

She was at home. She opened the door but refused to let him in. He placed his foot in the way so she could not close the door and began to play the big crying scene again. But then she gave a kick so that he had to pull his foot away and the door was slammed in his face. He rang the bell and pounded but she would not open it. Finally the doorman came and drove him out. Then Gun finally opened the door but only to beg the doorman's pardon and to thank him for his help.

Long after Per had left, Gun sat shaking with sobs and rage. Before, she had sometimes felt terror, a powerful fear of sharing her parents' fate. Gradually, the fear had been transformed to hatred. She never spoke of her childhood home and did not want to see her father. She denied the past, saw it as a contagion that could attack her and her children as well.

But she had thought that she had succeeded, believed she was safe. And then Per had arrived. The first times she had been weak, not been able to push him away. But now she realized it was necessary.

Not one öre would he get, never again. If he came back she would call the police. But, of course, she did not do that—though she didn't give him anything either.

Once upon a time Henning had wondered if Per could possibly be the much-discussed Sabbath Saboteur. Now he was pretty sure it was not so, Per was not that type. He was too drunk and scared, his desperation took other forms of expression.

The saboteur had been silent for a long time now. Maybe he had been frightened by the huge uproar the attack on Central Station had caused. It seemed as if the explosions would remain an unsolved mystery.

Then suddenly the detonations began anew the Sunday after Christmas. Some newspaper had calculated that the saboteur worked with a pattern. The different blast sites corresponded to the stars in the Big Dipper. Now that picture was being fulfilled with an explosion on Blasieholmen, and all the rumors and theories poured forth once more. The police still stayed powerless despite the promised rewards. And now people were wondering if there would be a New Year's explosion as well.

Henning celebrated New Year's Eve together with some friends from college days. He had accepted the invitation even though he didn't really feel like it. But there was no better opportunity and he did not feel like sitting at home either.

He felt how impossible and boring he was in the present company, that he could not put himself in the frame of mind to enjoy himself. He blamed it on not feeing well and he slipped away as soon as it was midnight.

As was typical of a New Year's Eve, the streets were filled with people. They lit sparklers and threw jumbo firecrackers, shrieked and hollered.

He walked in the direction of Sveavägen, thought it might be pleasant to walk through the whole town. He plowed through the crowds, saw a girl smile at him up close but he felt like he did not have the energy to smile back. Apparently it provoked her because he received a quick hard slap on the mouth—and then she disappeared.

Just then he heard the explosions, more muffled and substantial sounding than the usual New Year's noises. Somewhere from the Observatory heights, behind the Stockholm Public Library, he saw people rushing there and he followed them.

When Henning reached the site he only saw the back of a young boy who was being taking by the police toward the patrol car.

A boy, seventeen or eighteen years old. People were stating that it was the saboteur.

Later he was to read that they were three, young boys who had come up with the idea to create an explosion after listening to a radio report on the Bikini bomb.

No matter how stupid and dangerous the idea was, Henning felt sorry for the boy who was led away. He had provided a release for some of the anxiety that Henning himself also felt.

Suddenly, he got it into his head that he was in a hurry. He walked through the mist and the New Year's ruckus. Faster, faster, faster. Yet he did not want to come home; he was lacking a goal.

Or did he have one? Was he walking so fast because he wanted to arrive at Barbro's door?

But it was closed and dark.
Barbro, where are you now?

TO MAKE LOVE
WITHOUT LOVE

"Is there anything more?" the girl who was taking shorthand asked.

"That should be it," answered Erik Karge. He suddenly felt tired from the day's work and at the thought of everything that lay waiting. First the committee in the afternoon and then a meeting that evening again. Always meetings.

She left and he watched her leave. She was young, a good-looking girl, unbelievably small waist, hips that swayed gently. And she walked so lightly, almost glided. Expectant, smiling. Happy, of course, that he had not dictated more; now she would be done well before five. There was surely no boring meeting waiting for her.

A little envious. Not directed at her exactly, but more maybe at everyone who was young and free and had a life ahead. He was going to turn fifty in a few years. It seemed like a lot, as if the fun would soon be over.

He felt a little bitter. Though in fact he really had nothing to complain about. He had been more successful than most, more than many who had started with much larger resources. Now he was head of a company with ties to the popular movement, one of the directors of the labor movement, on the city council. He might feel that he was appreciated, a person to be reckoned with, listened to, and guided by. And then he was happily married, a beautiful wife, adorable daughters, a pleasant home, nice summer house. Everything that money, luck, and cleverness could attain. He had his health, too, was in pretty good shape for his years.

Of course, he had achieved success. Yet he had started from the bottom, had been born in the slums on the outskirts to asocial parents, had been tossed out into a life where early on he had been forced to manage on his own. Despite all the poverty, he had the topsoil in his pockets; he had a talent for doing business, to buy cheap and sell for more, to persuade and convince. Already as a boy he had run an enterprise in miniature, selling razor blades and contraceptives. As the years had passed the street urchin, street vendor, and revolutionary, Erik Karlsson, had been transformed into the distinguished director and city council member, Erik Karge. A rather good transformation act, he thought. To a certain degree it was a result of societal development—but surely his personal characteristics must have played some role? His brother, Bengt, had exactly the same origins but worked down there in the dark tunnels for his small salary.

Erik had spoken out for equality, and still did so. Nevertheless, he wondered if it wasn't an impossible dream. People were not alike, did not become equals even if one gave them the same opportunities. Even the labor movement paid its directors better than its janitors. And the directors' children went to high school and university while the janitors' children had to be content with going to elementary school.

He had met his son for lunch; they did that sometimes. Henning had certainly done well for himself, appeared to like it at the magazine. He reminded Erik quite a lot of his mother, the young Maj, the Maj whom Erik had once loved. Fair, thin, that slightly obstinate look in his eyes.

Henning had shown him some pictures; he was a photographer. He had taken the pictures one evening when the relatives were gathered at Emelie's. Erik had asked to keep a couple of them.

Now that he was alone he took them out and looked at them again. His relatives, the relatives that he never saw anymore. Maj's relatives more than his—even if his siblings were there. Emelie had grown old. Maj looked pretty much the same, even if you could see that she had gotten older.

Actually he had brought out the photographs to take another look at Elisabet. It might seem unnecessary—he did see her at the office from time to time. He looked for a magnifying glass that was hidden under some papers on his desk. How old could she be now? Not yet forty, thirty-six or thirty-seven. Well-dressed as always. And that standoffish expression, as if she knew that he was looking at her.

She was still in his memory, an irritant. In some way she had always goaded him, maybe because he knew that she had never really accepted him. He had felt a need to conquer her, to get revenge. And he had done that, too.

He had never gone after anyone so coldly and methodically. He had fooled her into being soft and warm. And then, once she had finally weakened, he had kicked her out, laughed at her.

It was to get revenge and she was worth it. Maybe she needed it pure and simple, needed to know that she was not flawless. Still, he felt a little ashamed when he thought of it; she was Maj's sister after all. But shame had its sweetness, memory its lust.

He looked at her through the magnifying glass. He had made love to her without love.

To make love without love. The combination was irritating. There must be something wrong with that; to make love and feel love were surely the same thing.

But there lay a truth in that, a truth that held for him. Now as he looked back it seemed to him that he had always been a lover but never really in love. Those innumerable mistresses he had had, already during his time with Maj. It had started with Irene, too, before they had gotten married. It had continued after Irene.

Lover, mistress ... the words were, of course, silly, but still fitting. A little bit of a gigolo, a lot of cheating. Silly scenes too sometimes— a husband who came home unexpectedly, tears and worry before an abortion was arranged.

But did the words apply any longer? Was there the same duplicity in his political life, in his work? To some degree perhaps this was so. A little crooked dealing, words lacking substance, gestures that did not correspond to actions. One talked about equality but held onto one's position. One took advantage of the concept of solidarity to sell one's wares.

One? Well—okay, me.

Of course, he had conspired, of course, he had utilized dubious methods at times. But he defended himself in saying that he had done it for the sake of the cause, in order to further the party's or the company's interests. Because he loved the game? Maybe the game more than the cause?

And there he had it again. The dealings more than the objective. A game, an act, a desire, a pastime.

Somehow he was too fond of the actual business dealings and being in charge. He liked mixing in politics and business and going to bed with women. To the point where he could be almost indifferent as to what kind of politics he was dealing in, what business he was promoting, who was the woman concerned.

Well, not exactly indifferent. The objective should be first-rate and neat and correspond to his ideals. First-rate politics, first-rate business, first-rate women. He had become more particular over the years, on all levels. He preferred not to think of the soap he sold during the first war … rat fat and dog poop, as they said then. And there had been a fair amount of rat fat and dog poop in politics and among the girls, too. Back then, a long time ago. Not now when he could afford to be more particular.

Growing irritated with himself he broke off his contemplations. Why should he always dissect himself and his motives? He was unfair toward himself, way too critical. Almost over-scrupulous. Here he wore himself out to serve the party and the company, took upon himself tasks of all kinds, probably earned less than if he had joined some privately-owned company. And then he chewed himself out because he didn't view working in the party and toiling for the company as a kind of punishment, but rather as something that he enjoyed and felt good about. Indeed, he did like doing business and being active in politics—so what? Was there anything wrong with that? And he liked girls, too. Shouldn't one take what life had to offer?

There was a damned puritan inside him, a killjoy, a denier of life. But for the most part that little puritan streak was rather nice and quiet.

He took a look at Elisabet. She was certainly good-looking. But at the same time she looked like that little puritan incarnate. As if she was very dissatisfied at the memory that she had once lived and loved.

Then he put the photograph away in one of his desk drawers and went to a child welfare committee meeting. After that he had just enough time to grab something to eat at a restaurant before it was time for a board meeting of the parish association. It was past nine o'clock when he got home.

The girls and Irene had bathed and the apartment was filled with warm femininity—the scent, the image, and the sound. The girls were growing up; there were a lot of women in the house. Lena was fourteen now and Berit would soon be eleven. And Irene was growing too, a little plumper with every passing year. Almost too much of the goodness when she swelled out of her bathrobe.

He sometime felt like a pasha when he arrived home to his harem. Lena slipped out of the bathroom, Berit jumped into his lap in her nightgown, Irene kissed him on the cheek. Soft and friendly, beautiful to look at. He felt a dizzying contentment after the day's work and meetings, so nice to finally be home, to have a home where one was welcomed like this. Now Lena had put on her nightgown and she came over, too, cuddling next to him on the sofa. Irene squeezed in on the other side and he sat there with the littlest one on his knee and the two others surrounding him.

"You smell like a whole perfume shop," he said. He sniffed the air around him, poking Berit's stomach with his nose until she squealed with laughter.

The thought she had been thinking before were long gone, his closest kin were so close. He felt newly bathed himself, physically and spiritually. Another person from the one who had been sitting at the office looking at Elisabet through the magnifying glass. A happy family man surrounded by wife and children, a man who had no need of other people, least of all other women. Though it would have been fun to have his son there, of course. But Henning would not be joined together with all this, he would have been a stranger if he had come. Irene became a little sulky if he even named Henning's name; she was totally jealous of his past. It had to be rubbed out, forgotten, and kept in silence. She had gone through a pretty hard time back then, when he had still lived together with Maj.

Did one have to lie in order to be happy? No, maybe just forget and keep quiet about what was not really pertinent. Henning existed in another context. It was right to leave the photos in the desk drawer at work; it would not be appropriate to paste them into the album that Irene kept. It would be all right with photos of his siblings, but never with Jenny and her daughters and Henning. In any case, his siblings did not fit in there either, they belonged to another world.

He sat in his own world, the happy, beautiful world that could be pasted into the well-kept family album. But the moment on the sofa did not last long; it was time for the girls to go to bed. He went along with Irene into their room, watched as she tucked them in, kissed them good night.

Happy girls and happy parents. Somewhere in the past, he could see himself and his siblings curl up together on a pile of rags and old quilts while their parents sat at the table and drank with some boarder. He hastily erased the vision; whatever was gone should stay that way. Only once in a while was he able to bring it out and exhibit it in doctored form, for example if the girls did not really understand how good they had it.

Irene closed their door and they walked into the dark living room with no lights on; through the wide windows he could see the light arch of Västerbron above the water outside. Irene stopped, turned around and placed her arms around him. He started to laugh, unbuttoned the few buttons still fastened on her bathrobe and took hold of her. When she bathed she always became a little light-headed, wanted him to come to her. And this evening he felt generous, the good husband family man who willingly and gladly fulfilled all of his marital duties.

"Chubby," he said and laughed again, giving her a little spank.

"Do you think I've gotten too fat?" She sounded so worried that he had to laugh once more.

"No … just pleasingly plump. So that anyone can tell that you lead the good life."

"I have my work cut out for me, too, you can be sure. Taking care of the place and the girls and … everything."

"Of course, I understand completely. But you can still lead the good life with that?"

Well yes, she had nothing to complain about. Except for possibly that he had so many meetings and so much work, so he seldom could be at home. But she knew that he had to do these things. Though it grew lonely for her sometimes.

"Let's sit on the sofa a while," he suggested. "Take it easy, be cozy. Do you want a cognac?"

"I'd rather have a little of the liqueur."

She turned on the light and sat down, pulling her bathrobe around her without buttoning it. And he went and got some glasses and filled them. He handed her one and they toasted, filling them up again after a time. He began to feel pleasantly sleepy, and also a little pleasantly aroused. Just enough to want in to her soft, round warmth a while, and then fall asleep without dreams.

She curled up with her legs under her on the sofa. Her bathrobe fell open, and the lamplight fell on her large breasts that shone like white lamp globes.

"Go to bed and I'll be in soon," he said, and emptied the last of his glass.

She went into the bathroom, and he put the glasses away, and turned off the lamp. He stood for a moment at the door to the balcony and looked out over the water and the street along the shore outside, remembering how he had stood out on the balcony and watched the car roll away with Elisabet inside it that evening.

Indeed, he had been avenged that time, been hard on Elisabet. But is one avenged against a person who is indifferent? In revenge there is hate—and hate and love can be very close to each other. Elisabet had always despised him. Until that time when he had decided to be avenged. And, then in the middle of the revenge and the hate, he had felt something else. Not just lust, not just bodily pleasure. Rather, something that resembled love. But since he knew that, that love was impossible, he had not given it a chance. Instead he had brooded about stirring her up, had wanted to do it, too. When love wouldn't do he had wanted to cause pain instead. Whatever it took: something that would be felt.

Once she had even lain on the bed in there; he had been shaken when he saw how beautiful she was. He had made love to her perhaps as he had never made love to anyone, not even Maj.

And then he had said that it was all in revenge.

Crazy? Or extremely wise? Most likely he would never have been able to take being with her for very long, nor she with him either. They were a good match maybe for sleeping together, but not for living together. In everyday life she was probably happiest with her calm, little, and all-forgiving husband, and he with Irene. But if he had been smart he would have arranged it so that they could still meet sometimes. Though, of course, that was probably impossible, she wasn't that type. You couldn't have it both ways, it had to be either or. Hardly even that. It had to be once and never again. It might feel as if Elisabeth had won anyway, as if she had forced his revenge. She was free of him but he was locked in the memory.

"Aren't you coming soon?" Irene asked sleepily from inside the bedroom.

"Yes, I'm coming now," he answered.

MEETING IN
THE SPRING

The winter had been unusually cold and long; people waited impatiently for the delayed spring. Everything happened so slowly, as if neither the cold nor the war wanted to relinquish their grip. Out in Europe, people were starving, barefoot children came to the food distribution centers to get their "Swedish soup." Mine sweepers were still at work. Several large plane crashes had occurred, and even if they were not directly caused by the war, it had the feeling of an echo of what had gone on before. And political antagonisms seemed to grow rather than diminish. Truman had promised American aid to all the countries that were threatened by Communist aggression, and in Greece a full-blown civil war as underway.

In Sweden, rationing continued and new things were rationed, such as coffee, which had been freely available for a while. The domestic economy was strained and there were warnings of inflation. But there was no unemployment and wages continued to rise—as well as prices.

The members of the discussion group that Henning belonged to continued to hold their meetings, to cultivate impatience. It was an ache inside them and they had a hard time finding an outlet for it. They were seeking action, the opportunity to do something more than talk. One became active in his union, another started his studies, some sought out political groups, a couple of them began to paint. Impatience demanded that they do something constructive, but there were so dispiritingly few real tasks. They wanted to change their existence but it was hard to get a handle on how. Anything they could do, was something they did instead of what they really wanted to do.

It turned to a topic of discussion that returned: are we being robbed of our power of initiative? People might complain that youth lacked initiative but what did people want? Was there any initiative to take? Everywhere the kind of people who knew better sat and would not allow any untried efforts to proceed.

They attempted to look around, discover any opportunities. The larger part of Europe lay in ruins, there was bound to be work to be done. Someone had heard that the Communists were going to send out work brigades; such a brigade was going to build the "Youth's Railroad" in Yugoslavia. That was a real job, an opportunity. Some of them signed up.

But not Henning. He had his work that he liked, and even if he still didn't think that he had really found his form and his style, he thought that he wanted to continue to write. That was his opportunity. And he still had the promise to be able to go abroad and travel in Europe. It was more than a promise now; it was beginning to evolve into solid plans.

Indeed, he was making plans and was happy about the plans. But it still sometimes felt like he was preparing for an escape after a failure. He had not found Barbro, not dared look her up. To meet with her could mean losing his dream. But each day that passed meant more risk that he would also lose his reality.

So he wrote at last, unsure and anxious. Only a few lines: if she wanted to get together with him she could come to the place where they met the first time. He suggested a day and time.

It was cold and rainy that evening. He went to the place he mentioned, up on Fåfängens Hill, stood for a long time in the rain and waited. She did not come.

Wet and chilled he finally walked away. The rain had begun to turn to clumps of snow; the city lights disappeared, drowned in the gray white fog. He sat alone an hour in a café, smoked cigarette after cigarette, felt once again the total bitterness of failure. He longed to be able to cry like a child but knew that his crying, too, had frozen and turned to ice.

Well, now his journey abroad, the so longed-for adventure, would be an escape.

One evening a week later, the telephone rang and Henning went and answered it. It was silent for a moment in the receiver; he thought he sensed someone breathing. Then he heard Barbro's voice. She had been away for a few weeks, had just gotten his letter. Did he still want to get together with her?

He half ran through the streets and his unbuttoned raincoat flapped in the wind. The evening felt warm and he felt that spring had arrived, a spring that suddenly had significance and meaning. Still, he did not dare rejoice completely. It might only be kindness, maybe she felt like she could not refuse to meet him. Maybe he would find out that she was seeing someone else, maybe their meeting would be a disappointment. But deep inside he felt something different that was like a conviction. Her voice, her tone gave him that.

She was standing in her outer doorway and saw him coming, walked toward him. He recognized her and didn't recognize her. Of course, she was the same, but also changed. She was someone other than who she had been two springs ago. Something in her eyes, as if her gaze had deepened.

In fact he would have liked to take her in his arms right away, in the middle of the street. But maybe she wouldn't like that.

They walked down Bondegatan toward the harbor and he tried to explain. Why he had just disappeared at one time and then not gotten in touch. That he had been frightened by her being so young and thought that it wasn't right of him to be seeing her. That he knew that he liked her too much to just be friends. Now he wondered if she could forgive him.

"Maybe you were right," she said. "I was probably too young then. It wasn't until long afterward that I began to understand what I had actually been feeling."

"What were you feeling?" he asked her in a low voice, almost inaudible.

"That we belonged together."

They sat down by the harbor pier on the round wooden bench that surrounded the columns of the lighthouse. Above them the light blinked across the water toward the inlet that welcomed all the vessels of the world. Barbro had crept in under his coat and he held her tightly against him.

"Now I will never let you go," he said. "Never again."

And she pressed herself even closer to him, and he held her even a little tighter. The closeness felt so important, as if otherwise they risked slipping away from each other, disappearing out into the darkness and never meeting again. In someway everything seemed to be new yet very familiar. Like coming home at last after being away for long time, like meeting the reality one had so often dreamed about.

They each told about the two years they had been apart. She had worked in various offices and most recently she had been in Eskilstuna for a while and helped a relative who had gotten sick. It was there in Eskilstuna that she had been when Henning wrote. Now her relative was better again. And Barbro would look around for a new job.

And that boy he had seen her with. They had been together for some time, she told about that, too. But it had been over for quite some time.

"And that was probably because of you," she said. "Because I saw you then, that time."

He felt no pang of jealousy, just fear: he had been so close to losing her.

"When I saw you I felt that you would come back," she said. "I saw that in you. So I waited."

He told her about all the times he had thought of writing, calling, how he had gone on errands past her door. And wondered why he had tortured himself for so long. Now it was over, now he had found her.

He kissed her again. But he saw how her eyes filled with tears and suddenly she was crying. He tried to calm and console her and question her. Was she sad, now?

She shook her head. Her tears shone like glistening small pearls and in the middle of her crying she had to laugh.

"I am just so incredibly happy. I have waited so long, still not knowing if I was going to meet you ever again."

"Barbro, Barbro...." He dried her tears, stroked her hair aside, laid his cheek next to hers. He felt, barely astonished: joy is pain, it hurts to like someone, not only when one misses someone, but also when one experiences the closeness. Every true experience is felt, and the one who feels strongly enough has pain. But that is when one first starts to live.

He wanted to cry himself. And at the same time proclaim his joy.

It took a long time to walk home.

They walked through the White Hills' dark park where one and another lantern shone through the as yet bare trees, and across the first blades of grass turning green.

Time after time they had to stop to embrace each other. They experienced the closeness, each other's touch, from the very lightest thrill of the finger against the palm of the hand to the pressure of body against body.

Now there was so much to experience and explore together, she shouldn't be afraid, not get hurt, nothing should be spoiled by rushing and excitement. Right now it was enough that they had found each other again and felt each other's closeness, just now they could barely take in more.

He followed with her at last to her door. She pulled a mirror out of her purse, wondered how she would avoid being found out by her mother.

"Just admit it," he said. "I want to shout it out loud, run in the streets and holler..."

"No," she said. "I want to have it for myself—just now."

But he knew about himself. Mama will see that I have changed, she will ask. Or not. But guess the answer.

He sailed away through the streets with his coattails flapping being him. With the feeling that he was flying above the surface of the earth.

Now his whole life was completely different, nothing that mattered yesterday was valid today.

The trip that he had looked forward to for so long now seemed like an obstacle, a danger. How would he be able to travel from Barbro just when he had won her back?

There was a solution, though at first it seemed too fantastic. He pushed the thought away a few times but it only kept coming back.

If they both went, if Barbro went with him.

But money?

He could not let go of the impossible possibility. There was one of borrowing money from his father. Absolutely borrow, not ask for. A proper agreement on repayment. Of course, it would be tough to do the paying back—but he could not skip the travel and he could not travel without Barbro.

Would she agree to it? What would her parents say?

It would have to be arranged. Nothing could be impossible now. And the very first thing was that she had to go and get a passport, for she very likely didn't have one.

Now he had to wait until tomorrow evening before he could find out what Barbro thought. How was he going to wait so long?

WAITING

Maj realized that something had happened to her son and could guess what. But she didn't want to ask and waited instead.

He was still restless—but in a completely different way now, a happy restless. He did not know how quickly he could get away, he glowed with anticipation. This was something different from his usual meetings, she could see that.

While she sat there at home, she felt a little abandoned. She knew: if Henning had found someone it meant that she was now losing him, that a greater loneliness than that evening's awaited her.

That was the way it was in life. Still, she had gotten to keep him unusually long. He would turn twenty-four that summer. When she herself had been that old she had been a mother for over a year. She had already begun to go with Erik by the time she had turned seventeen. At that time she couldn't, but now she could understand how they had felt worried sometimes at home. Emelie more than Jenny, in fact.

Maj felt like she had been more mature when young. As had Erik. They had not been particularly young parents. But she thought that Henning was still somewhat a child, needed fussing over. It was hard to hold back, although she could see that he became irritated, would fend her off.

"Have you noticed how much happier he has gotten?" she asked John.

"It's probably because he is going to go out traveling soon."

She smiled a little but said nothing more. John was kind—and wise—but he could not understand Henning the way she herself did.

It grew empty and silent at home when Henning disappeared, and John was quiet, didn't say much. He had become a little more silent with the years, more tired. His work at the warehouse had become heavier instead of lighter, more demanding; they had cut back on personnel. John had to toil with the enormous packages of upholstery fabric that had to go off and on the shelves, all the boxes that had to go out. He was no longer young. When evening came he was pretty beat, wanted mostly to sink down in a chair with the radio and a newspaper for a while and then go to bed early. He began an hour earlier than her in the morning, too; the warehouse opened at eight and the office at nine. So although they worked at the same place they never went together to work, only when they went home.

Maj had more energy, was almost ten years younger, too. She would have liked to go to the theater and the movies sometimes, get out some. But she knew how tired he was and didn't want to bother him. Though she did not want to go to bed as early as he did; she hated lying there hour after hour without being able to sleep.

The evenings Henning was at home she sat and talked to him. He was actually a real night owl, too. And when she looked at the clock later on she would have a guilty conscience; he needed to go to bed early the few evenings he was home. And there she was sitting and keeping him awake until twelve. But it was so much fun that she couldn't help herself and besides, she didn't know where the time went. Even when he was out she liked to wait to at least exchange a few words with him before they went to bed. With the same guilty conscience: now he was coming back even later.

Recently, when he had been out practically every evening, it had been so empty and quiet. And it would get even worse. When he moved away from home, got married. There were empty and silent years waiting for her; that was what remained of her life. Though she might still feel young, had a few years left till fifty.

But she had always been used to taking care of herself. Erik had seldom been home during the time they were together, then she had been alone with Henning for many years before she married John. She would probably manage. And she liked John a lot, was happy in his company. With his silence, too: it felt like a soft and warmth-giving shawl that she wrapped herself in when she sank down in an armchair with a book.

Maj read a lot, a lot more than she used to. She had time for it now. The apartment was easy to take care of; John was good in the house and often helped making meals and doing the dishes. She didn't have to worry about his clothes; he continued to do what he had done during his many years as a bachelor: leave them at the laundromat and the tailor's.

She could never have found a better husband than John. No one could be more helpful, less demanding. They had a good time together. She tried to mute the anxiety she sometimes felt. In general that worked, too. It was only now, while she was waiting for Henning's acknowledgement that she grew a little more anxious than usual. It was then the soft silence was more stifling than warmth-giving.

"Have you heard if Henning is coming along with us on Sunday?" John asked.

She gave a start. She put the book down that she had been holding in her hand without reading.

"He hasn't said anything yet. And I think I will let him tell us what he wants to do rather than asking. He knows we are going."

"Yes, well I think I'll go to bed," John said and got up.

"You go ahead. I'm going to sit here a little while longer."

He kissed her on the cheek. She stayed sitting there, wondering if she should wait up until Henning came home. She would have to see how long he took.

She closed her eyes and could see the sandy beach out there in the archipelago, the rocks and the path matted with pine needles that slipped between the bare pine tree trunks, the copse of leafy trees beside the cottage.

Especially now in the spring it was an adventure to come out there, to have a cottage to travel to, as well as knowing a piece of land. It was a new adventure; it had come with John.

The older relatives had never had this opportunity. A couple times she and John had had Emelie and Jenny out with them, but it didn't happen very often since the connections were bad and it was expensive with a car. Besides, neither Emelie nor Jenny were particularly interested; they were really strangers to nature. They did not know how they should sit and where they could walk, and they thought there were bugs and mosquitoes almost everywhere. In their day "ordinary people" could not have imagined having a summer place; even a community garden cottage at the edge of town was an almost unattainable luxury. It was not especially normal to have a summer place now either, and if John had not inherited that cottage they would probably never have had one.

The cottage meant so much to John as well; out there he could really relax and feel revitalized. His preference was to go out in the rowboat, he liked to sit somewhere on the inlet and fish. Sometimes, especially at the beginning, she had gone along. But talking and fishing did not go very well together, and sitting silent and still in a boat hour after hour was not her idea of fun. Things evolved so that she stayed at the cottage or on the beach. John had dug some garden plots beside the cottage where she spent a fair amount of time, especially among the strawberries, which were her pride.

They frequently asked Elisabet and Lennart if they wanted to go along; then Maj would have someone to talk to. John would take Lennart out with him in the boat.

Before, the sisters had had a little trouble understanding each other, they had not really enjoyed each other's company. There were many years between them, of course; Elisabet had also been somewhat contrary and difficult at times. But with the years they had grown to have more in common, and now in Maj's company Elisabet was usually nice. John and Lennart got along well together also—quiet and placid both of them, though otherwise so different. John was practical and down-to-earth, Lennart a little introverted.

It was going to be pleasant to get together out there on Saturday and Sunday, the first overnight of the year. But Henning would probably not come along.

Henning had told her now; it was as she had thought. Or perhaps even more serious. They were to be engaged at Whitsuntide, a couple of days before he left. A little speedy, he admitted, but it was because Barbro was going to go with him on his trip. Her parents thought they should at least be engaged before they went away together like that.

Maj was not bound by conventions, had lived with Erik and had Henning without being either married or engaged. But getting engaged was not the same as getting married; it was easier to change your mind and break it off. If it turned out they had rushed things. Of course, she had not seen the girl yet.

Henning and Barbro were going to come out to the cottage, but not until Sunday. And Henning had said that it didn't make any difference that Elisabet and Lennart would be there when they came; Barbro should get to know them, too.

But sometimes Elisabet could say things that … Maj would try to talk to her when they were alone, ask her to be cautious.

They opened the doors and windows to air out the winter's damp, lighted the first fire. Maj and Elisabet spread out the bedclothes as close to the fire as possible. It was necessary to get everything as warm and dry as possible before evening arrived and they did not have many hours before then. Lennart stood there a little at loose ends and watched.

When they had walked through the woods toward the cottage they had seen signs that something was going to happen soon out here— land was being divided up into lots. John had heard about it, too, and knew the person who was thinking of selling.

Maybe there was still a chance to buy a piece of land at a decent price. Once the selling process started it would undoubtedly become more expensive, the inhabitants would find that the land they owned was more valuable than they had believed. If Lennart and Elisabet were thinking about a lot, they would certainly get a good deal if they bought something quickly.

Of course Lennart had saved a little money but he was afraid of risking it. If something were to happen to him it was important that there be a sum of money for Elisabet and their daughter.

Buying a lot was a risk-free place to put your money, was John's opinion. Land never went down in price, not this close to a big city. If they ever needed their money they could sell half the lot and maybe get back more than they paid for the whole thing.

Elisabet grew enthusiastic. Even if they couldn't afford to build a proper house for several years yet, they could still throw together something temporary to live in. She believed John was right; there wasn't any risk. They could take out a mortgage as well.

John and Lennart took a stroll down to the fisherman who owned the land beside John and Maj's place. They got no direct answer; the old man wanted to think about it. But John was sure things would work out; he knew the old man and his method of doing business.

That was how they ended up talking more about Elisabet and Lennart's concerns than about Henning and his girl. And that was just as well, thought Maj.

They arrived already at ten o'clock, had started early and bicycled the forty kilometers from town. They looked so young and healthy, red in their faces from the effort and the sun.

As soon as Maj saw the girl she knew she liked her. She had been afraid she would be too severe in her judgment, that the knowledge that the girl was taking Henning from her would make her unfavorably disposed. But Barbro seemed so genuine. Fair-haired and open, cheerful and friendly. It wasn't a competitor Maj saw, but a new friend and close relation. Impulsively she gave the girl a hug, a little surprised at herself—she was usually more stiff and shy. She felt Henning looking at her, maybe he had been a little worried about the meeting after all, fearing that Barbro wouldn't be accepted—because no one could be good enough? But Maj was not that difficult.

When they had eaten Henning wanted to show Barbro around. They disappeared through the thicket down to the beach; just before they were swallowed up by the greenery Maj saw how Henning placed his arm around the girl's neck.

She watched them go, maybe watching something she herself had missed. She could not remember ever being like that … as if there was no one else besides the other person. She and Erik had never looked at each other like that … even though they had been just as young, younger. Erik had always had so much going on; she herself had not been so soft either and … alive? Not like Barbro. And when she had met John it had also been a little different, two middle-aged people could not shine with happiness like a pair of young people.

She could not begrudge them that, only feel happy. And maybe wonder how it felt.

"Young and in love," said Elisabet. "How long can that last?"

"I think they will stay together."

"Yes," answered Elisabet, "I think they will both get engaged and get married. But I mean, how long does one have the energy to stay so happy? Before one comes down to earth again. It can't be so very long?"

They came down to the inlet, followed the edge of the water, walked barefoot into the small, gentle waves that steadily rolled in. Their feet left imprints in the damp sand, traces that were quickly eradicated when the next wave rolled over them. He found a polished piece of planking that had floated ashore, let his hand glide over its smooth surface.

"Like your skin," he said.

She began to run along the edge of the water. And he had to dash to keep up with her. He caught up just as she was about to climb the hill where the water ended. And he held tightly onto her while they continued to climb up to the overlook at the highest point on the hill.

Up there it was windy. Before them opened the water, beyond the small islets and skerries lay only the horizon line.

"The world," he said. "Soon we will explore it. Together."

"I don't believe it's true," she said. "You're just lying to me."

The wind forced them down. There were flat stone slabs down by the water; the slabs were warm from the sun and their surfaces smooth, polished.

He took off his shirt and spread it out. He lay down.

"Come," he said. "If you lie down you won't feel the wind at all."

And she followed his request. Her face drew close. He only had to pucker his lips to reach her.

"It's so warm already," she said. "Like summer. Does it feel good to sunbathe?"

"Try it. No one can see you here."

"You'll see."

"Well, me, of course. But...."

"You may see."

And he rejoiced at the sight, his mouth and hands could hardly be sated. But she had to get used to him first, have as much desire as he did, come to him without fear.

He bored his face in against her breasts, weighed the soft orbs in his hands.

"Get used to being here," he said to them. "It is here you belong."

It was time to bicycle into town again. And the others, who were taking the bus, began to tidy up and close up the cottage. The bus had extended its line, now it wasn't more than three kilometers to walk to the nearest stop. And it was doable, especially when they were not bringing so much luggage back.

They walked along the road through the woods up to the main road, saw the white posts demarcating lots again. Some of the remoteness and isolation out here would disappear once the lots were sold, and cottages were built in what had once been a large wooded area to wander around in. Maj felt like she was already beginning to miss some of what had been.

She mourned a little over a solitude that waited and one that was about to disappear. Though mourn was too strong a word as far as Henning was concerned; she was happy, too, of course. For his sake, for the girl's sake. Could she ask for anything more than for Henning to be happy? Wasn't that most important of all?

It had been a fine Saturday and Sunday and now a whole lovely summer waited. She had much to be happy about.

THE TRIP
ABROAD

So they took a trip abroad into Europe.

Everything they were familiar with disappeared behind them. Their hometown with all its little pale yellow lights that glimmered in the blue spring evening.

They stood at the window for a long time in the corridor of the sleeping car.

Glittering lights streaking past, the spring night darkening outside. And their faces reflected in the pane, cheek to cheek.

Unreal reality, dream attained.

Everything coming at them was new; it numbed, almost devoured them.

Large white ferries that concealed the train cars in their innards shot across what looked like endless blue water. Trains belched out black smoke in the light green tunnels of trees, stopping at stations where rusty iron constructions that had once supported the glass roofs of the station halls stood like twisted, dead trees.

Destruction, chaos, and privation. Giant fields of ruins that once had been cities. Where hundreds of thousands of people still lived beneath the ruins, had lived during the past hard winter. Starving, begging children who had gathered beneath the railroad embankments and stretched out their skinny arms and dirty hands. War invalids with their crutches and occupation soldiers with their prostitutes, societies where anything could be bought for ten cigarettes.

At home, from a distance, it had been easy to draw borders. Around their own nation, between good and evil, around Nazi Germany which was now reaping what it sowed.

Up close it was harder. There the borders seemed shockingly temporary. A barricade across a street on the outskirts—and on one side of the barricade abundance and on the other destitution. On one side the good guys, on the other the bad ones? Was it so simple? Or was the border a lie, a barrier that should be torn down? And did that apply to all borders?

Henning wrote a lot of question marks, marks that could express both confusion and hope.

The war was over in any case and no one wanted a new one. Even if it took time, tattered Europe would be built up again and people would get food and work. The ruins were being torn down and scaffolding was being raised. If one wanted to live, one had to believe that there was a future. And he wanted to live.

That was maybe why he experienced the brightest aspects the most, why in spite of everything his reports to the magazine breathed so much hope. What would he have written about if he had had to travel alone? Would he have been able to see then that there were opportunities for life amidst all that death and devastation?

To hope is to defy, to revolt against death and defeat. The ruins were the result of the politics of the past, the judgment over the time that was.

The world of the future had to be different. He did not have any solution, only an ever stronger certainty of the necessity of a change.

The first part of their trip was quite hectic, crammed with impressions that had to be accounted for. It was everyday Europe and the lives of ordinary people he was to tell about. He interviewed, took notes. Took great joy in having Barbro there; what he described had been seen through her eyes and he felt like the articles were hers as much as his own.

Now they were really getting to know each other, together practically every minute of the day. Barbro was a good traveling companion, brave and hardy. Much of what happened to them was far from pleasurable, but she did not complain.

They lived cheaply, in small hotels and boarding houses. They usually shared a bed and sink; the rooms were small and gave no space for privacy. But they did not have any secrets to keep from each other now either. Still, there was some shyness left, or perhaps more a desire to show consideration. It existed in both of them and contributed to their still finding their love as something new and filled with possibilities.

In Paris he was going to file his last report; the rest of the trip would be vacation. They walked beneath the white bridges that reached out across the Seine's dark evening waters and suddenly felt at home, as if they had found again the city they had left behind. Though in a transformed state, as if in a dream. But wrapped in the same blue evening color.

Away—but still at home. And now he felt a violent longing to just be with Barbro, without having to think about articles to be written. Finally they had to find time for themselves and each other. Indeed, they had explored Europe, now they had to explore each other.

Maybe he was sloppier with the last articles in his series—but afterward he thought that they had turned out the best. Not so heavy and full of material like the earlier ones, more fanciful and playful and improvised.

He pulled the final sheet of paper from his typewriter. Now his work was done, vacation begun. After a few free days of their own in Paris they would head out to the coast in Normandy.

They found a place by the sea, actually a village with a single little country hotel.

The village was quite well preserved despite it having been on the coast of the invasion. Small gray houses along a dusty road that turned into a village street for a short stretch with some shops and a pub. And below the hotel there were groves of pine trees beside the beach and the water. The tides were strong here; when evening came the boats in the little harbor were lying on their sides in the sand and boys and men went out to look for crabs that had hidden among the bunches of seaweed beside the stones and islets that now stuck up from the sandy bottom. A disarmed mine lay there like a stranded sea creature, and a few rusty German soldiers' helmets sat poised on sticks that had been stuck in the sand.

Here, they thought, was where they found their first home. The rooms they had been in earlier had been nothing more than hotel rooms, temporary sleeping accommodations for travelers. Here was where they were really living and had finally unpacked their suitcases. Now they did not have to watch out for train schedules, there were no appointments.

The long, tranquil days gave them the opportunity to converse in a different way than when they had rushed from place to place and been so preoccupied with all the outward occurrences. They had to talk about themselves, about what had happened to them before they met each other and about everything else they had not had time for before. There was so much they did not know about each other that was new, and that felt it was important to find out.

But Henning was made anxious by the thought that now everything would soon be over. They had fled everyday life but it was still there at home waiting. When they went back, they would have no home in common any longer, there, they would have to each go back to their own home. Now he had gotten so used to continually being with her that it felt unbearable to think that they would live separately. That he would not get to fall asleep and wake up with her beside him, that she would not be there when he reached out his hand.

They would have to get married very soon and no one could prevent them from doing it. The difficulty would be in getting hold of an apartment. Economically it would work out; they would both work. He would write and ask if his father had any tips to offer; if there were anyone who could find an apartment it would be him.

It was morning but the room lay in shadow since the curtains were still drawn. He got up, pulled them aside a little and looked out. The sun was shining, the water glistened between the pines, and a tethered goat was grazing on the slope running down from the house. He opened the window, leaned out and listened to the lapping of the waves on the beach and the wind whispering in the treetops.

When he turned around and looked in the room Barbro had awakened, crawled out of bed and was now sitting in the middle of the wide bed on the spread out blanket. Like a flower, he thought, the white nightgown a cowl over the large quilt's heavy green leaves.

"To think that all this will disappear tomorrow," she said. "At least for us..."

"We have to get our own place soon," he said.

And for the first time during that trip he longed to go home, home to tussle with reality, to contend with getting the home they had to have.

SUNNY
SUMMER

The summer was more beautiful and warmer than any summer people could remember. The city dozed in the heat; people had a good time after the winter, which in exchange had been unusually long and cold.

Sometimes it was almost too good; the asphalt burned and bubbled, the grass lawns in the parks turned yellow, it felt stuffy on the crowded sidewalks and in enclosed courtyards. Then the most hardened city dwellers would long for shady woods and wind-swept beaches.

More often than not Gunnar would take the route past Emelie's and look in and talk for a while. The bond between the two of them was just as strong, though now he had Hjordis and the children. It was Emelie who had helped him to become who he was, who had once rescued him.

He tried to do what he could for her now. It was not so easy to do anything; she was always just as satisfied with her situation and claimed that she did not lack anything. She never asked for anything; if one wanted to give her something one had to come up oneself with what it should be. A really successful idea had been when he subscribed to a daily newspaper for her. It filled a lot of her time, and there were surely not many who were as well informed about everything that was happening around the world as Emelie was.

He had an errand on the way past her place and went up around twelve o'clock on one of the hottest days of the year. It was almost unbearably stuffy in the little apartment even though the windows stood open. Jenny was panting, mopping her face with a handkerchief and said, "Now it's almost to hot be in the city."

He hadn't thought of that before—they should go somewhere. He probably hadn't thought of it because it was hard to imagine Emelie anyplace else. From what he could remember she had never been more than forty or fifty kilometers outside of town. And the "real country" was probably not for her anyway. But, of course, there were other places ... where one could live almost like in the city, and walk on proper streets and roads and still get greenery and coolness. That vice president of a company he had done construction for recently, who owned a family hotel in Dalarna.... That was an idea. But he had to arrange everything first before he spoke to Emelie about it. It had to be contrived so that she would think she couldn't get out of going along. Otherwise, she would wriggle out of it, think it would cost too much, that he had to think of his own family first and foremost. She was so afraid of being a burden and maybe also a little afraid of new and unfamiliar things. But once she got away she would surely enjoy herself and feel good from it.

He made sure that Jenny would be free, and then he organized everything. He got them a room at the family hotel, ordered the tickets. Everything could be canceled in the worst case. But Jenny would surely say yes right away and together they would be able to convince Emelie.

It was like setting a trap. But it was necessary. If one wanted to give Emelie anything, one almost had to fool her into it. She always thought that anything that was given to her was an extravagance.

Emelie capitulated more easily and quickly than he had dared hope. Maybe because Jenny was so enthusiastic. She couldn't go and say no, because of Jenny! But certainly she was a little anxious at the thought of a journey and so many new things. How was she to behave so that Gunnar would not be ashamed of her? He knew that company vice president, too. Though the vice president would definitely not be there Gunnar said. He had several hotels and private hotels in different places throughout the country.

Worrisome—but adventurous, too. It would be so beautiful up there in Dalarna. Gunnar had bought a tourist guidebook that he gave her. It almost looked as it had looked here in the city in her childhood, wooden houses in the middle of gardens. She was a little afraid of the woods and rougher terrain, afraid of tripping and falling. But where they were going to stay wasn't any worse than visiting Skansen's historic open-air museum. And it was so pleasant at Skansen.

If there was anything she needed to purchase before the trip, then she just had to say the word, said Gunnar.

No, she didn't need anything. But Jenny thought Emelie couldn't go in that old summer coat. And that she could do with buying a new dress as well.

She went and bought a dress together with Jenny. But a coat—that would be too expensive.

Jenny was stubborn: Gunnar made good money; he wanted Emelie to buy what she needed. Finally Jenny had convinced her—Jenny dressed up in the old coat and pranced around and appeared so ridiculous that Emelie could not imagine looking like that when she traveled. Then Gunnar would truly be ashamed of her.

He came and got them in a taxi, drove with them to a coat store on Västerlånggatan, and impressed on them that it had to be a good coat. Let it cost what it cost, the main thing was that it be good-looking and well made and that Emelie feel good in it. When they were done with their purchase they were supposed to meet him at the coffee shop next door. He would sit there and read the afternoon papers while he waited.

It took them a long time to come and then they were wound up like a couple of kids. Emelie was wearing the new coat. And Jenny exploded with laughter when she told how they had tried on this and tried on that and didn't want to consider any coat good enough. Emelie had stood up for herself and said that her nephew wanted the coat to be really elegant.

Though, of course, it was frightfully expensive, too.

For Gunnar it felt like a liberation. Finally. Finally she spoke up, she would not accept just any old thing when it came to herself. For once she had not asked for the simplest and cheapest, but instead had dared demand something more and better. It was like a victory for human worth, he thought.

Indeed, the coat purchase had been a party. He seldom had so much fun with the money he earned.

He fetched them, made sure they got on the train, waved good-bye. Jenny had traveled a lot before, of course—but that was a long time ago and she was red with eagerness and excitement. Emelie on the other hand looked so small and pale, that for a moment he grew worried that the strain would be too much for her. Though once she had gotten her seat in the compartment and sat down she seemed quite pleased and expectant, too.

"I'll call tonight and make sure your trip went well," he said. "They have promised to pick you up in a car at the station. Let them take care of everything with the baggage, just give them the claim slips."

Their time in Dalarna was a completely new experience for Emelie. To be sure, she was a little uncertain and worried at first, afraid of being a bother. But everyone was so friendly. And there were plenty of people her own age; it felt like she soon knew some of them, almost like friends.

Most of all she liked to walk among the elaborately carved crosses in the old churchyard. It felt good to go there and think, about everything that had been, about all her relations who had passed on. She read the inscriptions on the gravestones, and observed how generation after generation slipped away. Felt how she herself was slipping with them. And Gunnar and his generation ... and their children and then.... Unrelenting, advancing, disappearing.

But Jenny came to fetch her away from there. They had not come to Dalarna to sit in the graveyard. Now they were going on an outing.

It turned into a kind of new home, and a new place she was familiar with and had feelings for. And she lived so well, almost so that she was ashamed. This was how only the wealthy could have lived before. Just being waited on, resting, eating, taking walks. She had never believed that she herself would experience this. But she did want to make her own bed in any case, let Jenny say what she wanted.

"If we save up maybe we can come here next summer again," she said to Jenny. She surprised herself at her own words. But Jenny took it as something natural. So maybe Emelie dared believe in it, too.

When they returned, Gunnar and his family were away, on vacation. But a few weeks later he called and asked if he could stop by and hear how it went.

When the doorbell rang Emelie assumed it was Gunnar. But the person who was standing outside was a stranger, a younger man.

"Aren't you Aunt Emelie?" he asked. "I'm Per, Per Berg."

He stepped inside, extended his hand and greeted her.

Emelie could hardly remember when she had seen him last. Probably sometime when he was little and had come here with Tyra, his mother. After that, of course, Emelie had sent a message countless times that he was welcome there, but she had never heard from him. She knew well that he had had his troubles, that he was a problem to deal with, too. She had heard Allan and Gun talk about him.

Now he wondered if she could help him. He had never asked her to before. He had been going through such a hard time and neither Allan nor Gun were in town, were probably on vacation. He had thought how Emelie had wanted to help him before, though he had not wanted to take advantage of her kindness then.

"I can certainly arrange so you can have a little food," she said.

That was not exactly what he had in mind, Emelie realized, of course. But according to what she had understood, Per had problems with alcohol and to give him money was just to make the situation worse. She knew how things had been with his mother's parents, even with his own parents, especially his father. If they got money then they just grew more depraved.

Per had often heard people talk about Emelie's helpfulness. But he did not understand that hers was of a different type from what he had encountered in most other people. Many gave not to help out, but to get away from the one who was asking. It was easiest to give something and then quickly close the door. They bought their peace.

Emelie had seldom had money to give away. Besides, she thought if someone really asked for help, you should really try to help and not do just the opposite.

But just now he could only get sandwiches and milk because she was expecting company. If he came back around six he would get dinner.

No, he did not want to be a nuisance. He had just thought that maybe he could borrow a few kronor.

She had so little money... But sandwiches....

Okay, just a cup of coffee, thanks.

Isn't Per working?

Not now, he said, it was so difficult to find anything suitable. He needed money for a night's lodging; he could get by with three kronor.

If she were only sure he was speaking the truth. But three kronor could hardly pay for any alcohol, as expensive as it was. Though a lot of beers, of course.

She took the risk and gave him the three kronor. Then he tried to raise it to five, but she pretended not to understand. And he could not count on getting money any more times; she made it perfectly clear. If he wanted food on the other hand...

The doorbell rang again—and now it was Gunnar.

Per looked at the newcomer. He could not recall that he had seen him before, though he must be his mother's half-brother. He seemed like a well-off guy, a new opportunity. There were apparently a number of relatives who were well-off, people he had never thought of as being related to him before, people who ought to be obligated to help him.

Emelie told Gunnar who her visitor was, told him, too, that Per was looking for work. Gunnar said he could probably arrange something. It happened so fast that Per could not come up with any excuses. Besides, he had actually thought of working again for a while, and now he would avoid going to the employment bureau to inquire in any case—and avoid hearing their sarcastic remarks.

He received a piece of paper with where and when he could appear, and then he rambled off. It wasn't until later that he began to wonder if he couldn't have possibly wheedled his way into an advance for the sake of family connections. But by that time he had already gotten so far from Emelie's place that he couldn't be bothered to go back.

"Be careful with that Per," said Gunnar. "He's not completely safe. Don't let him in when you are home alone. Don't give him any money—if you do that you will never get rid of him."

Emelie was not afraid of Per. But she did not believe that she could do anything for him either. She might have thought that for a moment, when he came. But then, fairly soon, she had understood, felt that it wouldn't work. Maybe she could have done something before, when she herself was younger and had energy in another way. But not now, she felt and acknowledged it. Not anymore.... But how come Gunnar dared give him a job?

The risk wasn't so great; Gunnar hardly believed that Per would come. If he came, then he would be treated like all the others. If he behaved everything would be fine, if he misbehaved he would have to leave.

But now he had to hear how Emelie's trip had gone. She had gotten a lot of color—and hadn't she actually grown a little plumper, too?

Apparently that had been a good idea of his. Now he only regretted that he had not come up with it earlier.

When Gunnar had left, Emelie sat down on the kitchen chair by the window; she usually sat there for the greater part of her days. She thought back about the weeks that had passed. If she got to go there again next summer.... It was something to look forward to when fall and winter arrived. She now had a goal that waited.

Gunnar did not know how much he had given her. He was much too kind. Even if she did not really want to admit it, she knew he would never give in before he would be allowed to pay for a similar trip again next year.

The streetcar rattled past down the hill outside her window, braking at the stop. When she leaned out she could see the green trees in the park farther down. It was still summer, a long way until next summer.

Eventually she turned back to the newspaper that she had not finished reading. She read one more time about the Gripsholm that had arrived in Göteborg with so many Swedish American tourists onboard. Some of them had been photographed, among them an old man who stood holding a photo of his relatives so that his sisters meeting him would recognize him.

Gertrud had written that they were thinking of coming, she and one of her daughters. This summer it seemed not to have happened anyway; now it sounded like they were thinking of undertaking the journey next summer. So maybe they would get to meet then—if they were both still alive.

But she could never help Per; she had met him too late.

NEIGHBORS
IN
NEGRO VILLAGE

The city grew continuously; whole new towns sprang up where before there had been woods and farmland. Now people were building mostly in the southern suburbs, in Johanneshov and Årsta and in Midsommarkransen and Hägersten. The housing shortage was considerable after the years of restriction during the war. And there were still a lot of the emergency tenements standing from the First World War on the heights besides Rosenlunds' old age home. But the real Negro Village was gone, that cluster of tenements had disappeared with the new Söder Hospital being built.

Something of Negro Village and its life would surely always be there in Per and his siblings. With Gun and Allan maybe it would mainly be something they would still be frightened of, a threat. Their childhood home had stood in the land outside the law, a wilderness where the representatives of the law had their hunting grounds and where the inhabitants were fair game all year round. But there had also existed a security there that they might miss: their mother's strong hand.

For Per, Negro Village meant—and he included the tenement buildings beside Rosenlunds as well—something more and better than for his siblings. It was his childhood and his youth, and it was there and then that he had had his time of greatness. Something of a king and hero, an unconquered fighter and a self-appointed gang leader. Back then he had both dared and been capable, back then he had not begged but taken.

Whenever he met someone from that period he could feel how the strength and joy coursed back into him, how he turned into something of the Per who had existed before they, society, had succeeded in breaking him.

He had worked for Gunnar a few days but pretty soon was fired. And with clear instructions that there was not one öre to be had from that direction anymore.

All his old possibilities began to dry up. He had tired them out, grazed on them all. Even Allan had grown tired and gotten mad.

So Per was obliged to look for work, in spite of everything. He rode as a bicycle messenger for an express service. It was heavy work and didn't pay well but gave him some freedom. Paid enough in any case so he could buy one schnapps on weekdays and a real pub crawl every Saturday. He didn't have any alcohol ration book; there was no point in even applying for one. Then he was obliged to use the taverns and bootleggers and those who used their ration book alcohol as a method of payment. Everything could be bought and sold for alcohol, it was hard currency. Per usually traded away his coffee coupons. The price was up to a kilo per liter now.

Others might be irritated that the wartime rationing had never stopped; he hoped it would continue forever. Though there was talk that coffee would soon be sold freely again.

He bicycled through the city on the hard-to-pedal three-wheeler. Despite it being late in the autumn, it was still beautiful weather and warm, though the trees were yellowing from lack of water. It had been such a drought that they had to ramp up electricity rationing. This was something he could not take advantage of so it hardly concerned him.

He was on his way to a printer's. He went the wrong way at first, had not read the paper so carefully. At the typesetter's they directed him to the bookbinder and gradually he got there.

He pushed the package over the counter, extended the delivery note to the woman standing closest. She took it, looked at him and suddenly greeted him familiarly.

Of course. He recognized her, too; they had lived as neighbors in Negro Village. Though they had not had much to do with each other, she was at least five years older.

Negro Village. It was as if he stood up straighter with pride, had become a little of the old Per again.

"Yes, goddam it," he said. "Those were the days." Did she ever see any of the old gang? Actually they should get together and talk about everything that has happened.

She hardly ever saw any of the old pals. Her papa was dead and her mom in a nursing home. But, of course, they could get together ... he could meet her, they could go out somewhere.

He had been sick and had it a little tough. Was so badly dressed, hadn't had enough money to buy a suit yet. Well then in that case he could come to her place and she would make him coffee. He promised to come. Though he wasn't at all sure that he was really going to do it.

He could just feed her a line; let her sit there with her damned coffee. But it had been a long time since he had gone to bed with a woman, and when one gave him an invitation he had better take her up on it. If she lived alone then maybe he could sleep there a few nights. Maybe she could wash and tidy up his clothes, too. He needed a woman for a while as a matter of fact, both for one and another reasons. But it didn't have to be a steady kind of thing just for that; he didn't intend to get stuck at her place.

He took out an advance of a few kronor and bought a pair of new underwear. The old ones looked so awful that he threw them out. In truth he should buy some rubbers, too. But he didn't have a lot of money and besides it was her job to make sure she didn't get knocked up.

Lilian didn't know for sure if she should regret inviting Per. He had not had exactly the best reputation at home in Negro Village, was known as a tough customer, a fighter, and a troublemaker. She knew about him taking part in a robbery, too, and going to serving time.

But he had probably changed, he didn't look so dangerous. More unhappy and mistreated, a failure. Most likely because there was no woman to take care of him, it showed so clearly on a guy when he was single.

He needed someone, maybe her. And she needed someone. Him? Two unhappy people could be happy.

Imagine getting someone to take care of. To get married and have children with. To no longer have to sit and wait—when no one came anyway. Sometimes it felt so terribly empty that she curled up in the corner of the sofa and wept.

She had had her stories, too. Believed she was in love and maybe also was loved sometimes. But most of these stories had not lasted very long. It wasn't her fault. She had still been there but the man hadn't come back.

Is there something wrong with me? She had asked herself sometimes. Do I look so bad? Why doesn't anyone stay? Why do they all disappear?

Those who had had the opportunity to choose had left, chosen someone else. But maybe Per did not have so many opportunities to choose. He had failed; you could see it on him. So then maybe he would stay, satisfy himself with her.

But did she really want him?

When the doorbell rang she still wasn't sure of the answer. Maybe it would have been better if he hadn't come; maybe she had committed something stupid when she invited him. But that he had just happened to come to her bookbinding shop—that must be fate, the inevitable that was bound to happen. She had read about such things. One could not escape what was written in the stars.

Per stayed at her place. That night and also those that followed. It just happened.

Lilian solved a lot of problems for him, was a convenience he had not really thought about before. Now he didn't have to go looking for bachelor hotels or other temporary lodgings. He got food and cigarettes and she took care of his clothes. Besides, he got her, too, and that could be good sometimes, even if he wasn't so dependent on women in that way.

She was considerably more dependent on having a guy; that he realized. She would have preferred to have a romp in the hay every evening—but he wasn't up for that. Otherwise she didn't demand much. Sometimes she whined a little if he told her to shut up or if he broke something when he got drunk. But he would wean her off of that, he couldn't stand whining. If she became a nuisance he would give her a real smack. Then they would see how that treatment worked.

Lilian paid for the rent—it was her apartment, of course. She paid for the food for both of them, too, and he thought that was as it should be; she should pay something for her entertainment. But he would not let any of his ration coupons go. She should be glad that she got to keep her own.

Even though it did not feel as vital any longer, he continued to run deliveries for the express service. Actually, she ought to be able to support a guy, but it might not be useful to become all too dependent on her.

Everything was pretty good. Except that she talked too much. He wasn't much for talking himself, didn't think there was so much to talk about. But it seemed to run out of her the whole time, prattle, prattle, prattle. Empty prattle.

Luckily he had a talent for not hearing. Her voice seemed to become part of the traffic noise, something you didn't notice once you had gotten used to it.

When he had lived with her for a few months, she came to him and said she was expecting a child. Of course, he should have given her a smack—to think that she couldn't take care of something like that! But at the same time maybe it was just as well things turned out that way, then he would be sitting more secure. Now that he had gotten used to his comforts it would be hard to go back to the old ways. So he didn't even protest when she said she wanted them to get married. She was to arrange what needed to be done, he would go accompany her only when absolutely necessary—to the parish office, for example, to ask to have the banns published and to the minister who would marry them.

Without really knowing how it had happened, he had glided into a new way of living. Now he no longer roamed the streets fighting for money. Instead he had the express service a few hours now and then, and spent the rest of the day in an old armchair that her sick father had sat in. The old man had even been sitting there when he died.

At Lilian's he regained some of his old self-assurance. Now he did not have to do the self-pity act any longer. When he could command there was no reason to ask. Lilian obeyed. She took care of him, gave him meals, brought home beer. Some of her father's old suits were still left; as far as clothing went he had never been very particular. He had never been able to tolerate snobs.

He found himself nicely settled. And Lilian did as well. Maybe she had dreamt of something different and better, but she had still found someone to take care of and someone to be dependent on. Per became a kind of substitute for her parents, an authority. She could grow a little afraid of him—as she had been afraid of her father once upon a time. Per was, of course, not really kind. But men weren't like that; experience had taught her that. He hit her sometimes—though not especially hard or often. In that respect her father had been much worse, as long as he had had the strength. My God, so many times she had been hit.

She told Per about her childhood. About her mother who had never wanted to do anything new, about how she herself always had to take responsibility for her siblings. She had never been able to be out with people her own age, like the others.

And as soon as her siblings could take care of themselves, they, too, had disappeared. She no longer had much contact with them, and did not understand why. She tried to invite them home sometimes, but they never had time.

While she talked, the snow was falling outside the window; the flickering whiteness grew denser, like a curtain that was concealing the wide avenue, Ringvägen, where the lights of the streetcars sometimes gleamed through the mist.

He came over to the window, stood beside her and looked out.

"Damn," he said. "You can't even see the lights from the café. I think I'll go over there anyway and grab a beer."

"There's some at home," she said.

"Yeah, that's true," he said. "But I'll get away way from your damn chatter for a while."

He left. And when the big chair was free she sat down in it for a while, as if in secret.

Just like Papa, she thought. He said that, too. And would go down and grab a beer, as long as he had the strength to go out.

THE
WHITE HILLS

The snow lay like a woolly sheepskin over the city. The White Hills finally lived up to their name, transformed into a billowing, white, snowy landscape. Sheds and ramshackle houses almost disappeared beneath the snow, turned into romantic Christmas card motifs.

From their window in an old apartment house on Skånegatan, one could look out across the white landscape with its small houses and heavy churches. Farther away the smokestacks of the factories at Barnängen stuck up alongside Hammarby highway. On the other side of the as yet open and dark water, the woods began, only nibbling a little at the edges of the built-up heights of Hammarbyhöjden.

Henning and Barbro had long looked for a place to live in vain. They had applied at the local housing authority, and become members of the tenants' housing association. Nothing had yielded a result yet. Not even Henning's father had managed to arrange anything for them.

But Mikael, Emelie's old childhood friend, had been in the hospital for a long time. He had hoped to be able to return home again, but gradually understood that it would probably never be. His apartment had stood empty the whole time. It was little, one room and a kitchen. But they were welcome to live there, he had Emelie tell them.

One person is dead—another gets bread. That rule certainly applied when it came to housing. Despite the fact that so much was being built, the lines only grew longer. A large part of it depended upon the fact that people now demanded a lot more space than before. Some ten years earlier at least four or five children had been required for a family to get to move into a little two-room apartment in a building with large families. Now they were saying that each person should have the right to his or her own room.

No matter how small and old-fashioned Mikael's apartment was, it was better than nothing at all. If they got that then they would get the chance to exchange it for something better.

Mikael died before the contract was completed but the landlord did not make trouble and let the oral agreement stand. Henning was able to go see him and write a new lease. He did it without having seen the apartment; Mikael's furniture was still in it. Mikael had not owned much, but he had still written a will. Emelie was to have what there was. The young people could have some chairs if they wanted them. Mikael had been a good friend of Henning's grandfather, Olof, and wanted to give something to remember him by to Olof's grandchildren.

Together with Emelie, Henning and Barbro went to look at the apartment and organize what was to be moved out of it. The stairway up was dark and there was no elevator; the building was old. The apartment was on the fifth floor and during the last period of his life Mikael had had difficulty going up and down. Emelie did not have such an easy time with stairs anymore either, she had to walk slowly and stand and catch her breath at every landing. Henning and Barbro really had to hold themselves back so as to not rush on ahead.

Ture Lindgren, stood the name on the doorplate. It was Thumbs's old doorplate that his son Mikael had taken over once upon a time. Thumbs had been dead for more than twenty years. Henning had a screwdriver with him and when he took away the old plate he could see the marks of others that had been there previously.

Indeed, the apartment was little; in a new building the kitchen would have been called a kitchenette. But it faced south, and outside was a wide-open view of the snow-covered hills. Mikael had kept it nice and tidy, even if the dust had settled during the long period he had been in the hospital. With Allan's help, he had repainted and papered it.

The decoration was simple, the furnishing spare. Mikael had been a seaman for many years, and gotten used to not having space for personal possessions. The old iron bedstead was not much to hold onto, nor the bedding either. But the chairs were fun and surely old. Henning inspected them and could not find one nail; that must be an indication. And Emelie remembered that the chairs had been in Thumbs and Matilda's old home on Åsöberget. There was not much left from that time, from her childhood home. She only had the little bureau that her mother had received as a wedding present once upon a time. A real antique, August had said. And it was in ... let's see now ... yes, it was in 1867 that they got married, exactly eighty years ago last fall.

Henning had a bundle of big cardboard boxes with him that he unfolded and fastened together with gummed tape. They began to take out what was in the drawers and cupboards. Some of it was only fit to be thrown away, other things Emelie wondered if the young people wanted to keep. Whatever was left over, Emelie would take home with her. In the attic storage that belonged to the apartment, were some boxes of letters and papers that apparently had belonged to Thumbs; it was best if Emelie went through them to see if anything should be saved.

There was also a souvenir from Mikael's many years on the sea. Mikael had designated a model sailing ship for Allan. Allan had lived with Mikael for a time and been so interested in that model.

Afterward they went home to Emelie's, were able to wash the dust off their hands and were invited to stay for coffee. While they sat in her kitchen she told them how it had been when Henning's grand-mother was once setting up house, how Bärta had invited home a gang of brick carriers who had helped her put together furniture from crates and plank ends. In those days people did not have the money to buy very much and there were no home loans either.

She showed Barbro the bureau that she had talked about. It was sweet, Barbro thought, even if it was a little clunky. And she also liked the story that Emelie told. About Lotten who had been promised a white wedding dress but asked to be given a bureau instead.

Barbro wasn't going to be dressed like a bride either. They were going to go to City Hall they had decided. They did not consider themselves Christians and thought it would be false to get married in a church. Afterward they were just going to have coffee at home at her parents' with their very closest friends and relations.

It was calm and cozy to sit and chat a while with Emelie. But they did not want to wait until Jenny came home from the theater, since they planned on being up late the following evening, when they were going to go up and clean their new apartment.

Finally! Finally a door to close, a place to hide, a place where they could be alone. Was it true?

They did not get much work done those first few evenings. First they had to find each other once more. Oh, it had been so long. Now they felt how difficult the period had been since they had come back from their trip. This was what they had dreamed of, a shack in their existence, a home in the world. It was happiness. They did not need anything more than this, which was how it felt now at least.

They went straight there after work every evening. They would usually stand a minute by the window in the dark room and look out over the white hills below, before they were separated for the evening again. No people, as if they were alone in the world, a shimmering white but dead world. Just now they weren't frightened by the thought.

Gradually, curtains appeared at the windows and paper on the cupboard shelves. They washed the newly bought china and put it away, filled the bookshelves with their books and the wardrobe with their clothes. The walls looked really bare for a long time; they did not have any paintings. Henning got a hold of some large posters. One was from a Danish music week and showed a plump female Pan. They put it up with thumbtacks.

They would have really liked to have a big and comfortable bed, one like they had in the little French hotel they had stayed in. But all their measuring showed that practically speaking it was impossible. With such a piece of furniture in the room they would hardly have space for anything else. They satisfied themselves with two ordinary beds without heads or feet. For everyday they could be pushed together. When they had company they could be placed separately and with the help of a few cushions be turned into ottoman sofas.

They day they got their furniture and rug they could finally see their work as good as done. The plants Barbro had brought from home stood on the windowsill; beside the bookcase stood the radio Henning had received as a birthday present some years earlier. It was a real home they had gotten.

Though there was one worry they would have, they realized this: heating. Wood was no longer rationed, but since both of them worked they could not light the fire until they got home and then it would be pretty cold inside. As long as electricity was rationed, using electric heaters was not allowed. But in a few months it would be spring and next fall maybe electricity would be freed up again.

Now they had kept the fire burning the whole evening and it had gotten quite warm. Still the cold was close by, it lay as if in ambush in the walls.

Laughing, they pulled the bedspreads off the fine new beds that were so primly made beside each other. They crept down under the thick protective comforters and hid there.

This was happiness: to have their little cave in the world where they could find each other.

Outside, the world was still cold and white and empty, and the clock up in the high church steeple struck twelve and died away.

Just under a week later they got married.

GÖTGATAN

Götgatan was the street of lights and youth, the goal of the evening. Irresistibly, people were drawn there, tumbling out from some of the dark side streets and standing there suddenly as if blinded and stunned. Here neon lights flashed and traffic bustled, lines encircled the movie theaters' ticket booths, and restaurants, coffee shops, and cafés filled up. Crowds of people milled on the sidewalks and jostled each other in front of the shops' display windows. Beside the terrace at Björns Trädgård Park the gang gathered. At what had once been called Södra bantorget, the new civic center with baths, library, and assembly halls had been erected.

Götgatan was the symbol of joy and free time. It offered a few blinking, roaring, and intensely alive city blocks alongside the many dark and narrow back streets with their sleeping apartment houses and work places, silent for the evening.

Something was always happening here. People met their friends, petty quarrels and arguments would arise, the news was pasted up in the news offices' display windows. Everything was well known and unfamiliar at the same time. You could point to every building or street corner and remember something that had occurred just there: in that store you could buy a confirmation outfit, at that movie theater they had a sign up, "Attention! Sound film!" longer than anywhere else, on that corner, a bolting horse ran in a display window. And while one remembered, one's gaze would wander anxiously to take in what had not yet happened, everything that could happen— and which usually did happen.

Some few evenings the street lay empty and quiet, with the normally open and empty establishments closed. Those who came there on such an evening, perhaps on a Good Friday or on Easter Day, might feel as if they were locked out of their homes. Where could they go if they could not go to Götgatan?

Good Friday—the day of death. Deathly quiet, deathly boring.

On previous Easter holidays, they had shown religious films or animal films. Even if the programs did not seem so appealing the audience came; they had to have something to do. It was *Golgotha* or *Bosambo* back then. This holiday it had been announced that all movie theaters would be kept closed on Good Friday and Easter Day.

Idle groups of people were hanging out on Good Friday afternoon at Björns Trädgård Park and outside the closed movie theaters and cafés. People were cold, there was a biting wind. But they stayed where they were, as if they could not really believe that Götgatan would let them down.

The gang grew, new groups appeared. People yawned listlessly, tried to laugh once more at old worn-out jokes, whistled at girls passing by. Everything without any pleasure or drive. Nothing was the same, the street was a different from the one they knew, foreign, silent, almost hostile. The Garden of Eden was closed.

Some of the drunken ones began to holler and quickly gained a large audience. At least something was happening, something that made the street and the day a little less dead. The hollering could be interpreted as something of a call to rebel, a protest against all those who were respectable and in authority.

A police car cruised by but there were not many who noticed it.

The police, who suspected that something was up, parked their car a short distance away and walked closer. But the increasing numbers that were gathering didn't want to miss the solitary little attraction of the evening. Grousing and squabbling, they followed the police who dragged the drunken ones off to their car. A few feeble and not really serious attempts to free those taken were made, but didn't lead to anything. The mood was more high-spirited than rancorous; the taking away of the drunks had its entertainment value as well on a day like this. Though when the people apprehended struggled and were shoved forcefully into the police car, the atmosphere changed, then people felt a sudden solidarity.

"It stinks like brass! Damned cops! Fucking pigs!"

The police had a hard time freeing themselves; one of them pulled out his billy club. The crowd surged back and forth around their car. Some found stones and threw them. And the police scrambled hurriedly into their car and took off.

Naturally people understood that they had called for back-ups. But now things had gotten going, now people did not intend to give up, now they wanted a rumble. And there came a whole lot more police and more youths were enticed to the scene by the cries and the din, and it took several hours before the howling crowds were at last dispersed.

The rumor of the disturbance spread and people waited for a continuation. On the evening of the day after Easter, the riots took on a tougher character. The police had armed themselves with sabers and riding whips, and it didn't take long before the entire Götgatan had been transformed into a battlefield.

Now was not a silent and closed Good Friday, but an evening where many people were in movement. The youths could slip in and out among the many people who were out on completely legitimate errands. Tranquil couples who had intended to go see Adolf Jahr in *The Poetry of Ådalen* suddenly found themselves drawn into a completely different drama. It reached its culmination around nine o'clock when large crowds were on their way to and from the many movie theaters. Police on horseback swung their whips and others charged about with sabers bared. People were forced to quickly plunge down side streets.

"Out of the way! Hurry it up!"

Panic-stricken people who barely comprehended what it was all about, were forced into wild flight, sought shelter in doorways but were driven out, hid themselves in the shadow of back streets; traffic was held up and rerouted. Howling mobs of youths swarmed across sidewalks and pavements, dispersed when the police advanced on them, regrouped, and pursued the retreating police. The whole street seemed turned into a frenzied sea where new waves ceaselessly rolled forward and crashed against each other. The police's hard methods against those who innocently happened to get caught in the middle angered many. Didn't people have the right to walk on the streets and go to whatever movie theater they pleased? Could the police deal with people any way they pleased? Many people went to Götgatan just to show that they did not want to give way to violence. Others were probably just curious. And the youths might feel that they had a responsibility as some kind of organizers. Here were people coming from all over the city and traveling from out in the country to experience the riots—therefore it was important not to disappoint them.

The following evening, an ordinary weekday evening, the street filled with people. A strange atmosphere, a mixture of expectation and dread, of carnival and revolution. Groups of howling youths pushed through the crowds, empty bottles whizzed through the air and were crushed on the cobblestones. Some of the youths had brought hatpins with them and tried to jab the police horses in their rumps. One gang took hold of a hotdog stand on wheels and rushed off with the stand and the enclosed proprietress who was screaming in terror.

Laughter and shrieks. Playing and hatred. Something of a bullfight. Youths who hooted with delight when they succeeded in throwing themselves out of the way of the lash as the whips cracked. Or howled in pain when they did not get out of the way in time.

Most of those directly involved were youths. Police had learned from the first evenings and from the newspapers' criticism, had become more tactical. Now they let the curious and the adult pedestrians be and concentrated on the mischief makers. They had also sneaked a large number of plain-clothes officers in among the onlookers; they could suddenly and unexpectedly step in or give those in uniform instructions.

Along with the many who were drawn to the disturbances were also individuals who hated and wanted revenge, who did not dare act alone but egged others on: "Stick it to those damned Nazis! Bash those fucking cops!"

For yet another evening the riots raged. The curious grew in numbers each time, and on the final evening it was estimated that ten thousand people had gathered.

Cars with loudspeakers drove back and forth, and a clergyman and a youth leader urged people through a microphone to keep things under control. But the youth leader inadvertently received a blow to the face from a policeman's billy club and had to be taken to the hospital.

It was being said that gang members had armed themselves with pistols and homemade bombs—but it was most likely only rumors. Despite the number of people it was not as unruly as the previous evenings. Maybe people had begun to tire; many of the most active had received their blows and scrapes.

The next evening, on the first of April, the police formed a ring around the central parts of the street. Many people had to take detours to get home and complained—but the evening stayed calm and the week of rioting was over.

Now people were asking: what had happened—and why? Had all that trouble really been brought on by nothing, by a dreary holiday's idleness? And then been blow up by the overdone and unsuccessful measures taken by the police?

Didn't there have to be something more—a deeper unrest, a hatred, a poison?

Henning had heard his parents talking about the hunger riots during the First World War. His father, Erik, had been very active, gotten a saber blow to the head, had been hailed as a hero in a tightly packed People's Hall.

At that time there were many powerful reasons for agitation. Poverty, food being supplied on the black market to armies on both sides, big oppositions. Things like that were over now, or at least not nearly as common anymore. In those days it must have been easy to protest, in fact necessary. Back then, one knew clearly what one wanted and what had to be changed. If one could not formulate one's demands with one's brain, one could feel it in the gut.

For a moment Henning could almost envy those who had it so easy, who without doubts could give their unrest a name and a label.

Beautiful labels with honorable words: radicalism, demands for justice, class consciousness. There was *freedom, equality* and *brother-
hood,* and *on with the fight against suffering.* They had banners, slogans and songs, plans and dreams for the future.

And now? Now they had nothing, only the lost howling and the
indefinable unrest. Others could apply labels: rowdy mentality, gang
behavior.

Couldn't one find some acceptable cause, some respectable reason?
Or at least some extenuating circumstances?

Henning himself had not experienced any of the riots. They had
spent Easter out in the cottage. Then he had been away for a short
reporting trip and gotten home the evening the police had formed
their ring around Götgatan. He had thought of taking that route
home to see how things were—but been stopped. Maybe they would
have let him pass if he had shown his journalist I.D., but he did not
bother to try; there seemed to be nothing to see.

Even if he had not experienced more than that of what had happened, he thought he had felt some of the atmosphere. The feeling of
an occupied city. He had not been spoken to the way the police spoke
to him since he had done his military service. He had kept quiet and
obediently taken another route.

But he had certainly felt the urge to protest, maybe even with violence?

He remembered the Sabbath Saboteur, how he himself and his
friends had been taken up with the pointless explosions. And then,
too, there had been some of this feeling of revolt, like during an occupation. People had set off explosions during the war like that, flum-
moxed the authorities.

It would soon be three years since the war had ended. It was easy
to recall the memory of the delirium of armistice day, but almost
impossible to understand that feeling one had had, that all their problems were solved and that everything could be different. Much was
still the same, he might think now. Yet still there was so much of the
war left.

What people talked about the most every day was all the rationing and restrictions that were still making themselves felt. But that wasn't anything that could have mainly upset the youths who had been the most active during the riots.

In their case it was probably more because peace had not yielded any true peace. Those who, in the delirium of the peace, had dared believe in a better world, must be disappointed now. Nazism's reign of terror had indeed been broken, the concentration camps had been emptied and the occupied countries liberated. Nazism as a movement could be considered dead. But its poison still remained: the methods, the incitement, the hatred, the violence.

In India, Gandhi, the prophet of non-violence, had been murdered by a religious fanatic. In Palestine, full-scale civil war was expected between Jews and Arabs once British troops pulled out from there. In Czechoslovakia, the Communists had taken power through a coup; many members of the government had fled or committed suicide.

But the concern about what had happened and was happening in the world could hardly be conscious among those who had been yelling on Götgatan. They were not mourning Gandhi, probably were not worried about the developments in Palestine or Czechoslovakia.

No, it had to be something else.

Perhaps because all norms had been dissolved by a war? The violence became not just accepted but glorified—under the requirement that it be turned "in the right direction." In film after film one could now relive the war in romanticized form. Brave invasion soldiers stole through the dark and stuck knives into the backs of enemy sentries, resistance fighters burned down houses and executed colluders with the enemy, partisans blew up troop transports.

It was easy and gratifying to romanticize the violence, almost a patriotic or civil duty. Film audiences could hoot with glee when unsuspecting German soldiers were stabbed in the backs. It was exciting and besides, one could imagine that one was part of the fight against evil as well, against the tyranny of Nazism.

Everything that one might believe was forbidden was allowed if it attained some goal. One could degrade and torture people, use all kinds of threats. The one who was in the right had the right to everything.

Wouldn't people be influenced by such attitudes? Maybe wish to play a heroic role themselves? If there were no reality that corresponded to the romanticized violence of this world picture, then they would create it. Police were apparently willing to help out.

Henning thought quite a bit about the riots as they talked about them time after time in his discussion group. But they could not come up with any real explanation for them.

The reasons remained hidden for his group. But the risks seemed to be even more clearly illuminated. If such tumult could arise without any actual reason or any organization behind it—what could be accomplished by organized forces, which could also point to reasons and goals?

The thought was unsettling. He said something about how fragile demonstrations were, how easily they could be misused. So little was required to put the masses in motion. And the world was full of leadership figures and demagogues who speculated on how such mass movements could be driven on and exploited.

And had he learned from Nazism's methods? Hitler was certainly a master of the subject; no one else had so quickly and effectively been able to whip up a worldwide storm.

Henning felt like the world was revealing itself, was showing how much of Nazism had survived the fall and demise of organized Nazism. Which maybe had always been there, in fact, and was inside every person? Not as a doctrine but as a mentality.

Nazism was maybe the wrong term, but it was the name that was easiest for him to give. Such was his experience and the time he had been living in. Others with other experiences might perhaps give the phenomenon a different name. He called it Nazism.

II

A TIME OF
TRANSFORMATION

The years after war are a time of ruins. Then come the new transformations: the demolition, the new construction.

Major and revolutionary events were being played out in the world. Empires fell apart and new states came into existence—India, Indonesia. In China the lengthy civil wars ended with a large Communist victory. Germany was divided into a west and an east state. The western powers joined together in an Atlantic alliance with the sting pointed toward the east; the newly conquered and disarmed Germans who were to be taught to be pacifistic, were provided with new weapons and were given a part in the task to defend Europe. In Korea, war broke out and the United Nations stood up for South Korea's defense against Communist North Korea. The Russians got the atom bomb, President Truman gave the order for the production of American hydrogen bombs, several big cases of atomic espionage were uncovered. Hostilities grew, a new world war was thought to be near.

In this unsettled world, Sweden lay like a calm oasis apart. Of course, it tried to participate, relief work continued and new actions were initiated; a field hospital was sent to South Korea.

But in that little oasis people were living in a time of transformation as well.

In just a few years, people had begun to emerge from the post-war crisis household economizing. One goods rationing after another was phased out; at last even the coffee coupons could be abolished. Salaries rose, new reforms were decided on: nine-years of comprehensive school, corporal punishment in schools forbidden, freedom of religion carried out. Some of the political figures in the foreground stepped down, Wigforss and Möller, and the Social Democrats led the government together with the Center Party. Gustaf V died and was succeeded by his seventy-year-old son.

In the city, some of the biggest streets lay torn up for several years; work was being done on the new subway system that was the means of transportation of the future and would connect the new satellite towns on the outskirts with the offices and stores in the central city. The first big green subway trains were already running between Slussen and Hökarängen. At the same time the number of automobiles was increasing, so many that a new feature was installed: parking meters.

A plan for the total transformation of large parts of the center was adopted; they wanted to "build for the centuries." From the rubble and ruins of the old Klara neighborhood, a new city of glass and concrete would arise. Like trumpets to the sky, five high-rise buildings would blare their fanfares over all the towers and the music of past epochs.

Transformations happened quickly now; the city's pulse beat ever faster. The person who wanted to keep up with the times soon felt rushed.

Henning did not feel like he was rushing but still felt how he kept on the move in another way from before. During the slightly more than four years he had been married, everything had changed: his demands and his everyday life, things around him, he himself. Barbro was still the same, it felt that way and he hoped and believed that it was so as well.

Before they got married he was a boy—now he had responsibility, had a child himself. They had a daughter who would soon be two years old and Barbro was expecting again. When they got married they had moved into Mikael's little lair, then they had changed apartments twice; most recently they had changed from a modern three-room in newly-built Årsta to an old-fashioned spacious two-room on Hantverkaregatan, where they were living now. It was the first time they had lived on Kungsholmen, and it was also something new and different, though in a positive way; in the suburbs he had never really felt happy.

When he had gone traveling with Barbro he had been a young and insecure reporter on his first international trip, now he was assistant editor-in-chief and sent out others on similar missions. In their first home they had barely had room for their beds, now they had a beautiful and well-furnished home. Back then they had not had a lot of money and had lived mostly on porridge and sausage; now at least they did not have to skimp when it came to food. At one time he had been happy when he had been able to afford a bicycle, now he had had a car for some months.

If someone had told him four years ago that he would be living this way he would have taken it as a good joke, laughed at the crazy idea. Now it felt completely natural, one quickly became accustomed. To the point where toward the end of the month he might in fact think he had it a little stressful and would probably have to ask for a raise soon.

Naturally they didn't live a luxurious life, only a life that he would have called so four years ago. They bought what they needed, without thinking too much. Well, the car in any case ... but there were so many who had a car and he could use it for work, too. They had not gotten their own summerhouse—though they could stay with his mother and John as often as they liked. John had even offered that they could build their own cottage on the property and he had promised to help with the construction. It had not happened yet, it still cost a lot.

At times he felt giddy at the thought of how quickly everything had changed. But usually he barely gave it a thought.

BRIEF REUNION

For many years there had been talk of Gertrud and one of her daughters undertaking a trip to "the old country." But time after time they had been forced to delay their plans. First for economic reasons, then because of Gertrud's illness.

Emelie had probably never dared take those plans really seriously, had not been able to believe that she would get to see her sister again. The distance between them was too great. One made such a journey only once in a lifetime, Rudolf had said before they left.

Of course, there were people who had come back, who maybe didn't like it over there. But for Rudolf that would have been the same as admitting failure; he would rather have tried once more in yet another foreign land. And Gertrud had always done as Rudolf wanted.

No, Emelie had always believed that the farewell she said to them one fall day in 1909 was a farewell forever. That the parting was as irrevocable as if Rudolf and Gertrud had died. Even though they were alive they were still lost. Sometimes it happened that Emelie said to herself that she was the last among her siblings. It didn't do to count the one who was so far away.

Then Rudolf had died, a number of years ago. And last fall Gertrud. So it turned out the way she had thought: the one who left did not come back.

Indeed, Emelie had mourned when she learned that Gertrud had died. Though it had not felt as hard as when August had passed away. August had been close by the whole time. The real sorrow for Gertrud no longer being there, Emelie had felt a long time ago, when she and Rudolf had left.

If she tried to be really honest with herself she had to admit: her brothers had been closer to her than her sister. Even during the time when Gertrud lived at home. She did not really know why. It wasn't because Gertrud had taken Rudolf from her once upon a time; she had accepted that as being for the best. Maybe more because Gertrud had never shown true solidarity with their brothers. She had condemned August and disowned him when he had been adopted by the wealthy Bodins. His difficulties, the deference he had to show to his new surroundings, these she had never tried to understand. And Olof, with his restlessness and his dreams of being an artist, she had never really understood him either, barely had more than contempt to spare him.

But probably all that was mostly due to the fact that she had always thought and felt precisely as Rudolf did.

It was forgotten now, forgiven, that which could be forgiven. Gertrud had not always had such an easy time of it either.

No, Gertrud she had never believed she would get to meet again. But that one of Gertrud's children was going to come was not as unbelievable. The old rules did not apply to young people; they traveled around in the world as if there were no distances anymore. Emelie and Gertrud had exchanged letters for all these years, had written a few letters a year. But at the last stage of Gertrud's life she had not been able to write by herself. Then Greta had done it, her second oldest daughter. Anna, who was the oldest, lived in Chicago with her husband. Greta somewhere near New York, like Gertrud. Rudolf had been with the streetcars in New York, a "collector" Gertrud had written, it was surely some kind of conductor. Here at home he had been a driver; Emelie remembered how grand he had looked in his uniform with the shiny buttons and the whip. When he had the whip he had actually been called a coachman; that was in the days of horse-drawn streetcars.

Greta had only been seventeen when they emigrated; she was married to an American now and probably never spoke Swedish with anyone. It had been hard to understand some of what Gertrud had written. Greta's Swedish was almost impossible to understand. Not even Henning, who usually helped Emelie with the deciphering, was sure what she meant all the time. Emelie had to ask Greta to write in English; that way Henning in any case could translate it and give a clearer meaning.

On her bureau Emelie had a framed photograph that she looked at especially carefully when she received the America letters. It showed four generations: Gertrud and Greta, Greta's daughter Jane, and Jane's firstborn, Gladys. The little one must be ten years old now. Neither Jane nor the girl spoke a single word of Swedish. They were completely American.

Recently Emelie had looked especially carefully at the picture. Now Greta had written that she and Jane were going to come to Sweden at the end of July. Greta was going to celebrate her sixtieth birthday in the city where she had been born; the trip was a birthday present from her husband and children. Jane was going to go along to keep her company, but their husbands were going to stay conveniently at home.

Emelie had been at Greta's birthday celebrations before. The last family event she had celebrated together with Gertrud's family had been, in fact, Greta's seventeenth birthday. There had not been much celebrating, of course. It had been a few days before the big strike broke out. In truth, Emelie had gone to discuss the strike with Rudolf; she had not been really sure if she was going to strike or not. She was the manager at the perfume factory at that time. Greta's birthday had been a pretext. She had given Greta a fine bar of soap that she had been able to buy cheaply at the factory.

Then the strike came and after that Rudolf could not return to the streetcar job. That was when they emigrated.

Now Greta was coming home to turn sixty. A little slender and frightened girl had become a rather commanding and substantial middle-aged lady, she was a grandmother as well. There was not much to recognize in her features.

Naturally it wasn't just Greta who had changed. Emelie herself had not yet turned forty when they left; now she was over eighty. It was lucky she had sent pictures that Henning had taken so that Greta was prepared.

They were going to stay at a hotel. It was probably best that way; in America they were surely used to more space than Emelie could provide.

If Greta was coming, then she would naturally want to meet all her relatives, even August's children who were her cousins, of course. Emelie understood it was something she would have to try to arrange. It wasn't so easy, she hadn't seen them since Ida's funeral. It did not happen very often and the only one who kept in touch was Karl Henrik; he usually sent a flowering plant at Christmas and called sometimes to ask how Emelie was. Emelie had a bit of a hard time with the telephone. She did not hear very well. And she always thought that calling him herself was difficult; you never knew if you were bothering him either.

Jenny solved the problem, in her way.

"We can ask Gunnar to call," she said. "He will gladly do it, they have business together, too."

And after a few days Gunnar was able to report that it was all arranged. Karl Henrik's sisters were apparently away, but he would be home.

Gunnar would be in town, too, and promised to come for an appropriate occasion. But he didn't speak English. The best thing would be if Henning could be there. Elisabet and Lennart could also manage with the language.

It wasn't until then that Emelie really understood she would not be able to talk to Gertrud's granddaughter. With Greta it was certainly different; she probably spoke Swedish better than she wrote it and in any case she would surely understand most things.

But the distance had been so great: they didn't even speak the same language. One could get that far from those one thought of as the "closest kin."

She had to at least ask Henning what hello and welcome and please were called in that language, and learn it. She could not just stand there like a fool when she, for the first and most likely only time, was to meet Gertrud's grandchild.

They arrived, by boat to Göteborg, and from there by train to Stockholm. The same route that the family had taken when they emigrated, though in the opposite direction, of course.

When Emelie stood on the platform at Central Station and waited for the train, she could for a moment imagine that the years that had passed had been erased, and that she was standing there to wave farewell. Together with Thumbs and Knut, Rudolf's father and brother. They were both dead now. Knut's children maybe still lived in Göteborg; Emelie didn't know, never heard from them.

Back then it had been a steam engine that had billowed steam and slowly puffed away; now an electric train softly and almost noiselessly glided in. Rows of cars and shiny glass windows rushed past before the train stopped with a little lurch.

Were they on it? Would they miss each other in the bustle?

But then there was someone who was waving through a window that had been pulled down and calling: "Aunt Emlee! Aunt Emlee!"

In the photographs Greta had appeared commanding, almost stern. It was evidently an expression for the photo; in reality she was plump and soft, in fact almost wet. She cried in happiness at seeing them again, she cried when she spoke of her mother's death, of her children's weddings, of her grandchildren. Then she took Emelie and Jenny, each by the arm; she had met Jenny, too, of course, long ago.

Henning had to take care of Mrs. Jane Wardner who was his second cousin. She seemed cool and slender beside of her mother, elegant in her gray traveling suit, almost pedantically well groomed. She asked in what way they were related and he tried to explain, though he couldn't think of the word for second cousin in English. Before they arrived at the car they had gotten to the point where they were calling each other Jane and Henning.

As they drove across town, Greta declared that she didn't recognize anything at all; everything had evidently changed. It was something of a disappointment; she had believed that for the most part everything would be the same as before.

Then there were a few hectic weeks. Greta puffed and perspired in the heat, but had endurance. She had to see everything. The Stockholm

Palace, the department stores, the museums, Skansen outdoor museum and Drottningholm Palace. And naturally what was left of the neighborhood where she herself had grown up.

Henning tried to take as much time off as possible, and drive them around in his car. And since there was a lot of material for reportage in Greta's experiences, he got subject matter for new articles at the same time.

Afterward he would be grateful that he had taken the time and the trouble. He got to hear a lot he had not known about earlier days—or that maybe he had heard but forgotten. About Emelie herself and her siblings and their parents. Greta asked and Emelie told. They were down at Nytorget and saw the house where Emelie and Gertrud's mother grew up once upon a time, and where the two sisters had also lived for a period; their mother had moved home to her childhood home with them and Olof when she had become a widow. They were out on Åsöberget and Emelie showed them the cottage that her parents had moved into as newlyweds, and where she and all her siblings had been born. And they went to the part of town that had once been called Siberia, and found the neighborhood where Rudolf and Gertrud had lived and where Greta had lived as a child and a youth. So much was left, still. They could even find what remained of the cosmetics factory that Emelie and Gertrud had done piecework for when they had lived on Åsöberget—part of its office was there in Skansen's historic city neighborhood. But the house that Emelie had moved into when Gertrud got married was gone; Katarinavägen went through there now.

Everywhere Greta asked and Emelie told. The more she told the more she seemed to remember, the past came to life. Henning had to try and help Greta translate as much as possible so that Jane would know what was so significant about the tumbledown dwellings and slummy buildings they saw. Then he had to take the time to take photos also. Greta wanted to have pictures so she could show everything to her siblings and children when she got back home.

Henning had not been especially interested in what had happened to his relatives in a time that was past; he had a rather foggy image of their existence. He who was young was so caught up with living in the present, viewed the past as something dead and of no concern. Now that he had grown more settled, he could listen in another way and find that what was being told concerned him as well.

The most remarkable thing indeed, was seeing Emelie's transformation, how she revived when she got to go back to the past, how her eyes shone with the reflection of her memories, how her voice grew younger, warmer. It was a different Emelie than the old and somewhat quiet one he thought he knew, it was a person who once had lived as intensely and as engaged in life as he himself.

One day Karl Henrik played the host.

Truthfully, he had not really intended to meet the America relatives for more than a lunch and afterward maybe arrange to show off some of his buildings to them. But then he and his son were alone in town, his wife and daughters were out at their summerhouse, and nothing in particular demanded his presence at the firm.

Maybe he had a little guilty conscience, too, knew that his father had liked his old sister so much. He should have gotten in touch with Emelie a little more often now that both of his parents were dead. She and his half-brother Gunnar were in fact the only close relatives he had besides his siblings and his own family.

At one time he had been a little ashamed of these poor relations, preferred not to remember that his real grandfather had been a simple workman in the Bodin Company. He felt a kinship with the Bodins, with those who had adopted his father and not with those who had given him life and birth. But over the years—and maybe because his own self-confidence grew—his viewpoint changed. It made no difference who his father's parents had been, the important thing was that he himself was who he was: the administrator of the Bodin Company and largest shareholder. It was the same with relatives as with grades earned at school—such things only meant something when a person was unknown. One did not ask to see a prominent architect's grades before one engaged him for a construction project. It was just as unlikely that there would be any conceivable situation where someone would cast aspersions on Karl Henrik Bodin because his grandfather had been a herring packer. Just the opposite; many bragged about their humble origins. It gave an extra effective background to their own successes.

He inquired as to who would be coming along. Together with himself and his son they would apparently be ten people. Henning was bringing his wife and his mother, and Gunnar could also take the time off. That meant three cars. Besides, he would let his son Claes manage the whole thing and make the arrangements; it could be a useful task for him to practice doing.

His son was ambitious; it turned into a huge program. He wanted to present a picture of how the city had grown in recent decades. He showed maps at their office that gave a clear picture of how construction had extended beyond the old tollgates more and more, he had the cars drive to sites where work was going on that would make the city's continued growth possible. They saw how a new bridge, Liljeholmsbro, was being built; they saw how preparations for a new bridge that would lead Södergatan's traffic in toward Tegelbacken were underway, they saw the construction of the subway. Then Karl Henrik invited them for lunch at Operakällaren Restaurant, and afterward they continued out to the new town of Vällingby where lots of little houses were shooting up from the mud of fields and farmland. It was going to be an ABC town, a new type of suburb, Claes told them. A, workplaces, B, homes, and C, a planned town center. Everything would be here. And here, where new things were emerging was where Bodins was, naturally. He proudly pointed to the buildings with the sign: Bodins is building here. And they had to walk around in the new buildings and see how fine the apartments were going to be. Lastly the day ended with dinner at Djurgårdsbrunn Restaurant.

Henning discovered that he and Claes were the same age and had friends in common from college days. They felt almost like old friends themselves, could talk to each other easily and bandied words about happily.

Emelie observed them, their simultaneously friendly and disre-spectful way toward each other. Karl Henrik himself did not seem as if he felt left out in any way either, just the opposite. He chatted with Jenny and Greta and Maj and Gunnar as if they were old friends, and everyone used the familiar forms of speech and were on a first name basis with each other. It was certainly only herself who had a hard time leaving the old respect for the upper class behind; she could not really forget the large Bodin office, the money, all the people who must be dependent on Karl Henrik. He was a company director and she had always anxiously curtsied to such people.

These were different times. If it was due to the times or something else, it was still clear that the abyss that had existed between the dif-ferent branches of the family was not as big as before. Here they were sitting together, Gertrud's child and grandchild, August's child and grandchild, Olof's child and grandchild. The descendants of all three siblings. That was something new, something she never had believed would be able to happen. And it made her glad; it was as if all the dif-ficulties that had happened at one time were now forgiven and blotted out. For maybe the first time, she felt like she had really succeeded in keeping her promise to her mother, that she had taken care of her sib-lings—even though none of them were alive anymore.

Now she could actually die at peace. Though just now, of course, it was also a lot of fun to get to live.

She had been sitting quietly a moment. She thought she felt some-one looking at her and looked up, met Gunnar's eye. She nodded, smiled—he smiled back. She remembered how she had held his hand when he was little and frightened. Now he was so big and calm, she could feel little and also a little frightened herself. She knew that Gunnar would lead her to the car. At that point she would take his hand and feel safe.

The day together with Karl Henrik was the highlight of their trip. A few days later Greta and Jane left. And Emelie understood that she would never see them again. But it would be fun to get letters from them, even more fun now that she had met them and could seem to hear their voices behind their words.

And even if she were never to see them again, their visit had still meant that she had grown closer to them. And besides that, she had found a new friend. Karl Henrik, who she had never really known before, began to be a faithful guest; he called regularly and asked if he could come by. Gradually, she completely forgot that he was a big company director, and felt like he was just "one of the boys."

FOREIGNERS

Elisabet knew that she was difficult, she admitted it. She got irritated easily at trifles, judged too quickly and harshly. And demanded too much of her existence, always wishing for more than she got. She often felt treated unfairly, maybe not by people but by life. She thought she belonged to a generation that had had it harder than others, first from the years of economic crisis, then from the war.

Still, at last things were finally going all right for her. She had an interesting and well-paying job as head secretary. And a kind husband, and a healthy and well-behaved daughter. They had bought a summerhouse, gradually they would manage to get a bigger apartment, too. She could buy things that she wanted for their home, and dress well and not too cheaply. When it came to clothes she had always been particular, spent more than she maybe actually could afford. This meant that Lennart covered more of their common expenses than he really should have. But on the other hand, he had such small needs of his own; she had to really nag him to buy a new suit. And besides, shouldn't a guy cover most of the expenses anyway? Many women stayed at home and pottered about and didn't earn anything—in which case it was only fair that a working woman also get a little extra pleasure out of it.

Yes, of course, things were pretty good for her, she had to admit that. And she could understand that those who lived close to her had a hard time understanding why she was so irritable and difficult, that sometimes they undoubtedly wondered what they were guilty of when she showed her displeasure. If they asked her she usually avoided answering. Maybe because there wasn't any real answer, because the reason was so paltry that she was ashamed to name it.

Without wanting to, she gave them a feeling of shame. They became so cautious, barely dared act without asking her opinion first. But this irritated her; then she became the one who felt guilty. She wasn't that difficult! They should do precisely what they wanted as far as she was concerned. Lennart, too. He did not in the least have to be self-effacing the way he was, just the opposite. She wanted him to have his own will, didn't like how he always came and asked for her approval before he decided anything.

She had not bothered to meet the guests from America, even though her mother and Emelie had asked her to come. She had muttered something about them not being her relatives—and they weren't either. It had naturally been thoughtless of her to say so—Jenny had been hurt and would, of course, get the idea that Elisabet somehow felt left out and shunted aside. That was not the reason at all; she had just been annoyed by the fact that Karl Henrik had not invited her and Lennart. Of course, she understood that there could not be an unlimited number invited, and that Maj, who had met Greta before, was closer. And not that she and Lennart would have taken the day off from work either, even if they had been invited. But she could have been permitted to say no thank you in any case. And Henning had been included, too...

He had, as a matter of fact, taken the whole week off to drive around with them, could apparently take time off here and there as he wished; ordinary people could not do that. She and Lennart would never be able to take such liberties despite their working so many years. Lennart was there at his old printer's and had to punch the clock every morning and evening and every break. And he received a salary according to his contract, not one öre more. It was as if his abilities meant nothing—he didn't have any piece paper to prove them. It was as if Henning, who had gotten his high school diploma and gone to university for a few years, had landed in another social class. He earned good money, too, and had bought a car. He got to travel abroad.

But Lennart stayed where he was.

She should not get mad at Lennart, did not want to get mad, had promised herself never to do it anymore. It was after that thing with Erik had happened, which seemed so incomprehensible now. It was not only incomprehensible, but also unforgivable. But Lennart had forgiven the unforgivable and therefore she had to forgive him everything.

To forgive Lennart... It was hard since he had never done anything that needed forgiving. He was never mean, he never snapped at her, he tried to do everything the way she wanted.

No, she never had to forgive him. What was needed was something that had to occur at another level. That he look for a new job... That he take advantage of his abilities in a real way. Now he was reading books in English and German and French, he even read in Latin. He brought home stacks of books from the library and had a whole cupboard full of notebooks with notations. But he did not earn a cent with it; everything he knew was of no use.

He always stood aside, as if he was hiding. Already by his clothes, one barely saw that he was there. If he was in a large group he seldom said anything, could almost appear dumb.

At one time she had thought that they were so alike. Now she felt surprise that two such differing people had been able to find each other.

She wanted to decide—and he let her decide. But sometimes she could also long for him to make a decision and say: This is what we are doing. Now we aren't going to discuss it anymore.

Maybe it was because she had fallen for Erik that time. He knew so well what he wanted, resolutely took the burden of deciding from her, just said: Come! Lie down! Go! It was as if she had thought it felt good to be degraded, had asked to be walked on.

Sometimes she had wished Lennart would be hard on her. That he would not always give way, but would be immovable. But at the same time she knew she would not be able to handle it, in fact she would unquestionably leave him if he were hard on her.

Gradually, she had found that in spite of everything there was something hard inside Lennart. It took a while before she noticed it; it was so deep inside the soft exterior. But he was hard on himself. He bicycled to and from work, in all kinds of weather to save streetcar fare, seldom bought himself anything, sat long into the night reading and taking notes, even when he was tired or sick. And when there was something that really concerned him, he held on tight regardless of what others said and thought. Even regardless of her?

It was the same with his studying, maybe with his work, too. She had nagged and wanted to get him to live differently; he had neither protested nor become irritated—but had continued in the same way as before. She did not discover how serious this stubbornness was until it came to Joseph Schönlank.

Joseph was a refugee. A professional refugee he himself was able to say. For twelve years he had fled the Nazis and he still wondered if he had reached his goal. Sweden was certainly good in many ways, but he did not really feel at home there.

He was born in West Prussia during the First World War in a Jewish family. His father was a craftsman. The family had succeeded in fleeing to relatives in Austria before Hitler came to power in Germany. Then it was as if they had been swept before the giant German extermination broom, to Czechoslovakia, to Holland, lastly to France. Most of his relatives had in one way or another disappeared en route, tried to hide, been found. Most likely all were dead; he had not heard anything from any of them. He himself had been imprisoned after the French surrender, put in a concentration camp—but through some strange twist of fate, he ended up being among the few survivors. He had been driven to Sweden in one of the "white buses" shortly before the end of the war and been given care and food, returned to life again. He had a photo that had been taken by some newspaper photographer at the time of his arrival. It was impossible to believe that the emaciated man in the picture was the same as the rather well-fed compositor who was showing it to them.

Joseph had learned Swedish and returned to the work he had sporadically been able to do during his years of flight. He came to Stockholm, got temporary work at the printer's where Lennart was employed. He proved to be good at hand setting type and making up forms, liked it there and stayed.

It had taken some time before Lennart and Joseph became more than just work colleagues. It probably started during a period of overtime when they stood side by side and together did the make-up of a union newspaper. Joseph had asked Lennart for advice since Lennart always was in charge of that particular newspaper. Then they had continued the conversation during the meal break and soon found that they had many interests in common. Joseph read a lot, too, and had missed having someone to talk to.

Sometimes Joseph got so excited that his knowledge of Swedish did not really suffice for him; then he might switch to German or French. That pleased Lennart; he had read a lot but spoken little and now he got to practice and also get his pronunciation corrected.

One evening a week they went together and ate at some simple restaurant, sat there a long time and talked over a cup of coffee. Joseph was renting a furnished room but hoped to eventually get his own small apartment.

Most of the time they talked about things they had read about. Sometimes Joseph might also tell about his family and his life in different countries. But he never spoke about the concentration camp and Lennart didn't ask.

Joseph Schönlank! Elisabet already disliked the name. It sounded so silly, undependable almost. Besides, she didn't understand what he was doing here now that the war was over; it would be a lot better if each and every person stayed in his or her own country. Not because she had anything against foreigners, but there tended to be trouble and fighting when people came into unaccustomed situations. Besides, they would need work and food and places to live. Somehow that would mean they were living at the expense of Swedes, that there would be more to divide up and choose from if those foreigners weren't here. If one only thought about apartments, how long she and Lennart themselves had waited to get to exchange theirs for something bigger. Would someone like Schönlank now be able to come and get ahead of them in line?

Still, it was okay as long as she herself didn't have anything to do with him. He and Lennart meeting at work and out somewhere shouldn't cause her any worry. Though she really couldn't understand why Lennart should choose a foreigner and a Jew as his friend. People who saw them together must wonder, suspect that something was amiss there in any case.

And now Lennart came and said he wanted to invite this character to their home.

She felt the urge to blow her stack, tell him no. A person she didn't know, they didn't know anything about what he had been involved in. Some of those people the Nazis had put in jail must have been guilty of something or other. And people had read how horrible it had been in those camps; surely people who had lived there had gotten all kinds of illnesses. Of course, one should be kind to them, but it wasn't necessary to bring them home, to risk anything.

Of course, she was being unfair, of course, she exaggerated—she admitted it. There was an unreasonable fear inside her. Of what was foreign. This was true for adventures and experiences as well. She was not only afraid of suffering, but also of the one who had experienced it. She did not despise just the filth, but the one who had once been soiled as well.

Maybe that was why she had despised Erik so much at one time, for his talk of "rat fat and dog dirt," because he wanted to take hold of her with hands that worked with things like that.

What must Joseph not have taken part in? Hauled dead people, scrubbed crematoriums and privies, captured rats with his hands, crushed lice between his fingers... Everything was possible, nothing unthinkable. And she was to take care of him, he was going to drink out of her cups, eat off of her china. Did Lennart know what he was asking of her?

She wanted to shout: no, no, he cannot come here. But she checked herself and said: yes, of course, if you absolutely want it.

He came. And in spite of the fact that Elisabet had made up her mind to dislike him, it was hard to do. If one saw Joseph in a crowd one would not think there was anything special about him. A little dark maybe, with dark hair. But otherwise just a completely normal, rather short but robust man of thirty-five. Simply, but well dressed. He had a bouquet of flowers for Elisabet and a bag of chocolates for Monika. Elisabet checked the bag in private; they were completely ordinary chocolate bars that he must have bought in some shop close by.

They offered him a simple dinner. Any grander preparations were out of the question when they both worked during the day. But Lennart had bought a bottle of wine and the mood turned quite festive. Which without a doubt was due to Joseph; he so clearly enjoyed the meal and the environment, really radiated friendliness and delight. Even if he didn't speak Swedish perfectly, it was easy to understand him and he drew his hosts out of their usual stiffness and quiet demeanor. His stories were funny; he had charm. Elisabet found herself sitting and laughing and really having a good time. It did not feel at all like Joseph was a stranger—more like an old acquaintance. There was nothing scary about him; even if his experiences had been unusual he seemed to be a completely normal person.

And later on in the evening she saw Joseph and Lennart sit in the two armchairs and look at some of Lennart's books. They looked like they had fun together, Lennart who otherwise was so quiet and tranquil, laughing and talking away. Indeed, suddenly he began sentences in French and Joseph answered and it sounded almost like they were putting on a play together.

She felt the difficult uncertainty. Charmed but not conquered. Joseph was probably good, good for Lennart, too. But still a foreigner, despite everything. And he transformed Lennart into something of a foreigner to her, too, like when the spoke French together and she could not understand what they were saying.

As if she had ended up on the outside. For the first time she felt like she was sharing Lennart with someone, that there was a part of him that she no longer owned completely. Faced with his reading she may have felt something of the same, but books were dead things. Now there apparently was a person who meant a lot to him. And with this other person he possessed a world that she really didn't know.

But she had her world, her friends. Though with Lennart it had been different, he had only had her.

Now there was something more and it felt like a threat. Perhaps also like a defeat: she wasn't enough any longer. After Joseph left she washed herself carefully and took a little more pains with the dishes than usual, for safety's sake. This happened during an inner debate; at the same time as she was ashamed of her terror of bacteria, she warned herself that in spite of everything, one never could be careful enough.

Lennart dried and put things away.

"You liked him a lot, right?" he asked.

"Yes," she conceded. "He was okay. Very nice."

"He is one of the finest people I have met," said Lennart. And she felt it like a reproach, like a comparison that ended up to her disadvantage.

"I don't know him very well," she replied. She hurried to add: "Oh, it's getting late. I have to go to sleep if I'm going to be able to get up early tomorrow."

She got into bed quickly, pretended to be asleep when Lennart came in. Now he doesn't need me anymore, she thought, now that he has found "such a fine person..."

"Thank you for this evening and good night," said Lennart and patted her arm. But she didn't answer, was pretending to be asleep. She lay awake for a long time and thought how now, for the first time, she had really felt how hard Lennart could be. Even though he must have felt her resistance, he had invited Joseph to their home and would continue to meet with him. In fact, he even wanted her to admit herself defeated, to like Joseph. And now she didn't know what she herself wanted, whether she wanted to protest and scream that she didn't intend to have anything at all to do with that Schönlank. Or if she was happy that Lennart had showed his will at last, and if she would go so far as to suggest herself that Joseph accompany them out to their summer place next week.

PIONEER
ONCE MORE

The city had grown like a tree; annual ring had been added to annual ring. Settlement had been added to settlement, streets extended farther and farther, sheds and small industries vanished to be replaced by tall buildings. It was a natural growth and it had been going on for centuries; on the maps one could follow how the streets' grid stretched over continually new areas.

The city's distinctive feature had been proximity to many opportunities, anonymity among many people, protection from the dark, cold, and wind. The city had been concentrated, compact. The distances usually not farther than what one could walk to workplaces, amusements, and friends.

That was how it had been—but it was not that way any longer. For about ten years they had been building following other patterns. The natural growth had been interrupted and now they were designing instead. They talked about the need to break up the big city into smaller pieces, created a kind of settlers' society out in the woods surrounding it. The time was ripe for experimentation since the lack of housing was great: they did not have to fear any backlash. As soon as the new villages stood ready, they were filled by people looking for housing, mostly young people. In this way, the designed villages also got specially designed inhabitants where the average age might be around twenty years.

Often the constructions never really got fulfilled. They planned town centers with stores and institutions, but did not have the funds or the possibilities to build them. Sometimes the new communities were too small to sustain the businesses that the town planners had sketched out.

The city as it had existed had been encircling, with connecting rows of buildings that created wind-protected streets. The new towns were made up of sparsely set out clusters of buildings between track-like winding roadways for cars and green thoroughfares for the pedestrians.

Eventually, they seemed to find that the experiment was not completely successful. Communications became difficult and could not be solved before a there was a subway network built. But even then there were to be problems. If all the new communities were exclusively made up of housing units, the traffic structure did not work as it should. There were lines in to the workplaces in the city center in the morning, and lines out to the housing in the evening.

They came up with a new solution. The aim was to create larger construction projects; communities which would contain both housing and workplaces, and build a foundation for real town centers.

The first of these communities was Vällingby, which was now being constructed very hastily. Already from the start the town would have a subway in to the city. In the advertising brochures, companies were urged to "give their company air" and move out to Vällingby; it was spoken of as "the future city of business."

Erik Karge was fascinated by the drama, by the construction process. People's victory over nature, the possibility of building up a whole new society, to be able to build with social ambitions, create a scientifically correctly designed milieu.

In fact, the city was nothing more than an article of consumption, he thought. A machine which hundreds of thousands of people wore down every day, and like all other machines had to become worn out and exchanged. If all those who screamed about preserving everything old got to have their way, then the whole city would become a dead museum.

People had been satisfied with patching and repairing for as long as possible, changing out small sections, adding on. Now the time was here for radical transformations. Entire new towns like Vällingby. The tearing down of larger sections of Norrmalm. Old junk and refuse should go, everything he thought of as a sign of the old, rotten society, the city of the poor.

The city that existed was built for horse-drawn vehicles and families with seven children in one-room apartments, and Östermalm's old gentry in ten-room apartments. Tear down the whole lot, let sun in the city with wide streets, so cars can get through!

A new view on humanity demanded a new city. The old should have been buried together with Oskar II.

With a special delight he threw himself into city council debates when city planning was involved. If there had been a chance he would have preferred to be elected to the housing committee. He had managed to get off the boring child welfare committee some years back.

He was there when the subway between Hötorget and Vällingby was dedicated, and watched as Prince Bertil cut the blue and yellow ribbon with a large pair of scissors. And he began to inquire about the possibilities of exchanging an apartment on Norr Mälarstrand for one in new Vällingby. They needed something bigger; the girls should each have their own room and he needed a room to work in. And now it was really time to change; they had almost lived twenty years in the same apartment. He had gotten stuck, he thought, grown apathetic.

He went out to Vällingby and looked around.

Fantastic! A few years ago there had only been fields and meadows and one and another red cottage and barn out there. Now they were working everywhere, giant groups of buildings were springing up around muddy tracks. Across from the subway station the town's center would come up in a few years—with sidewalks that were wider than many of the inner city's business streets.

The get to experience the actual creation, the transformation; to get to see how the new city came into existence... Almost like becoming young again, to get to feel like a pioneer. It was an opportunity for rebirth that he could not miss.

To his surprise, it did not end up being difficult at all to exchange a five-room apartment in Vällingby for a three-room on Norr Mälarstrand. People were apathetic, he thought, did not understand the value of what they were being offered. Just to come close to nature, see the woods from the windows. And the nature preserve at Judarn had been spruced up; it was not far from Vällingby. As a matter of fact, he should get a dog, have a reason to get out and exercise in the mornings.

When he announced his decision at home, he found that he was met with a certain resistance. Irene give him a little trouble that he had expected; he had to promise her a monthly pass on the subway so she could ride into the city and to her department stores. But, the girls ... whined so and wanted each their own room. Out in the country, away from everything they knew, far from everything ... it sounded like that from the girls. But the subway went into town in a jiffy ... well, a half hour.

They had no true pioneer spirit, were, of course, a little spoiled. It didn't even help if he tried to tell about his own childhood, how hard things had been for him But they would have to resign themselves. There would be movies and a theater out there, and several department stores and sports centers.

His enthusiasm was irrepressible; they gave in at last.

But once he had forced the decision, he was perhaps still a little ambivalent. He maybe wasn't so completely onboard with that pioneering either. Of course, he wanted to move. He wasn't so old, fifty something. He shouldn't feel his age. He had to admit that he didn't keep going as vigorously as before. He was not so hard on women anymore, as if it really wasn't worth the trouble. He took it a little easier at work, too; things went well anyway. He had declined a number of projects.

It felt good to be spared some, take it easier. But maybe that was also a bad sign. Was he finished? Incompetent soon? If one was going to stay at the fore, one had to have the will for it. And he didn't want it as badly as before. But maybe that was because he had grown apathetic, gone so long in the same tracks. It would probably be better when he arrived in the new environment out there, got to feel like a pioneer again. Maybe he would start to take long walks before he went to the office, become really fit.

One could see by one's children that one was becoming old oneself, as the saying went. Indeed, he was actually a grandfather now that Henning had become a father. But Henning was a little outside, someone they didn't talk about at home. In any case, he could see it daily by his daughters. Lena nineteen now, Berit sixteen. Soon adults. Small children, small troubles—big children...

No, there wasn't that much trouble at any rate. But it was harder with girls than with boys, riskier. When his daughters were out in the evenings and were late, he might wonder what they were up to, sit and think about everything he had been up to when young with girls their ages.

But the girls he had met had surely been different from his own daughters, he consoled himself. Though it was a little grim to hope at the same time that they would meet different guys from the kind he had been.

When he saw the girls at home he thought they were only kids anyway. Way too childish for any normal guy to become interested in them in that way. And if he thought about how they had been just a few years ago ... playing ball, playing hopscotch...

They had never joined the movement; he had not succeeded in engaging them. It was naturally wrong not to. Though sometimes he might think that it was just as well that way. Political youth were radicals and there was nothing wrong with that—but along with radicalism came often a freer view on love as well. All right, that was surely fine, that, too; marriage was naturally not the most ideal form of living together, "a ring in the nose like the Zulus do." He remembered how one had discussed free love in the Communist youth club he had belonged to. And not just discussed.

The girls were not mature enough yet, neither for love nor for politics. But children can play dangerous games sometimes. And it wasn't good when children had children, that much he had learned at least from his work on the child welfare committee.

Lena had been together with various different boys, just now there was no one special. But Berit, the little one, had, of course, a steady guy, which was probably why she did not want to move.

It was an unusually unpleasant autumn, nasty weather every day. When they moved, too. A lot of things had time to get wet before they were covered up on the moving van. The wind whistled around the spread out buildings in Vällingby, large puddles grew on the as yet unfinished streets, mud sprayed around the car's wheels. In the fog and evening darkness, they could see nothing of the green woods that Erik had spoken so much of, and the way from the subway station to the building where they were going to live seemed long and difficult, even now when they were coming in a taxi.

Outside the entryway, children stood in boots and jumpsuits and jumped so that the mud splattered against the building facade. There were plenty of kids in the stairwell also; a lot of families with children must be living there, too. It seemed as if one could hear every sound in the building, at least it was much more filled with sound than the solid and quiet building on Norr Mälarstrand.

Irene was tired, unhappy about everything that had gotten wet and maybe ruined, irritated by all the noise. Lena was in a bad mood, too. Berit was staying in town until late in the evening; when she finally came out she could not find her way home and wandered around growing furious and soaking wet.

Erik tried to keep cheerful. He offered wine—they should toast the new apartment. He tried to get them interested in how they would furnish it, got the girls to choose which room each of them would have.

Berit's anger worried him, or rather calmed him. He recognized so well her temperament; it was his own. She would surely feel at home out here; there was a bit of the real pioneer in her. Lena was perhaps more lackadaisical and lax, like Irene. She might not like it before everything was put in order, most likely wanted to trot around the streets in high-heeled inside shoes. That wouldn't work here. For himself he would have to buy galoshes, though he would have preferred not to use such things.

It took some time before they got things in order; after several weeks it still seemed as if they had just moved in. Curtains had to be made and hung, some pieces of furniture were almost impossible to place anywhere; a whole lot of supplementary purchases had to be made. Irene had never been especially quick, and now it was as if she had been crippled. She lacked the will, almost didn't care how it turned out.

He tried to cheer her up. As for himself, he liked to walk around in the half-finished community, had a little pamphlet he brought along and would look at the drawings in it and try to imagine how everything would be. The theater there, the restaurant on that corner, the department stores, the church. He tried to get Irene to go along, wanted to show her everything. But she refused to go out and look, had enough of it she said. She sat up to her ears in mud and construction trash all day long. When Erik was free she wanted them to get out of there, in to town or anywhere at all. At least draw the curtains and not have to see the wretchedness outside.

He had to walk alone, once in a while he could entice Berit to go with him. But he never got as far as the woods; there weren't any real woods close by anyway.

Right after New Year's they received visitors to the country; Irene's sister, Maria, and her small son paid a visit. Now it was good that the apartment was so big that the sister and the boy could have a room to themselves; they took the one that was Erik's workroom.

Irene and Maria went into town and shopped every day. The visit was evidently good for Irene; she grew more cheerful and liked it better when she had company in the daytime.

One Saturday evening, they were going to visit a friend of Maria's. She lived in Blackeberg, so it was not so far, only two subway stations away. They stayed a little longer than they had intended and, as so often on a weekend evening, it was hard to get hold of a taxi when they were going to go home.

"Let's walk," Erik suggested. It was not far at all. Not more than a kilometer, no longer than Drottninggatan. He would carry the boy who was lying down and sleeping.

It was snowing; the roads turned beautifully white. Around the apartment buildings in Blackeberg it was calm and quiet; that town had been built a few years earlier and had real streets built around it.

But when they came to the wide Bergslagsvägen, they were met by the wind. Bright lights shone down on the roadway. Headlights came out of the fog of snow; like phantoms the cars appeared, flew rumbling past, and disappeared with their small red lights peering out of the mist.

Sleet blew in their faces. The boy who Erik was carrying began to wail. The road seemed endless, a straight motorway across the field. The cars belonged to another world, the person who walked was just as alone and left out as a hiker who wandered around in the mountains.

They tried to turn up their collars and wrap their handkerchiefs as protection around their faces. And they struggled on.

No taxi available, far to the subway station. It would maybe have been better to go back, turn up one of the more sheltered streets again and take the subway in Blackeberg. But to turn back was also unappealing; then they would have struggled in vain. So they continued on, gritted their teeth, set themselves against the wind. Sometimes a gust came along and pressed them back; Irene gave a shriek a couple of times when she thought she was going to be thrown out in the road. The child only sniffled now. But he began to be heavy to carry; Erik felt that he wasn't so young any longer.

"Drottninggatan!" hissed Irene. "Like walking down Drottninggatan!"

Cars shined their lights on them time after time, whooshed past, pulled up clouds of snow, sprayed slush, disappeared.

"I will certainly freeze my legs," said Irene. In some way she almost sounded satisfied, as if now she really had managed to show what a mistake Erik had made when he forced her out here.

And Maria slipped and was about to fall. She, who was the sister-in-law, did not dare protest as loudly as Irene. But when she moaned it was still as a supporter.

Finally, they had gotten so far that they could turn off from Bergslagsvägen's wind-whipped racetrack. Now the main thing, first and foremost, was to cross to the other side. They tried to look out through the snow, find a safe enough opening between cars. Then walking up the hills was next; the wind whistled there also, but it still felt a little safer and better. And walking between the half-finished buildings and scaffoldings was really safe. They trudged on, almost staggering through the last few steps. Finally, they reached the doorway to safety.

Erik offered a red wine toddy, told them to drink up, and get warm. As for himself he felt aching all over. Irene and Maria drank but did not say many words. Irene seemed on the verge of tears. Erik decided not to go into their bedroom before she had fallen asleep; after this ordeal he didn't have the energy for more complaining.

He sat in the kitchen and drank one more toddy, wondered what could be wrong in the new community. One could not apparently walk out here; the road they had walked on was absolutely not suitable for that. One could come here on the subway and then stay in one's own community. In fact, he had begun to grow tired of the subway; of course, it had been more pleasant and easier before when it had taken him ten minutes to walk to work. It took him, for sure, three quarters of an hour to get there now, at least one-and-a-half hours a day commuting.

It was not so easy to be a pioneer.

But there had to be some solution. He thought about the pioneers in other wildernesses. They must have had horses to get around on. Which in his case meant that he should have a car. Then he would be independent in a completely different way, sweep past like those drivers out there on the roadways, sit inside in the comfortable warmth and feel sorry for those poor people in the dark and cold outside.

That was the way it had to be. Except for the fact that he didn't have a driver's license. He had not grown up in a time and an environment where one had cars. He had never planned on getting one. Out here it was apparently necessary. And he would surely be able to learn to drive even if he was not so young anymore.

Then he would get out of walking to the subway, too.

SHADOW PLAY

The winters were worrisome for Emelie now. It was then that her back and limbs ached and she had a hard time moving around. She couldn't go out, not even to the closest store, instead stayed sitting at home like a shut-in. But she was a few years past eighty now, and it was maybe natural that infirmities had arrived.

Aches and the forced isolation made her think more and more often of the end. And she got prepared, in her way. Her survivors would have as little trouble as possible. In the top drawer of the little bureau that she had inherited from her mother, she placed the papers they might need: the minister's certificate, her retirement letter, and her health insurance book. And her bankbook. Thanks to the money she had been left by August, there was enough for the funeral. It shouldn't cost them anything to put her into the earth.

She showed Jenny where everything was. But Jenny did not like thinking of unpleasant things, she barely wanted to look. Since, in addition, Jenny was very forgetful, Emelie showed the papers to Maj, too. Maj was calm, took it naturally. One could talk with her about things Jenny didn't want to listen to.

Emelie continued her preparations. She went through what she owned, all the smaller and bigger things she had collected through the years. She had thought she had thrown away a lot, but now it still appeared that so many useless things were left.

A lot could be disposed of and she did that now; she was strict and she sorted through things rigorously. Even though, there was also a lot that certainly never would be of use anymore but that she still wanted to keep as long as she was alive. Like the old handkerchief with an embroidered forget-me-not that she had been given by her father on her eighth birthday. It was so fragile that it split when she carefully lifted it up out of its wrapping paper. But she placed it back inside and wrapped a new piece of paper around it. She pondered it, and was not really satisfied. Now they would have some inconvenience anyway. But there was a possibility she could write instructions on the outside so they at least could avoid opening it and looking inside to see what it was.

An old handkerchief, she wrote. *Can be thrown away.*

There ended up being many brown packages. A bar of soap and a pass card from the 1897 exhibition, an envelope with a ration card from the First World War.

Practically everything she kept, but did not use daily, she wrapped in a package and tied string around. Old knives and forks, which were no longer used, clothing that she seldom used, photographs of old work colleagues and workplaces. It grew quite empty on the hangers in her wardrobe, but well filled on the shelves above, full of packages in brown paper and with instructions as to what they held. And most with the addition: *Can be thrown away,* or just: *To throw away.*

Gradually, she also went through the boxes that had been standing in Mikael's attic and that contained things Thumbs had left behind. She had gone through them once earlier and thrown away some of them, but now she did it more thoroughly. There were a number of newspapers that she bundled together; they were so old now that maybe someone might think it was fun to look at them. That became one package. Then there were a lot of letters and papers that had to do with working conditions and labor unions; that became a package as well. There were letters from Rudolf and Gertrud, too, and she tied them up with string and wrote that they could be sent back to America.

When she was sorting through Thumbs's papers, she found a sheet that seemed to be torn out of some old weekly magazine. It was folded in half and when she opened it up she saw something that interested her. It was a picture of some ships down along Stadsgården; some dockworkers were occupied with unloading while a well-dressed gentleman stood and looked on. In the background, you could see piles of sacks; one could make out some men who were carrying sacks, as well. And a wagon driver with a pair of horses.

Thumbs had written some words in pencil in the margin. His style had never been easy to read; it took a moment before she could make out the text: Young Lundström watches his slaves.

Apparently the well-dressed gentleman was the son of the stevedore Lundström who once had been the big man down at the harbor; the firm was certainly still there. But who were the slaves?

She tried to study the picture more closely, noticed it was getting dark, and stood up laboriously and turned on the ceiling light. She sat down and looked again. Surely one of the men in the foreground looked like Thumbs, the young Thumbs. And the other, who was almost kneeling from under the weight, who seemed so fragile and thin... Could it be? No, that would be unbelievable. But maybe still...

She grew excited, had to go in to Jenny in her room and ask to borrow her magnifying glass. She tried, with the help of the glass, to come in closer, see the features.

It could be her father. He had looked something like that. It was only a drawing, of course, maybe the artist had not succeeded in portraying the features exactly right. Soon she was thinking that there could be no doubt about it. It was her father.

Once again she had to stand up, this time to tell Jenny about her discovery. And they sat together and looked at the picture, discussing if it really could be as Emelie believed. Emelie tried to remember his features. Her father had died when she wasn't more than nine years old; her memories were blurred, shadowed by the years that had passed. And now there was no one left who had known him. To think that Thumbs had never said anything, that he had never shown her the picture. But he had always been so caught up in the present. Probably he had found that page in the magazine sometime and stuffed it in among his papers and forgotten about it.

Henning got to see the picture, too, when he came to see her; he asked if he could borrow it—would have part of it enlarged. A few days later he arrived with the result; the small faces now filled a surface area as large as the entire original picture. Every little line could be seen, the features emerged out of a field of shadows. And even if the enlargement maybe made the figures more unreal, Emelie felt even more sure, of course, it was her father. Didn't they see how Henning resembled him?

Indeed, the likeness could frighten him, almost so that he wanted to deny it. The harbor worker was sick, haggard, worn out. As for himself, he did not suffer from lack of anything. Still, they did look alike and that made him think that he could have looked like that if circumstances had been different. That was how he could come to look if they did change.

He remembered Emelie's stories about her father, everything he had talked about when Greta was here. How he had toiled to take care of his family, how he had gotten sick. From what Henning could understand, Emelie' father had been an ordinary, decent, and hard-working man who had done his best. But he had lived in a time when that didn't help. He himself was also pretty decent and rather hard working—and that had yielded him a completely different dividend. Circumstances could mean that much. And then a little willpower and personal effort?

There was Henning Nilsson bent under his burden, worn out by hunger and sickness. Didn't anyone see how bent over he was, didn't anyone guess he soon would collapse?

And here sat Henning Nilsson at the coffee table, well dressed and well nourished, his car on the street outside.

Shadow play, circumstance's game. So much depended on when and where. Born then or now, here or there. It did not determine everything but most of it.

He had several copies of the picture made. Kept one himself. He showed Barbro; she did not think that the likeness was especially striking. Still, it bothered him.

Maybe it depended on the fact that, for the first time in many years, he really had a reason to worry. As if anything that had some tie to accidents and suffering scared him now, gave him a feeling that such things could also be inherited. He wanted so much to be sure he lived in another world and time from the old Henning, wanted to believe that those closest to him and he himself would not have something that bad happen to them. But then he suddenly found that suffering, sickness, and death always exist. That every person's life had to be something of a tragedy, since death always provided the ending to the drama.

When he was younger he had sometimes felt too completely protected, wanted to free himself from his mother's care. Now he found that there was no protection and that he missed it. The successes he had came so easily and quickly, could give him a feeling that he had been given some kind of guarantee for a happy life. Suffering and difficulties could strike others—but not him.

And then suddenly to find that nothing is secure and protected, that happiness is readily susceptible, that danger lies close at hand.

Barbro was not really healthy. She had given birth to their second child, a son, a half year ago. The delivery had been difficult and she was still weak. Anemia, that much they knew. Maybe something else as well. It seemed as if the doctor could not pin down what it was. Or—what if he knew but did not want to say it? That thought increased his worry.

Whatever it was, she had to get away and rest for a time. The doctor had suggested a place that was something between a guesthouse and a rest home.

Naturally she did not want to go—but understood that she had to. It was hard to see Barbro sad. When he thought of her he always saw her smile first, the sparkle that was in her eyes. Now she was crying even though she tried not to. And her cheeks had gotten so thin.

She cried when he drove her out in the car, cried when he left her.

They had to hope, dare to believe. If nothing else then for the children's sake. He forced himself to. Now it was he who carried all the responsibility for them a while. Their son was so little that it was absolutely necessary to get a nurse for him and, as luck would have it, he managed to get hold of one. It was not easy to manage the whole thing, economically speaking. He would be tied down also, had to be home evenings and on Sundays, arrange it so he didn't have to travel abroad for the magazine. They were understanding there, so it would probably work out. And his mother and John were prepared to help out in any way.

But as much as possible he wanted to shoulder things himself, without any help. He felt like it was his part, what he could do for Barbro now. She at least would not have to be worried because of the children. No, she only had to think about getting well. She had slept badly at home; the boy had woken up often during the nights.

It was a gloomy time for Henning. He was torn between his duties and his wishes: he wanted to take care of the children, wanted to see Barbro, wanted to do his work. Every time he did something he neglected something else.

Still, it was his work that kept him going, he thought. If he worked intensively enough some of the worry could be turned into energy, get him to forget things for a while.

On Sundays he tried to go out to see Barbro with the children. Then someone had to come along to sit in the backseat of the car together with them; usually it was Barbro's mother, sometimes it was his. And, of course, it was nice to see each other. But it was hard, too. To sit for a few hours in a strange room or walk in a garden where many sick and weak people were strolling with their visitors. There were so many reminders here of how things could go, how it could turn out for people.

And then the farewell, the bitter farewell when he and the children had to leave her, in a way abandon her.

Despite everything, hope still grew. Barbro felt well from the rest, had gotten a little color from the sun. She was in the city for a visit to the doctor and found out that everything was going in the right direction. But that she should still be careful and rest a while longer.

Even if Barbro was going to be completely healthy again, Henning knew that he had lost something. Maybe something that should and had to be lost. That feeling of invulnerability, of being safe and protected. The person who has once experienced the chill of sickness and suffering's shadow can never again feel really safe. To have been in the shadow once was to become conscious of life's incompleteness.

He slept poorly at night, was sometimes woken up by the boy, dreamed more than he usually did. One night he dreamed that he was walking across a marsh. It took some time before he noticed that it was a marsh, he walked so calmly and securely as if he were walking on a path in the woods. But then he noticed suddenly that he was stepping from tussock to tussock and that it was bubbling and rising between the tussocks. Then he grew afraid and when the fear came he lost the ability to move forward. Then he tripped, stepped sideways, managed to pull himself up, went down again. And he woke up, afraid that his crying out would have woken up the children.

He went out into the kitchen, tried to calm down with a cigarette. Wondered: were the good years over now? Maybe not yet; to be aware of the dangers might not in and of itself be a danger but rather an aid. It was the feeling of panic that was dangerous. If one could avoid that then maybe one could even live under dark shadows.

He fetched the picture that he had enlarged, sat a while and looked at the two shadow figures. A Henning who was trying to hold out, who was such a person that the memory of him now, more than seventy years later, was capable of lighting up his daughter's eyes.

That Henning had surely lived his life in the darkest shadow. And still not in vain.

Then he himself ought not to let himself get frightened. Barbro was better, the doctor had said. She was weak, they would have to adjust themselves accordingly and remember. They should not think of any more children. But they would probably be able to live a long time yet and in a way that they and their children would find joy in it. The fear of losing each other should not become so great that the joy disappeared. He had to learn to understand and to accept that life is always lived in the shadow of death.

The consciousness of limits, happiness's and life's, could be turned into something of value. Now, when they were separated from each other, he felt even more strongly than ever how they belonged together. And joy that they had found each other.

ON THE SIDE

The city celebrated its seven hundred year jubilee. Huge crowds of people thronged into Kungsträdgården, the canons thundered their salute from Skeppsholmen, fireworks blazed against the early summer sky, fountains played out on the water.

The day that was designated the real jubilee, the seventeenth of June, demonstrating East Berliners were shot by Russian tanks that rolled into their city; the same day the city hall in Magdeburg was stormed by thousands of worker who were demonstrating against the Communist regime. Festivities in Stockholm. State of emergency and court marshal in East Germany. In Korea, they were discussing the possibility of a truce after three years of war.

The din from the city and from the world only reached the cottage in the archipelago in the form of the newspaper headlines and articles. They did not have electricity out there and thus no radio either.

Although Henning was now there in the calm surroundings, the city's unrest was still inside him and he felt some irritation, felt sidelined from all the events. The silence was unnerving, seemed unreal. Didn't one have to be near the happenings, at least close to the news sources?

Naturally he was nervous. It had not been easy for him to manage everything while Barbro was away, take care if the magazine during the days and the children during the nights. He had slept poorly. Had worries about money. Been irritated by the nurse who had such decided ideas about how everything should be.

Now he could hope at any rate that the most difficult time was over. Barbro had been allowed to leave the rest home. She still had to take it easy and he had been able to arrange for his vacation to begin at the same time that she came home. Now they could spend his vacation together in the cottage. When Henning's time off was up, Maj and John would begin theirs. Then Barbro and children could stay and get help from Maj.

With John's help, Henning had begun to build their own cottage on the same lot. It would only be a little summerhouse, nothing special or big. Still, its construction presented a lot of difficulties for him, who was unused to that work. But John had been of good help in the beginning; he was handy and in addition had many good contacts. He had come across some demolition timber and some used windows and doors that Henning could take over cheaply.

Despite it not being heavy timber, the work was tiring, especially now when John was not out there helping him. But it also felt good to tire out his body, throw himself into it. And also the work yielded a visible result.

Time after time he had to take a few steps away and stop and look at the result. It wasn't really perfect but it did look pretty good anyway ... and later once it had paint on it...

Writing in the magazine was like writing in sand, he thought as he stood and looked at the growing house. Words disappeared. But what was built remained; to build was to create something lasting. And when he was occupied with building, much of his worry disappeared; the cottage was something so tangible, like a sign that they would get to live and dwell here many summers, that Barbro would become really healthy again.

When he worked like this, it almost felt like this work in some way contributed to Barbro's getting better again. It was a notion, an idea he had gotten, maybe because it felt so hopeless and frightening to know that one could not do anything. Then one seized onto superstitious fancies, that working became the same thing as stroking a talisman. He had worked so that the sweat ran down him, half-running with the bundles of boards, hammered as if in a fever.

Maybe almost forgetting those he was working for? Barbro and the children had been alone a few hours now, maybe she needed his help with something. Maybe she had even called out to him without him hearing it.

He hurried off. They were still there inside John and Maj's cottage.

The boy had fallen asleep in his little box under the shadow of the pine trees, Barbro was playing with their daughter. Henning stood a minute beneath the trees nearby and watched them while he caught his breath.

Then he went forward and sat down beside them. Barbro leaned against him and turned her face up toward the sun. And he heard her heart beating, felt that she was alive and was close to him again.

He thought: one of the rights of human beings must be to get to pull oneself away from everything that is happening and sit here on the side of events, get to turn one's back to the world a moment while the sun shines and the heart still beats.

During recent years he had been working too hard, all too seldom had time for or given himself time to sit like this. But what did one get from life if one ran through it, if one never gave oneself time to sit down and let it in?

On Saturday morning Henning had gotten so far with the cottage that he could move their beds over there; they could live there even if it wasn't painted yet. It was practical to sleep there on Saturday night since John and Maj would be coming out on Saturday evening. At the same time, Lennart and Elisabet came, too, with their daughter; they had their own lot and cottage. But they usually got together and ate.

Maj told them how she had gone with Emelie and Jenny to the train; they had traveled to Dalarna as they usually did; Gunnar had arranged everything for them as always.

"It's only we who don't go anywhere," Elisabet said in a dissatisfied tone.

Then she sat silent; if she had to answer a question she only replied with a few brief words.

Of course, they could have gone somewhere if they had wanted to. However, that wasn't what she wanted, but something else, something that she had planned for a long time and almost achieved until it was yanked away from her.

It was a car that she wanted. A new car, not something old that other people had used and gotten the best out of. And it should be bought with cash; she did not like having debts. She was just about to begin taking driving lessons and counted on buying the car as soon as she had a driver's license. It shouldn't take long; she thought she knew exactly how to do it, that she had the aptitude in her hands, as if they were made to drive.

Lennart had no driver's license and probably wouldn't get one either; it was too hard, by the way, to imagine him as a driver. But she could see herself at the wheel of her own car. Not a big car; a small, shiny, and preferably red one.

She earned roughly the same as Lennart and he paid for most of their common expenses. Still, it was he who had saved the money and not she; she wanted to be well groomed and nicely dressed, and the money she earned went toward that. Lennart lived in a completely different way, needed so little.

It wasn't that he was stingy, only that he did not have the same needs. He only changed his clothes the few evenings they went out or when they were going to have company, otherwise he went around in an old worn-out suit and boring gray shirts. It was good enough for the printers, he said. He bought a number of books, of course, but most of them he borrowed from the library. Maybe it was out of consideration for her that he did not buy more; she thought that books gathered dust and sometimes complained that his old volumes smelled like dust, too. For that reason, he had stuffed most of them in the cupboard.

They had used a large amount of the money he had saved through the years to buy the lot and a prefabricated cottage. It was a purchase that Elisabet had maybe forced but that she could be proud of now— a successful piece of business. No more than six years had passed since then, but people already had to pay at least double as much for land out here. Still they were almost fighting to get to buy and the sellers had to ration it.

Now Lennart had saved so much that there would be enough for a car. He would have preferred to leave the money sitting in the bank, of course; if something happened to him it might be good for Elisabet and their daughter to have some money. It was naturally a considerate and kind thought. But surely he would be alive... Finally she had gotten him to go along with the purchase; he had seen how much she wanted it. It would be so convenient to drive out to the country then. But the whole thing would make for expensive trips; he had objected.

Then something had happened. Something that did not thwart the purchase but which postponed it.

It was Joseph Schönlank's fault. Joseph's wishes had come before hers. Lennart preferred to make Joseph happy rather than her.

She had said this to Lennart, blamed him even though she had once decided to forgive him everything he could possibly do. And even though she felt that she was wrong.

That was certainly bad—but the disappointment was so great, she didn't have it in her to beg, felt like she had to spit it out to not be poisoned by the grief.

"But this is concerning a person!" Lennart had answered. "You can't weigh a person against a car!"

Maybe not. But Joseph could have solved the matter another way, asked someone other than Lennart for help. One should not use one's friends as much as one pleased.

"Joseph has never used me."

"He's doing it now."

"But I want to help him. I would do it even if he hadn't asked."

"But you couldn't care less about what I want, even though you know how much I've wanted it."

"It will only be for a few months."

"The whole summer will have time to go by. And I hate that crush on the bus and the schedule you always have to keep track of."

She could remember every reply; they stuck like they were branded in. The first time they had really argued. She had indeed quarreled with Lennart sometimes but it didn't become a real quarrel if no one answered back in the same tone. And he hadn't done that before now.

He had not given in the least bit. He did not want to understand her. He said mean things—like that about weighing a person against a car.

She had never meant that either. She only meant that each person should take care of his or her own affairs. This was nothing that she and Lennart needed to concern themselves with. It wasn't strange if people said they couldn't lend money because they had big expenses themselves. Even Joseph ought to be able to accept that. There had to be one single person other than Lennart who could help him. And they didn't need to and couldn't very well feel responsible for a person they had never seen.

The person in question was Joseph's mother.

For a long time he had believed that all his relations were dead, exterminated by the Nazis or died fleeing them. During the years that had passed, he had done what he could to gain certainty. But it had been difficult to get definite answers. Still, he had received confirmation that his father and some of his siblings had died.

Then he had suddenly found out that his mother was still alive. After her husband's death she had become completely apathetic—but friends had helped her escape the German occupation troops and she had lived under a name she had taken in a southern French town. Those who knew her and had helped her had perished, but in some miraculous way she herself had succeeded in surviving, despite being severely ill.

It wasn't until now that she realized one of her children was alive. Joseph had traveled down there immediately. And returned to obtain a residence permit for her in Sweden. After his many years in the queue for an apartment he had also been promised one, so he would be able to bring her there.

But the trips and the moving cost a lot; he had to buy furniture in addition since before he had been renting a furnished room. His mother had some debts she owed to the people who had been taking care of her, she needed new clothes. Before Joseph went down to get her he had asked Lennart if he could lend him ten thousand kronor. He would get the money back, at the latest in a few months.

It was nice that Joseph had found his mother and could bring her to be with him. Elisabet had nothing against that—even if it was a foreigner who would be living here. She did not even say anything about Joseph getting an apartment, though they themselves had not gotten anything bigger yet. But when they took the car from her, too, then it was going too far.

No outsider had ever helped her, she had had to take care of herself, work her way up. But that she would stand ready to sacrifice herself for others, people she had never seen—it was unfair to demand that of her.

"We can buy the car in installments in the worst case," Lennart had said at last.

But she didn't want that. Maybe because she wanted to be a martyr now, feel slighted, shunted aside by that remarkable Joseph.

Henning had a car. Gunnar, too. Erik had recently gotten one, she had heard. Everyone who wanted one had one. Except her.

She felt the tears beginning to come. Then they would wonder, maybe ask. But that thing with the car was something that concerned only herself and Lennart.

She slipped away a moment, stood at a distance from the cottage and heard the buzz from inside, saw the light from the windows. No one would understand her if she told them what was going on, no one would understand how she longed for that car, that she already felt it like a part of herself.

Just now she had felt worked up, thought she would burst into tears. It was so warm in there, too. Out here in the cool of the evening she felt calmer, some of the heat and the anger disappeared. Somewhere far out on the inlet a motorboat could be heard. The moon was up; a little of its light was reflected in the metal of Henning's car that was standing between the trees behind the cottage.

She walked closer to the car. It was old, not at all as good-looking as the one she was thinking about. It had gotten its scratches, in fact it wasn't much to envy.

While she stood there and looked at the car she thought how she actually felt sorry for Henning. Not because of the car, but because Barbro had been sick for so long. And she felt sorry for Lennart when she was so difficult. Sorry for Joseph and his mother. And for John who seemed so tired, and then for Maj, too. Unwillingly she had to admit that she did not have it so tough herself, that maybe she should not feel sorry for herself.

And now she had to wonder what was wrong with her.

Suddenly she felt regretful, wanted to make everything all right again.

She dried her eyes, just to be sure, before she went back into the cottage. Now the warmth felt welcoming. She sat down beside Lennart, took his hand in hers. He looked at her a little surprised, then he quickly patted her hand.

No one knew what had happened, why she had come about. But they accepted it gratefully, the mood lightened, the danger was over.

TO COPE
WITH FREEDOM

But time disappears and life, it changes shape,
And roads and sorrows, they change as fate decrees.
Soon comes the time when one marches from the fortress,
From thieves and rogues, from want and sorrow,
Out to freedom again, to a glass and a friend.

The melody was inside Berg, in his head. He tried to hum it—the Svartsjö song. But it sounded terrible. His singing voice had apparently completely disappeared during the years that had passed.

Finally free.

"This time Berg will nevertheless try to cope with the difficulty of freedom," the little female welfare officer had said.

"Yes, you won't get to see me here anymore," he had answered. And the time he had spent in institutions ought to be enough. Almost half of his life. He would be seventy-five next time; it was getting time to take it a little easy.

Out to freedom again,
To a glass and a friend.

It still went on in his head. But he had to be careful with the glass if he was going to keep himself on the outside. And he did not have a friend anymore, had really never had anyone other than Tyra. If only Tyra had been allowed to live... Though, in fact, it would not have been so different in that case either.

He should say hello to the kids anyway. It was only Allan who kept in touch sometimes. Allan had told him that Per was married now, too. All three married, all had kids, too. But Stig had died. It was probably Stig he had liked the most. Stig would have gotten his accordion.

The train slowed down and David Berg stood up and took down his suitcase from the luggage rack. It wasn't big but it contained everything he owned. He had never really owned very much—though he had still had somewhat more before. It had disappeared, slipped out of his hands like everything else, like his life.

Rather neatly done actually. He smiled his crooked smile. To be able to live for seventy-five years without amassing anything. If he dropped dead now there would hardly be a trace left behind—other than the papers of the authorities, of course. They had probably scribbled even more there.

In spite of everything, he thought that he felt more secure than usual when he came out to freedom this time. He was a retiree now. He had been one for several years now, of course—but did not feel like one and instead gone on as usual. Even if the money one received wasn't a lot, one should be able to exist on it. One could get a housing allowance as well. And of the kids Allan at least would give him something every month; Allan was kind. Gun didn't dare to because of her husband. Per was out of the question.

The future could be quite worry-free. A retiree doesn't get scolded for being asocial because he doesn't work, a retiree has the right to rest. That bit about work had never really been his thing. Those moneybags, poor moneybags, worked and toiled so that they passed out in time for retirement age. As for himself, he had not wasted his energies and ought to have most of his strength left.

He placed his hat on his head, a little at an angle, and caught his reflection in the mirror. He didn't appear to be as old as he was. Not like some kind of damn inmate either. Actually rather dashing.

Out to freedom again,
To a glass and a friend.

What could his old buddies be up to? Now that there weren't any ration cards to do double deals with any longer. And they were saying that liquor was going to be freed up, too. People were crazy. But it didn't concern him anymore if his meal tickets dried up. He was retired, as honorable a retiree as anyone else. Though he had not paid one single öre...

He wandered out into the big station hall to see if everything was the same. Yes, indeed. People who were taking the train, loafers, some con men and pimps, the police. One of the policemen was an old acquaintance, had nabbed him once. Just here, by the way. When he had almost succeeded in selling a clock to a country bumpkin. Though, the cop almost does not catch any bandits.

David passed by the policeman at close range just for fun, wanted to see if he would be recognized. It didn't seem so. If the cop, contrary to his expectations said anything, he would respond: "The constable is surely not going to accost an old retiree who has just arrived on the train. The hall is, of course, meant for travelers? For that matter, for those as well who have just arrived on a one-way ticket from an institution."

One-way ticket—that was the best, that one. No return, not on leave but discharged to go home.

Though he had no home. It would be a bachelor hotel to begin with. But you didn't get housing allowance for that. So it was important to find a room so he could get the allowance. A retiree should not throw his money away, rather he should say thank you and accept when the state is treating.

He exited onto the square in front of the station, stood a minute and squinted against the sharp, autumn sunlight. Everywhere around him was rumbling and booming. Almost to the point where he understood how the bumpkins felt when they came to the big city. The traffic swarmed over wooden bridges and between the gaping holes; they were extending the subway under Vasagatan now. And the railroad yard was gone; he had had a lot of fun there once upon a time. Now it was one big, mud porridge that some guys were trying to sink some giant-sized concrete foundation footings into. And out in Norrström's current, jagged iron struts stuck out above the water.

Large trucks with gravel came splashing out of the holes of the tunnels. Everywhere there was only work going on.

New and unfamiliar, everything. Here a figure like David Berg had no residential rights any longer. Though he had been born and raised in this city, a true child of the gutters. And now they had even taken away the railroad yard!

The fat cats, the crazy fats cats. They were so full of energy that they didn't know what to do next. They could just as easily kick themselves till they were tired. The city was fine the way it was, it was good enough for him, and it could be good enough for them, too. But they always had to change everything, didn't think it was good otherwise. Like building apartments tens of kilometers outside of town, and then sitting and riding for hours to go back and forth to their jobs. Buy themselves cars and new furniture and then work twice as hard to be able to pay for everything...

Poor old fat cats; he felt sorry for them. They didn't even have time to sit down in the sunshine and have a beer. They just slaved away, just kept on running—until they got a heart attack and died.

Out to freedom again,
To a glass and a friend.

But the melody sounded strange here; it was also drowned out by the rumbling. And David felt a longing for a small dark café where he could hide from all the efficiency for a while. Sit and sniff the musty smell, look at the yellow brown walls that were impregnated with the odors and smoke of decades. As a matter of fact, there was nothing as cozy as those small shabby cafés. If he tried to calculate where he had spent his life, then the cafés would come in next after the institutions. But where the institutions represented compulsion, the cafés symbolized freedom. To be free—that was sitting at a café.

There were—or at least had been—many pleasant cafés and eateries in the old Klara district. He had to make sure that they were still there.

The first signs on the way were worrisome. Klarabergsgatan was unrecognizable. The narrow street had been transformed into an enormous open stream of traffic. On the north side, the old houses were still standing—but they seemed to have been blinded by the daylight, exposed, been stripped of life for the most part. On the south side, the moneybags were building with their new blocks, encircling the churchyard with boxes that looked like margarine crates.

Alongside Hötorgshallen market hall, a lot of buildings had also disappeared, but the hall was still there as well as the many stands out on the square. Beside the Concert Hall the enormous holes were gaping again; they were digging down for the subway there, too. But at Mäster Samuelsgatan and Beridarbansgatan there were some neighborhoods that still looked the same; he found a café there and slinked in.

While he drank his coffee he leafed through his notebook where he had written down some addresses. Gun and her family had moved. Somewhere south of Söder. Hökarängan, that's what it was. Allan was still living in Hammarbyhöjden. And Per on Ringvägen.

If he were to begin with Gun … and save the best and the worst. But it was too early to go yet, he should get there in time for dinner, then they could hardly avoid inviting him to stay.

It was only the kids—and hardly them—that he could turn to anymore. Dora was no longer alive, and besides had always been impossible. The old buddies it was best to try to avoid, if he was going to "cope with freedom," as she, the little welfare officer had said. Tyra had a brother who was real accommodating as well. What was his name again? Bengt, maybe. He would ask Allan for the address.

He put down his notebook, stuffed his glasses in his breast pocket. He sat and felt well being, calm joy. He was home again, free. And calmer than before, without any howling needs. This time he would for sure be able to cope with freedom, as if the burden had become lighter with the years.

Two lines ran from the subway station in the dark pit beside Katarina elevator, 18 to Hökarängen and 19 to Stureby. There was hardly any chance of taking the wrong one. It was fast going out there, didn't take much over a quarter of an hour. As a result he got there a little earlier than he had intended; he strolled around a little bit in the new community.

So this was the way they were living nowadays. The buildings were so alike that he wondered how people could find their way home, especially when they were a little tipsy on a Saturday night. A few neon signs turned on, it began to glow, and mist rose up from the big field. If there were towns on the moon then they must look like this, he thought, unreal, square, lifeless. Though there were still people, small dark figures against the light walls of the buildings.

He began to grow cold, had not gotten around to getting an over-coat yet. He would find out if the city mission could help him with it. Maybe it was time to ring the bell now. He had made note of which building it was.

They lived on the ground floor. It was Olle who came and opened the door. He looked surprised and hardly welcoming.

"So you're out," he said. "Out and moving about."

"Yes, I'm home now. For good. May I come in?"

Olle moved aside. Just then Gun came out into the entryway; she paled when she saw who had come.

Weren't they even going to ask him in?

"I just thought I would see how things were with you," he said. "It's been a long time."

"We're just about to eat," Olle said. "But there's enough for one more. If you will take it like it is. Like a regular worker has it, not exactly any luxury."

He extended his hand toward Gun. She took it but dropped it quickly, looked like she was about to start blubbering.

Otherwise she was looking like Tyra more and more, though not as lively as Tyra. And she had kids, too, three. The boy was seven now, then two little girls. The youngest was only a few months old; she was asleep and he couldn't see her.

Gun set the table for one more in the kitchen.

It was mostly only Olle and David who talked; Gun kept quiet and listened, shushed the kids when they wanted to say anything.

The boy had just begun school. Their apartment was fine but they had not really settled in yet out there. Noisy, loads of kids, shotgun apartments where emergency cases from the housing waiting list had to live.

People who could not take care of themselves....

Olle's hobbyhorse. He talked about how things used to be, how poor he had been when he was growing up, how hard his parents had worked, how many siblings he had had.

And still we turned out to be real people!

David nodded and agreed—things were different once upon a time. Of course, they had been up to a lot of mischief back then, too, and not always been little angels ... but somehow it had been honorable trouble they had gotten into. Like stealing apples from the trees and such. But nowadays they were different, harder, more polished.

And he thought of Per. Maybe Per would invite him for dinner, too. There he would probably get a beer with his meal, not just milk. For sure Per had been both hard and polished—still getting caught anyway, or course.

As for himself, David had had a little bad luck in life. But surely he had turned out all right, too; he had never committed any big crimes. He had had a little trouble with alcohol, he had to admit that. He had peddled bootleg occasionally and done crooked deals with ration coupons—but one had to do something when one didn't have any work. He could agree with Olle in good conscience now.

Yes, yes so true, as it was put. They were surely too indulgent now, should take charge in a different way, put a stop to the mischief.

Gun still barely said anything.

While David drank coffee he came up with an idea that put him in a good mood. Naturally they thought he had come to beg money from them. But he would fool them. Pretty soon he would thank them for a good dinner and pleasant company and leave. Without saying one word about money. Then they would be taken aback for sure.

Even if it felt difficult, like throwing away money, he was successful. He even gave the boy a twenty-five-öre piece as "startup capital"
from the institution.

A friendly smiling grandfather said good-bye.

"It has certainly grown cooler," he said. "I'm going to go out and
get an overcoat tomorrow. Isn't this hat nice? I got it for only three
kronor secondhand at The Ants...."

He sat down in the almost empty subway car, caught his reflection
in the dark pane: the hat looked really good.

He had to laugh to himself again, now they were really flabbergasted.

But it was still a little more than a joke. An attempt to live a new
life, cope with the freedom she had talked about. The little welfare
officer. In truth, he had probably done it for her sake, so that she
would praise him. Like she had done those times he had come back
sober and tidy from a leave. For her sake, almost. To receive her
praise. It felt really empty to not have her anymore, to not come to
anyone and tell how he had not asked for one öre, and had instead
given the boy money.

"Wasn't I good?" he wanted to ask. And he looked at his hat ... and
his tie. "Don't I look handsome, like a fine old retiree?"

Tomorrow he would try to get in touch with Allan. Mostly to ask,
"Wasn't I good? And the hat?"

Allan was a little too clumsy, not as sensitive at comforting and
praising as the little welfare officer. But he had to do. Somebody had
to comfort him anyway if he was going to be able to bear up, be able
to cope with this damnably heavy freedom.

FINDING AN ARRANGEMENT

When Per had moved in with Lilian he had been broken, laid low. Afraid of being incarcerated by society again, prepared to beg and plead.

Under her care, he regained much of the force he had once had. The force he had owned and recouped was brutal. If Lilian had imagined that she had taken care of a sick companion dog, she now found that it was a wolf.

He accepted that she was there and that she took care of him—but not much more. He did not ask her for anything, he commanded. If she tried to ever raise an objection she only heard: *"You heard what I said!"* Then he would strike her.

Still she was not actually afraid of him. She was forbearing and not unused to being hit. She would never receive from Per as many blows as her father had given her. He would never go to so much trouble.

The difficult part was not that he hit her, but that he was so uninterested. That was different from her father; he had been red in the face with rage and exertion. He hit her because he cared about her, cared about what she did. Papa hit with feeling but Per didn't; that was the difference.

As if Per did not even have an interest in tormenting her, as if he was totally uninterested in her. She got a slap on her ear so she would obey or a shove in her back so she would move. He never spanked her like Papa always had. It was as if he didn't want to touch her. Sometimes he approached her in bed, after they had turned out the light. He would only take her fast and hard. And then pushed her away, freed himself, fell asleep. Usually he was really drunk when he approached, as if he needed to anesthetize himself to touch her at all.

They had had two children, in any case, two boys. He was not kind to them either. They could not be in the living room when he was home; he wanted peace. During the day she put them in the "crèche," she had to work, of course. Though she was barely allowed to be in the living room either.

Once he had eaten he usually went out, as good as every evening, sat in the beer parlor across the street. He had friends he met up with there. But he never brought them home; was he so ashamed of her? She knew that she wasn't exactly beautiful, that she talked too much. Still, she didn't look any worse than people do for the most part, did she? And talk … one had to be able to say something sometimes?

One day the doorbell rang as she was fixing dinner. Since Per never opened the door, she turned down the gas, wiped her fingers, and went out to find out who it was.

The person standing outside was an older fellow in a dark overcoat; he looked a little refined. At first she didn't recognize him, but then she saw that it was Per's father; she hadn't seen him since they lived in Negro Village.

"An old acquaintance, I believe?" he said; he apparently had recognized her, too. She nodded but did not dare say anything, did not know what Per would think. If he ever mentioned his father, it was with a curse word at what "the old devil" had done or was doing.

"Come in and I will tell Per," she finally said. She closed the door to the vestibule—it was unnecessary for the whole building to hear if there was any trouble. Cautiously she knocked on the living room door, opened it, and slipped inside. David could hear her whispering but could not make out the words.

"What the hell is he doing here?"

It was Per's voice.

She whispered again.

"Let the devilish creature in then."

David hung up his hat and coat and stepped inside. Per was sitting in the old armchair; he didn't get up. David walked over to him and reached out his hand. Per greeted him unwillingly.

"So, they've let you out now," he said. "But you're not working, are you?"

Lilian pulled over a chair and David sat down. Then she disappeared out into the kitchen; he heard the sound of frying and wondered if they would ask him to stay for dinner. He had come in time, as he had calculated.

"No, now I am retired…. I rent a little room, get by. Isn't this suit nice, by the way? I got it second hand at Little Crumbs…."

"I don't give a shit about the clothes, and don't go thinking you will get anything here."

"I don't intend to ask for anything either," David said. "I just wanted to hear … well, how things are going for you all."

"That's none of your business."

"One is always interested in one's own children. Allan has two kids now—and Gun three. And you?"

"Two."

"And you are working … and everything's good?"

"The hell it is good. It will never be good."

"I recognized her out there. She was one of those who lived diagonally across from us, Nordins, right?"

"That may be."

Once they started talking about Negro Village it was as if Per loosened up anyway. Suddenly he laughed.

"Do you remember when the old lady broke her leg and went to the hospital? What a hell of a party we had. Rutan got completely wasted. And the old man, Farfar, sat at the kitchen table and licked up the beer that was running down the oilcloth. Yeah, it was something…."

David remembered it was then that Stig had left, it was then that he couldn't take it any longer. And even so, Stig was still … yes, he was the one who was to have the accordion.

"We're going to eat," Per said suddenly. "My old lady will have to put out one more plate. But you can't have any brew; I have nothing at home."

"I'm not drinking anything anymore," David answered.

"Don't talk shit," Per cut him off. "I'll bet you slurp up whatever you can get a hold of."

Lilian wanted to offer them coffee after dinner. But Per was going out.

"Sit here and drink that dishwater," he said to David. "But you won't get any money here, you know well. So don't try with Lilian."

"No, no. I'm fine. I have my pension—and then I get a little from Allan every month."

"Yeah, that stupid devil is easy to fool."

When Per had left, Lilian was transformed. Caution and fear disappeared; now she dared to speak. David was almost buried beneath the rush of words.

David himself liked to listen, also to listen to others speak. It was mellow and friendly, homey. He felt quite lonely, did not meet many people, in any case many who took the time to talk to him. The old buddies were in institutions or lying in the hospitals and graveyards. He actually felt best at Allan's home, but he couldn't be there all the time. At Gun's it wasn't as good; listening to Olle was like listening to an old prison warden. Lilian avoided anything that might be unpleasant for him, only talked for the sake of talking. It was soothing, almost sleep-inducing.

She washed the dishes and he helped with the drying. He had not done that since the old days when he had wanted to be really nice to Tyra. Actually he had only done it when he wanted to go to bed with Tyra, then he had jumped in and been eager, wanted her to be done quickly with her household chores. Not that he had needed to be ingratiating to Tyra; she had never been like that. Only that it had been fun to do it, to be there and bump into each other a little and give her a little slap on the rump in passing.

Strange, there were so many who he thought reminded him of Tyra these days. Lilian, too. Not at all in her face. But when he saw her like this, a little to the side and from behind, then it was like it was Tyra who was there and pottering about. The slippers, the sturdy legs, the wide backside, the slightly stooping back. He almost felt obliged to give her a little comforting spank.

"Don't be sad, my girl," he said. "Everything will take care of itself."

She turned around and looked at him. She looked like she was about to blubber. For a minute he was afraid that he had done something foolish when he had given her a spank like that. Maybe she took offense all the same.

"Do you really think so?" she asked.

"One can only hope," he said. And patted her on the cheek, saw that she needed to be consoled. "We certainly can both be friends...."

Then the dam broke, she dropped the dishrag and threw her arms around his neck. She was taller than he was; her face lay against his shoulder and he thought, now my suit will be spotted from her sniveling.

"There, there." He tried to calm her, regretting what he had gotten himself into, she was probably hysterical.

Finally she took the towel from him and dried her eyes and nose.

"Please excuse me, David," she implored. "But I am so unused to anyone being kind. I am not even allowed to speak. Can you come back soon? It is so nice to be able to talk to someone."

She stood in the doorway and waved as he left.

It was like seeing Tyra standing there. In some way it was as if he had gotten Tyra back. Though naturally he wouldn't get up to any hanky-panky with Lilian, of course, not. He was too old for that. But still—it was almost like having a person to be attached to.

David was limping a little when he walked; his leg had begun to bother him again. It was a wound he had gotten when he had been drunk a number of years ago. And then it was something with varicose veins as well. In the institution, he had gotten a little help with it; it was hard to take care of it alone. He would probably be obliged to go to a doctor. Maybe the doctor would send him to the hospital.

In his younger days, David had been an expert in wangling his way into the hospital; it felt good to take a few days to recuperate when his life got too difficult.

But that had been a long time ago. Now, when it might be a question of something serious, he wasn't quite as sure if he wanted to go there. He remembered an old guy with sore legs he had known; they had cut off one of his legs finally. It was probably best to stay away. Or else safer to consult with them before it was too late?

He walked up to Söder Hospital on a weekday when it grew too painful. The doctor thought that he needed to be admitted as soon as possible. Before a week had passed he was admitted.

The hospital lay approximately where Negro Village had been located before. For David Berg it almost felt like moving home. The view over Årstaviken and the railroad bridge he recognized so well from before. Though he had never had it as nice at home as it was here, of course.

Home. It had occurred to him that he actually even longed for the institutions, for his friends, for the little welfare officer at the last place. For the irresponsibility and for just giving in. He had never had such an easy time getting by out in life; there were so many temptations, so much that enticed him. Work was something he had never actually done. And since he had to live in any case, he had occupied himself with other things. And as a rule would go to the hospital after a while, of course.

The hospital was, in fact, ideal. A person was a free person yet still was established, a combination of institutional constraint and freedom. One was taken care of, had people to talk with, could go out into the smoking room and sit there for hours with the other old guys.

Here it wasn't hard to accommodate oneself to the daily routine; he had been in worse places. And here he had significance; here they were kind and friendly toward him. He had always been a little smooth in his manner; that fit in well here—a good and grateful patient. But if young girls, students and nurses' aides, were brusque with him, then he would go to the head nurse and complain. They couldn't treat an old retiree just any old way.

Yet it was pleasant with so many young women; it was a change from the institution's wardens and guards. It smelled clean and nice around them, they were fun to look at. He would have really liked to touch them, too—but they didn't like that.

Quickly he sank into the hospital's world, into its environment. He had never felt so good in any other place. Now it was just a question of being able to stay there, avoiding having to come out again. He had found an arrangement that fit.

MEETING, TRYING OUT

The personnel director came and introduced the two new employees. One of them was going to work together with Elisabet and she wondered who it would be. She took stock of them quickly, hoped it wouldn't be the little, over made-up one. It wasn't either; she was going to the cashier.

The other one seemed much better, almost a little shy, a tall dark-haired girl of about twenty.

"So this is Miss Karge who is going to assist Mrs. Eriksson," the personnel director said.

Elisabet gave a start, felt how she grew pale, had to restrain herself in order to greet her in a friendly manner. But noticed how she didn't really succeed; the shock and anger could not be hidden.

So typical of Erik—to get his daughter a position here. And not bother about the discomfort it could bring with it. But had he really counted on this—that it would be Elisabet taking care of his daughter? Probably not, even so.

She would see Erik sometimes when he stopped by to talk to her boss. For quite a long time she had thought it was disagreeable to run into him, a reminder of something she wanted to forget. Now it hardly had any effect on her; the old occurrence was maybe not forgotten, but it was meaningless. She was indifferent to him. But Erik would be most attentive when they bumped into each other; try to turn on the charm. He got nothing for his efforts; she was never anything other than coldly correct.

This situation was more difficult. The girl was going to work for Elisabet. It would be unnatural not to use the informal mode of address with her, not to talk to her like everybody else. The way their work was laid out they would have to have continual contact, get along. Otherwise things would become both ineffective and unbearable.

He came in the afternoon to see where his daughter had been placed. He seemed a little sheepish when he discovered it was in Elisabet's office. She left the father and daughter alone and went in to her boss with some letters that had to be signed. When she came out from there, Erik was waiting for her in the corridor.

This time he did not try to play the charmer.

"This wasn't intentional," he said. "I only knew that there was a position available in the cashier's office. But the other woman who began at the same time had, of course, better qualifications for that work."

"Have you said anything about Maj? Does she know that Maj and I are sisters?"

"No," he said. "That's surely unnecessary."

"I will tell her. It's better that one of us says it than that she finds out some other way."

Us. That word had a disagreeable aftertaste; it intimated that they once had had something in common together.

"As you like," he said. "Though Irene won't like it, she's a little jealous of my past. But, good God, it's been twenty-five years since Maj and I had anything to do with each other—it must be outside the statute of limitations by now?"

"Your daughter ought to know anyway."

"Indeed, you're probably right. But remember that it really wasn't my intention that this would happen. Try not to punish her for my old sins, okay?"

There was a lot to answer that with, but she kept silent and walked away. He stayed standing where he was and watched her leave, marveling over the fact that she still seemed so young. It was unbelievable that he had had her at one time—and that he had let her go.

This business with Erik's daughter irritated Elisabet, made her nervous. But there was something else that was bothering her.

The dream of the car seemed difficult to turn into reality. Elisabet was almost beginning to despair. It was not dependent on the money any longer. Joseph Schönlank had paid back what he had borrowed a long time ago. The loan had hardly led to any great happiness, Elisabet thought. Joseph's mother had died only a few months after she got here. But, of course, Joseph had gotten to see her and be with her when she died.

No, it wasn't the money anymore. Now it was only Elisabet herself it depended on. And the petty driving inspector.

Strange … she had imagined what it would be like to drive, thought she knew so well how it was done. She had seen herself behind the wheel, sensed her ability, her confidence.

The theoretical instruction had not caused her any concern in the least. She threw herself into what she was assigned, had always had an easy time of learning. But learning to drive was definitely something else, something harder. At first she had been all too confident, thought she knew exactly what she should do, barely wanted to follow the instructor's directions.

Driving a car could not be so difficult. Even Allan who wasn't the brightest bulb had learned to do it. Though he had had a lot of trouble with the theoretical part.

It seemed obvious to her that other people would accommodate her, leave room for her. They saw that she was driving toward them, they could wait until she had passed.

The driving instructor kept at her incessantly that she had to be more careful, show more consideration. And she also had to have gentler movements, not try to force the gears in place, not brake so suddenly.

Gradually, as she sensed more and more that she was failing, she grew bewildered and lost faith in her ability. She did everything wrong though she knew so well how it should be done. Maybe she had a temperament that did not go with driving a car?

She failed her driver's test. Movements too jerky, too little caution— she knew this herself, sensed her mistakes. It was because she wanted to appear confident and overdid it. When she continued with the lessons she felt more insecure than ever.

And now this complication at the office had arisen.

In the middle of a lesson she stopped driving, gave the excuse that she was sick and went home. That evening she cried a long time and then she told Lennart about her new work colleague, too; she hadn't said anything before. As if she was ashamed to say Erik's name.

After that, it was several weeks before she showed up at the driving school again and continued her lessons. By then she felt calmer. Things were going well at the office; Lena Karge was easy to get along with, did good work. And the girl couldn't help that she was Erik's daughter.

It wasn't until the beginning of May that Elisabet got to take a new driving test. She passed this time. After more than forty lessons—she hardly dared calculate how much it had cost.

A few days later she went together with Lennart and bought the car, a shiny little red Volkswagen. The dealer had to drive it out to the street and then she sat at the wheel and had to go through the gear changes a few times. This car was quite different from the Volvo they had at the driving school.

They pulled away from the curb with a jerk. But already after a little while she felt like she was used to it and secure, that everything was exactly as she had dreamed and thought it would be. And still unbelievable, fantastic. Her own car, to feel how it obeyed her least hand movement or pressure of the foot.

Joy and pride almost blinded her, she drove through a red light at a crosswalk, and she almost collided with a car that came up on the left. Luckily, nothing happened in either case. That would be just great if she came home with a dent in the new car, it would have been too completely mortifying.

Lennart seemed worried from where he sat beside her. "Not so fast," he said. "Look to the left! There is a stop sign here!"

She laughed at his nervousness, felt unassailable.

She parked the car on the street outside the building where they lived. Then she had to go to the window time after time to look at it. To see that it was still there, that no sticky-fingered kid had been poking at it, that no one had parked too close so that it would be hard to get out.

Eventually the streetlight was turned on above the building entrance; it shone on the car's newly polished chrome.

Lena Karge was in fact a very good work colleague. And a good person, too, Elisabet thought. Not that quiet at all once she had gotten used to things; they could have a lot of fun together. Elisabet was quite a bit older, but she hardly thought of that; it was as if Lena was the same age. They began to eat lunch together, there was always a lot to talk about regarding the company, and besides, they got along well together.

Naturally they got to talking about their private lives sometimes. Elisabet told about Monika who was in second grade in school now. And Lena might say one thing or another about her parent. Papa had so many meetings and then he was sitting up half the night because he had to read for his many duties in the city council and various boards.

It was funny to think of Erik as "Papa." But gradually Elisabet got used to the thought. She could laugh to herself; it was as if Erik had become tamer, less dangerous, older. Old Papa who sat with his papers, that was a different Erik from the one she had known. Back then he had always seemed so alone, during the time he was together with Maj as well. A roving animal on the prowl, hungry, fierce.

It was Papa who had been so eager for them to move out to Vällingby. Lena liked it a lot there, but Mama still thought it was just as out of the way and inconvenient. She took the subway into town as often as she could, met her girlfriends, and went to the department stores.

If someone else had told her that, Elisabet would have snapped and said some spiteful words about housewives who wasted time with nonsense. But where Lena was concerned she didn't feel she could, instead she became tactful and tolerant.

They usually did not talk about Maj or about Henning, who was Lena's half-brother in any case. But one day when Elisabet had gotten some photos she had developed, she thought she ought to show Lena what the cottage in the archipelago looked like, she had indeed talked about it at times. And then it happened that she showed her the other pictures, too. In one of them were Henning and Barbro with their children, in another Maj was there.

Lena looked at the pictures quietly. But a minute later she said: "It must be so strange having something important that we can't talk about. I have only heard Henning's name a few times. I know that he exists. But it is as if Mama denies it, as if she can't acknowledge that he exists. That's why Papa never talks about it. That must be wrong, then one just gets a big empty space, something one has to go around all the time."

She had happened to see her father and Henning together one time. Papa had asked her not to say anything to Mama, it would only uselessly upset her.

For the first time it occurred to Elisabet that one could maybe feel sorry for Erik, too.

"Do you think badly of Papa ... because he left your sister?"

"Well, no. It was probably she who left him just as much. They did not go well together. And it is a lot better to recognize one's mistake than to continue."

"But you two seem ... well, sort of a little reserved when you see each other."

Elisabet felt unmasked, wondered how much the girl could guess, how much one showed without knowing it.

"It just happens that way," she said. "It is hard to get away from the old stuff."

"That's too bad," said Lena. "For, in fact, you two would get along well together and could have a lot to talk about. Papa can be a lot of fun, especially when he is debating. But Mama doesn't really under-stand that, she thinks he is serious and gets upset. Even though he is only having fun."

One day when they were eating at their usual lunch place, Joseph

Schönlank came in. He approached them and said hello, and asked if he could sit down. He wanted to thank Elisabet for her recent hospitality; he had been with them out in the country over the weekend.

Now he had been to the dentist in the building next door and was just going to drink a cup of coffee before he went back to work.

Elisabet introduced him to Lena. She wasn't really sure if she liked him sitting down with them; Lena might wonder what kind of odd person he was. But Joseph was pleasant and it was always easy to talk to him.

A few days later he was there again. He joked that he would make sure his treatment went on for a long time so he would get the same nice company at lunch several times.

Afterward Lena wanted to know more about Joseph, she was markedly interested. And Elisabet told her. But she also said, a little in jest, that Joseph was way too old for Lena, surely over thirty-five.

He had to come back one more time, his last visit to the dentist for now. They knew which day it would be. Lena was in a hurry to leave for lunch on time. But Elisabet was held up by her boss and took longer.

That irritated her a little. She didn't know if it was so good to leave Lena alone with Joseph. If he wanted Lena and him to meet, then the girl would not be able to resist. Lena had been too completely interested. And Joseph was still a foreigner, had grown up in another country, had encountered such terrible things. Lena was a completely ordinary Swedish girl, without any experience at all of life. She and Joseph could never go well together.

Elisabet didn't make it down to the lunch counter before Joseph had already left. But Lena sat there smiling to herself.

BROKEN HABITS

For someone who has grown old, every change can be felt as a danger, a forced step closer to the finish. Habits give security, become something to hide inside. The pattern of every day living can feel like handrails, something to hold onto, something that gives security.

But sometimes the everyday pattern can slowly, almost unnoticeably shift. And when one suddenly notices it, one can feel fooled, deprived of an illusion. Nothing is as it has been, dreaded change has snuck in under concealment, hollowed out the handrails like woodworms.

Emelie continued to read her newspaper as regularly as before. But it told about a world ever harder to fathom.

There had not been any real peace after the big war. In Korea, it's true, they had called a truce at last, but in Indochina they were still warring. And both of the major powers had hydrogen bombs now; distrust only grew.

In Sweden, of course, things were calmer. Kings and presidents came on visits—and the Russian navy.

It was not as rewarding to read the now as before. Emelie saw so much worse. The fine typeface blurred together and became unreadable; often she had to guess what was written. A lot was incomprehensible, some of it she surely misunderstood.

It took time so she did have something to occupy her. And that was nice now that she could barely do anything useful anymore. But it was as if the newspaper had betrayed her, was not hers in the same way any longer. It was for younger people with better eyesight. As long as she could see the headlines she would try and read anyway. If, for nothing else, then for Gunnar's sake, since it was he who subscribed to it for her.

Emelie seldom got out anymore; the stairs were a problem for her and there wasn't any elevator in the building. And she did not long to get out in the same way as before. She was actually most content at home, in her habitual place, among what was familiar.

She was not sick, could certainly live a few more years. But her legs were bad, as if she felt a stone chill in them, the memory of all those years she stood on the drafty stone floor in the Melinder factory.

Jenny had started rehearsals again, she had gotten a little part in a comedy that was going to be on in the fall.

In truth, Jenny ought to admit that she was a pensioner; she was a few years past seventy. But she wanted to work so much, and so it was actually nice that she had gotten this job. There had not been so many roles for her these past few years. She was still lively and agile, though she maybe had a little harder time remembering her lines, she complained about it sometimes.

It had been a long time since her last role. And for that reason extra nice. And a little anxiety provoking, too.

The character she was going to play was an old acquaintance.

"I've been doing old harpies since I was twenty," she told the director. "As soon as there is one like that they think: that's a role for Jenny Fält."

"This one you should do a little differently," the director said. "Though it should provide a splash of color, of course."

He liked Jenny. She was easy to work with even if she had perhaps gotten a little flighty over the years. Willing to take risks. Naturally a little primitive, a type, not a real actress. But people recognized her, knew what she would deliver, laughed as soon as they saw her. Not the young people, maybe, but people who were a little older. Heavens, he hadn't been more than ten himself when he had seen her for the first time, at a movie matinee, *Anderssonskans Kalle*. She had played her role so that the film resounded with it. He could still laugh when he recalled her. If he saw the film now it might not be as funny; she had surely overacted, pure slapstick.

She would hardly be able to handle a bigger role, probably never had one either. But in supporting roles she was good, as she was at

The Oscar Theater years ago. And wonderful to have for a little splash of color. That was her function here. And his task was to see that the effect was not all too glaring.

She was to come running through a door, down three steps, and shout.

She was nimble, fit. No risk letting her dash about, she could manage it, had more energy than many young people. She did exercises during the breaks; one of the girls had seen her doing a handstand in the loge.

"Let's try it again," he said. "Jenny, can you come a little more to the left, cut across a little more when you come from the steps. Then you stop just about here."

"Sure thing." She got it.

She stood behind the door and waited for the reply that was her signal. Now it came—and she thrust open the door and almost flew out. Cut across a little more, that was it.

She didn't see as well as she used to maybe. Or was too eager, started across too soon. Her foot missed the bottom step, she lost her footing, felt: now I'm falling. She fell over.

Jenny had fallen countless times, was almost a specialist at that kind of thing. This time it came so unexpectedly, she didn't have time to get prepared. And also her body was no longer young, it had calcified despite the exercises. She felt the pain and cried out. Tried to get up but couldn't.

They hurried over to her, were going to help her up. But they found it was best to let her stay lying down. It was pretty likely she had broken something.

"Now you will have to go find another old harpy," she said. "This old harpy is apparently done playacting."

"You'll come back," the director said.

She didn't say anything. Felt bewilderment but hid it. She tried to pull her large mouth up into a smile, it wasn't successful at any rate, it only turned into a grimace.

"Someone has to call home," she said. "Don't give up if no one answers; let it ring long enough so that someone will finally come."

"Take it easy, boys. This lady is old," she said to the ambulance men.

She waved to her colleagues from the stretcher. As if she was still playacting.

"She'll probably never come back again," someone said.

"Hardly a chance," said the director. "She's probably gone now. But she was a splash of color in any case."

While Jenny was at the theater Emelie sat alone in the kitchen as usual. She usually didn't open it if someone rang at the door. She didn't intend to answer the phone either, was hard of hearing. And it was almost always calls for Jenny.

But then it rang so terribly time after time that at least she went into the other room and lifted the receiver.

They had to repeat the message a few times before Emelie heard and understood. She managed to pull herself together enough so that she could note which hospital Jenny had been driven to.

She had been standing while she spoke, now she sank down onto a chair in the room. She sat a while completely still, while slowly the whole significance of the conversation became clear to her. Jenny at the hospital, Jenny not coming home to her. There was no point in her sitting and waiting any longer.

She went out into the kitchen and turned off the fire under the coffee pot.

Jenny in the hospital. Jenny who had been so happy about this role. How would things go now?

And she herself? She sank down onto a chair again. She had never felt so completely abandoned before. What happens now? How will she be able to manage alone?

The telephone numbers for Gunnar's house and Maj's house were written in large ciphers on a pad of paper by the phone. But both of them were surely at work now. Maybe she could find the number for Maj's office in the phone book, with the help of a magnifying glass. But Hjordis was probably home; as a matter of fact, she could try to call Gunnar's home first.

Hjordis answered, she would call both Gunnar and Maj. Emelie should just stay calm, everything would surely work out.

It took only a half hour before the doorbell rang and this time Emelie opened it. It was Gunnar.

Along with Gunnar came calm and security as always. Even now when her whole normal and safe everyday world seemed to have collapsed.

He wanted Emelie to stay with him and Hjordis while Jenny lay in the hospital. It would only be difficult and inconvenient for her to be alone. Wouldn't it be a nice little change and fun to get away from it all for a while? And fun for them to have her. It was so beautiful in the garden now; she could make the most of the summer in a completely different way out there. It was easy to get out in the fresh air. Emelie could live in one of the rooms on the ground floor so she would not have to deal with the stairs. It would be fun for Hjordis, too. She took care of some of the office work for Gunnar's company but this time of year there wasn't much to do.

Emelie didn't really know what she preferred to do. Maybe it was her duty to sit in the apartment and wait for Jenny, to be there in place. But she wasn't doing any good that way.

She felt that Gunnar meant what he said, that he wanted her to come.

Only once before had she stayed out there, even if she had been there often to see them. That was the time she was unemployed and was going to help Hjordis with their first child. Mary was born in 1922; that was thirty-two years ago. Mary was married and had children of her own now.

Emelie accepted, would gladly come if she wasn't too much trouble. But not until the following day. Maj would come up later that evening, could help her pack what she needed. She would manage fine until then.

Gunnar offered to help he pack. But he wasn't allowed to. A man wouldn't understand that sort of thing so well; it was better to wait until Maj arrived. In any case, Emelie could pack most of it herself; there wasn't so much she needed to take with her.

He left and Emelie stayed sitting there.

There was no real reason to turn on the light; she sat at the window and watched how the dusk sank slowly over the street outside. Was Jenny in severe pain now? What if she never came home? How would it be then? Emelie had never stayed in the hospital, only been to visit. Also, the hospital felt like something alien and dangerous that lurched a little closer, threatened what was normal and secure.

She was still sitting in the shadows when Maj arrived. Maj had her own key and didn't need to ring.

Maj had been at the hospital and been able to see Jenny. It was a broken leg, as they had thought. Despite everything Jenny had been in a pretty good mood, was joking with the nurse. But cried a little bit when they were alone together, said she was probably done with performing; now she would probably never get another chance.

Jenny had had such high hopes for this role. But she had them every time, had always hoped for a breakthrough.

Emelie was sitting ready when Gunnar arrived, with her coat on and her suitcase by the outer door.

Even though she understood that what was happening was for the best, she left her home with anxiety. There was a fear that she would never come back, not have her own place any longer. Without Jenny it wouldn't work; alone she could not take care of herself anymore. And if Jenny got sick it would not go well either; then they would have to apply to someplace for both of them.

She looked around one last time. Would she get to see everything again, how long would it be?

But she shouldn't look sad now; then Gunnar might think she didn't want to go with him. And she did really want to, as long as she knew that she was going to be able to come home again.

They drove past the shop where Emelie had worked. Gunnar asked her and Emelie told about times gone by and became so enthralled by the memories that she almost forgot Jenny for a while.

Out in the house on Tistelvägen, Hjordis welcomed them with the table set for breakfast. They had fixed up one of the rooms on the ground floor for Emelie, with a bed and a reading lamp and an armchair and everything she could need. And flowers from their own garden.

There were so kind that she had to shed a little tear, despite all her good intentions to avoid doing so.

Each and every day Emelie was able to sit out in the garden; she liked most to sit in the light shade between the fruit trees.

She remembered so well how it had looked the first time she stayed there. At that time, what now was the garden had in fact just been a plot of muddy land. Every evening Gunnar had dug and planted, worked until it grew so dark that he couldn't see anymore. He had put in trees and bushes, sown grass.

The gooseberry bushes she remembered especially well. They were still there; whether or not they were the same bushes or possibly new ones he had planted. Gunnar had been so fond of gooseberries; they had had some bushes in the little garden that belonged to their house on Fjällgatan. And Gunnar had gotten to help Emelie pick them there; she had had a milk bottle and he a cup that he would empty into her bottle now and then. When he was done picking he had been allowed to eat some berries. She could see him in front of her, he was small and thin then, how he took the berry and bit off the little nub and then he pressed it against his lips and let it explode into his mouth. How pleased he looked, how he licked his mouth afterward.

And now he came to her and said: "Do you remember the gooseberry bushes on Fjällgatan?"

She could only nod.

He fetched some berry baskets in the kitchen, moved a chair as close to the big bush as possible, helped Emelie over to it. He took a stool for himself and sitting beside her, began to pick.

A moment of happiness, of memory, and fellowship.

CLOSER TO
LIFE

Living out at Gunnar's was like coming a little closer to the world. Here there was a lot more activity, here so much more happened than at home in her own apartment. Every day Emelie received reports from life, from a world that seemed more alive and pressing than the theater world that Jenny usually talked about.

Gunnar's children, who were both married now, came to visit with their families. His son worked in the carpentry firm, and he and Gunnar discussed the parts of the city that were being built and businesses that they were setting up out there. His daughter was married to a radio dealer and talked a lot about the new television and its future. Last spring, in May, it had had its premier and large crowds of people had gathered outside display windows and in movie theaters and department stores to see broadcasts that came from the Royal Institute of Technology.

Sometimes Hjordis's sister, Asta, came out; she had a tobacco shop in the Klara neighborhood and told many stories of famous people and others. And with Gunnar, Emelie could discuss the newspaper stories; now she got a clear explanation of much that she had had a hard time understanding during her incomplete reading. And then there was Hjordis, there, too, all day long.

If Emelie felt like she was getting a little too much of the good things, she could go and sit in her room and rest a while. But usually it was just fun. Like old times, when it was always so lively at home.

She was sitting and doing a puzzle with one of Gunnar's grandchildren when Maj came. The last pieces were just fitting into place. They had not looked at all like they were going to fit at first, but then one fit and then it was just as if the others slipped in after. And the picture was complete.

Maj came out once a week and called almost every day. It had turned out so that she had the closest contact not only with her mother, but also with Emelie.

First and foremost, Maj always had to tell how Jenny was doing. Things seemed to be progressing; after a rather short time in the hospital, Jenny had been able to go to a convalescent home. The doctor believed she would have a full recovery even if she should expect to walk with a cane for a while. Jenny was quite happy at the home, was already some sort of minister of fun there, knew everybody. But, of course, she longed to go home.

This time Maj also had a strange story to tell. Elisabet and Erik were working at companies that had quite a lot to do with each other, and now Erik had gotten a job for his daughter at Elisabet's company. The girl, who was called Lena, and Elisabet had become such good friends. And through Elisabet the girl had become acquainted with a good friend of Lennart's, Joseph Schönlank. And now Lena and Joseph had gotten engaged.

It was like the puzzle pieces that Emelie had just fit together. They didn't seem to fit at all—and then suddenly they fit into the pattern, formed a whole.

But that was really strange ... Elisabet, who had always disliked Erik so much, who had been so unjust in her condemnation of him many times. Completely irreconcilable, as if it had been her he had betrayed. And now she was good friends with his daughter.

Maj had also met Joseph; he had been out at their country place. Nice, but not so young, must be significantly older than Erik's daughter.

Maj spoke entirely calmly about Erik. She had nothing against meeting either him or his daughter, she said. It wasn't unlikely that the girl would come out to the country next Sunday.

She began to laugh. How small the world could be.

Otherwise Maj did seem tired, not especially happy. John was unwell, had a hard time keeping up with his job. Heavy, a lot of lifting. In other places the work could be mechanized, there were lifts and trucks. These days there were surely not many who carried as much as the one who worked in a warehouse with fabrics.

A little bit after Maj, Allan and Daggan arrived. They came out to Gunnar's to visit sometimes. Allan was not working at Gunnar's company any longer, now that Gunnar had stopped building houses. He was a heavy laborer, a "heavy" as he himself said, and didn't like to stand inside in a carpenters' workshop. He would grow nervous, feel closed in.

He had bought a car a while back.

"Only an old used jalopy," Allan said, but it was good enough for them. Almost every evening he took Daggan and the kids out for a spin. But this evening they had gone alone; the kids were no longer as enthusiastic. Besides, Daggan might need to get away from them for a while.

So they almost felt like newlyweds, he said. Out on the loose.

"That's right. I'm pinched completely blue," Daggan said. "He's crazy."

Maj had to think of what Elisabet had to say when she had seen Allan and Daggan swimming out at the country place: elephant seals' mating dance. Of course, that was mean, but it as right on target, too, they were so uninhibited; Allan hugged and spanked his Daggan and neither one of them cared if anyone was watching. She had become really plump and big, something to grab hold of, Alan said.

"You're crazy," Daggan said again.

Allan could seem coarse, insensitive when he laughed his enormous laugh, bellowing. But as so often happened, the first superficial impression and the reality did not match, thought Maj. Allan was gentler than most people, liked to keep in touch with those who had helped him at one time, he was loyal. Loyal to Emelie and loyal to Gunnar. Now he regularly visited his father who was in the hospital again. As far as the children went he was almost womanishly tender. And always anxious about doing something wrong, making someone upset. But he knew what Daggan could tolerate; she liked the slightly hard-handed play.

They had been on vacation in Denmark. Well, only one day, in Copenhagen. He had left the car in Malmö—he didn't dare drive it in right-hand traffic. He went to Tivoli with the kids, drank real beer, ate red sausages that were called pölser, and picked at some things; it was shrimp. And seen a tattoo parlor. He had wanted to send Daggan in; it would have been fun to have her decked out with flowers and leaves here and there, but she had refused.

And Daggan had bought a cloth with the mermaid on it. And the sandwiches they had eaten and the coffee that was undrinkable.... Though it was very hard to understand what people were saying.

Just think how people could travel now, so much they were able to see.

Emelie, too, could certainly go to Copenhagen, Allan thought.

But then Emelie laughed. No, it was too late. She didn't want to go that far anymore.

Hjordis came with the coffee. Gunnar and his son, Torsten, discussed the building sites with Allan now.

There was so much that had changed in recent years, most of it for the better. Before everything had been carried. The mortar women had carried mortar but that was a long time ago, before Allan and Torsten's time. The brick carriers could still be seen on less modernized construction sites. But they, too, were in the process of disappearing to be replaced by lifts and cranes.

Cranes, that was the future, according to Gunnar. They were used more abroad but were beginning to come here, too; several years ago they had imported a number of cranes from Germany. Now the effort at Swedish production was underway; a "climbing crane" was in the works, which would be able to climb along as the building grew in height. Once they had reached the top it could be disassembled into pieces.

And then everything was being made in components now. Not just windows and doors, but large sections of walls, floors, and roofs, whole roofs and pillars. Soon they would be able to build buildings like children played with construction sets. And then the construction workers would be an engineer or a machinist who directed the machines.

A lot of the heaviest and the hardest work would disappear, the raw exertion. But still people would be well exposed to weather and wind, would have to clamber through slush in rain-soaked sites, stand in the draft and feel the icy chill in buildings where the windows had not yet been put in, try to get a grip on tools with fingers frozen stiff. Toil would be replaced by haste, with the help of the machines people would get twice as much done as before, but the pace would be hard. Those who whistled over the high wages of construction workers ought to try the job themselves a few days, then they could see if they wanted to change jobs.

Emelie listened to them and thought back. It was like hearing August and Gunnar once upon a time. Now it was Gunnar who was the oldest and best informed. Not a boy any longer; he had turned sixty-five a ways back.

Gunnar's mother, Allan's grandmother, had been a mortar woman at one time. Now there weren't mortar women anymore. Except for one standing as a statue up at the union headquarters, Allan said.

Even if not everything was so good, things were better. People were not worn down like before, they got to live in another way. They had the energy to live, Emelie thought.

Maj got a ride home from Allan. She got the whole back seat of the car to herself, otherwise that was where the kids got to carry on. There were traces left of them: a teddy bear lay on the seat and a half-licked peppermint striped lollipop in the back window.

Daggan got in beside Allan; that was her spot. Though, of course, he explained that she always sat in the way so that he had a hard time reaching the gearshift and the handbrake.

The autumn evening was lightly misted with fog. They drove through the area with older houses, came out on broad Nynäsvägen, seemed to be lifted up by the giant bridge over Skanstull. Neon signs glowed beside the industries along Hammarby Canal. On the other side of the water, where the city gardens had been, they were soon going to begin construction of an enormously tall building. Allan pointed, he was going to start working there on the first of November;

it was SENTAB who was going to build it for Folksam. They were going to remove all the park's dirt before they could begin blasting. He would be close to his job; they were still living at Hammarbyhöjden. He would even be able to make it home for his lunch break and give his old lady a few pats for a while.

"He's crazy," Daggan explained. "He drives me nuts."

Of course, he was going to drive Maj all the way to her door. It was fun to drive.

He glided up to the curb; Maj stepped out. Allan and Daggan hollered and waved as the car pulled away again.

Maj still felt as if numb from the commotion when she came up. John was already in bed, he was probably asleep. She took off her shoes and walked quietly so as not to disturb him; he needed to sleep the times when he could.

A book was lying on the shelf and waiting for her. But this evening she didn't really feel like reading. It was better to just sit, let her thoughts wander.

Allan and Daggan, their almost unnatural naturalness. Like children, or elephant seals playing, as Elisabet said. Close to each other, close to life. Maybe she was a little too proper, a little boring.

Strange actually that both she and Elisabet had become so proper. They weren't like Jenny at all—she could fling herself around like Daggan—no matter how unalike they were in general. In this respect, Maj and Elisabet were in fact more like Emelie. Though when young Maj had been quite free, not afraid of shocking anyone either.

And Elisabet, who had gotten to be good friends with Erik's daughter....

Now Maj could smile at the thought, the combination. At one time she had certainly been bitter. Felt betrayed, affronted. Erik had begun to see Irene while he and Maj were still living together.

Back then, a long time ago, it would have felt unpleasant to meet a daughter of Erik and Irene. Now she almost wished she could get to see the girl. Something of a souvenir of the past, a half-sister of Henning. Could the girl and Henning be alike? Didn't Elisabet say she had dark hair? Henning was fair, like Maj herself.

Of course, she had liked Erik at one time, he had been the love of her youth. But hadn't it always been so, that he in some way was cold—despite all his hectic ardor? He was eager, engaged—but only on the surface? He changed women, changed parties. He had his ideas and ideals—but was it more than a superficial pattern? Did he ever give himself the time to stop and sink into something? Didn't he always have to live on the surface to be able to quickly move on after one of the new goals that he coveted?

So different with John. He was tranquil, too tranquil she might think sometimes. He stayed put, at his job, with her. Also at the cottage; his family came from that area. A little bit of inertia maybe, but more of security. There was a calming, pleasant warmth, around him.

With the years she had attained some of that calm herself, even though she had been so restless when young. The best thing she knew was to go out to the cottage and just walk around there and potter about with small things. Rake leaves, straighten out a plant, find some mushrooms. Live close to the soil.

She could see the path between the trees and the low, sharp, autumn sunlight that cut through, that glistened on the pine needles, on the trunks of the pines. The tufts of mountain cranberry bushes with their shining berries, the boat that lay pulled up on the sandy beach, the stern lapped by the small waves that glided in and out with a light, frothing sound.

The sun glittering on the water, almost blindingly.

She looked up; the light from the floor lamp shone in her eyes. It was probably time to go to bed now.

PARTY
IN A SUBURB

The Sunday before Advent, the fourteenth of November, Vällingby Center was going to be inaugurated. Erik waited impatiently for that moment while he, day after day, followed how department stores and boutiques rose up from the rubble of the construction. He met his brother, Gunnar, who had a lot of interior jobs out there. They talked a while, about Jenny who got to come home from the convalescent home, and about Emelie who had also moved back home now.

And the work here?

Well sure, it would probably be ready on time even if it seemed unbelievable just now when you looked at all the mess.

Fine. The important thing was to create a center as fast as possible; that was necessary if people were going to like it out here. Otherwise the subway was going to work like an escape hatch, tempt more and more people in to the lights and life of Kungsgatan. And Vällingby would just become a dreary and quiet bedroom community, like so many other communities had become.

The meeting with Gunnar—a reminder of all the others, of Maj and of Henning. It was like touching a sore spot, an old boil that had to be lanced now. He had been too lenient—or perhaps too slack?

It was that Irene could not come to terms with his past, did not want to be reminded of it. He never talked about Maj or Henning at home, when he saw Henning he did it without Irene knowing anything. It had been easiest that way, no trouble. At the same time it was naturally wrong, modern people did not behave that way. He had divorced friends who got together regularly with their former wives. It was outright unacceptable to behave as he had done. Now he was going to invite the boy home, whatever Irene said.

Something had to be done, soon. For Lena's sake as well. Irene had taken it hard that she had become a workmate and good friend with Maj's sister. And that the girl had then gone and gotten engaged to an acquaintance of Elisabet was, of course, even worse.

Irene and he had, needless to say, met Joseph a few times; he had been invited home. A decent guy though rather old for Lena. On the other hand, he probably suited her better than any young whippersnapper. Lena was so serious, had always been a little advanced for her years.

Irene had managed to take hold of herself and had been very nice when Joseph had come. For Lena's sake, of course. Lena was everything to her—he himself was fonder of Berit.

Both Joseph and Lena socialized regularly with Elisabet and her husband. And through them Lena would surely meet both Maj and Henning soon.

It felt wrong and in some way humiliating if Lena was to meet her half-brother for the first time at someone else's house.

He tried to explain this to Irene. Now it was high time that he get to introduce his children to each other, before someone else did it. There was no reason for her to be jealous or upset, that time with Maj was an eternity ago. And Maj was not the type who would try to get in between; she was honest.

As he had expected, Irene became hysterical. And naturally it was he who was the culprit. How could he ever have let Lena start working at that company....

For the girl's sake, he implored her. Irene had to try and look at the whole thing calmly, she couldn't let Lena suffer for his old sins.

That helped some, she calmed down. And finally she became much more reasonable than he had ever dared hope. She certainly didn't have anything against his son, she said. It was only the memory of that awful period that stirred her up, back then when Maj and Erik were still living together and Erik had not wanted to clear everything up.

Inside himself he had to wonder if he ever would have married Irene if Maj hadn't left. He had not been at all so sure that he wanted to live together with Irene at that point. But maybe it was best as it had happened; he and Irene had a good life together.

But he had definitely been much too afraid when he hadn't faced up to this situation. Or maybe he was just not engaged enough? He had gone along all these years and cheated, so all that was needed would have been for him to say how he wanted things. Irene had given in, she would have done that ten years ago as well, twenty years ago. He could have seen Henning normally the whole time. If he had wanted to badly enough.

He had not really had time for the boy. He had had so much else. Work, politics, his home. And the women he saw on the side, all the ones that Irene did not know about. Though he was almost done with that by now.

In any case, they would settle the matter now. Henning could bring his wife and children with him and come eat dinner the same day the town center was going to be inaugurated, for example. They could get together outside first and look at everything that was new, and then go home and eat. There were sure to be fireworks, too, in the evening; in which case they would have a good view from the windows in their living room.

He felt quite satisfied with the plans that he laid. His old talent for organizing was still there.

By the tens of thousands people came out to Vällingby, by subway and car. Every imaginable parking space all the way out toward Blackeberg was taken. And people crammed onto the broad sidewalks and in the shops open for Sunday, which had been built above the subway. A lot was still missing—such as a school, theater, and church. And the square shopping corner still stood surrounded by half-blasted mounds.

Yet it was something new they had created, the first real living, and to a large part self-supporting, suburb.

Irene and Lena didn't care about going along. Irene was going to prepare the food and Lena stayed and helped her, waiting for Joseph.

But Berit went with Erik to meet their guests at the subway. She really wanted to get out of the housework, and besides she was both interested in the festivities and curious about her half-brother.

It was fun to go with Berit; Erik felt young once again. The girl was pretty, dressed more daringly than Lena. There was something so fearless about her in general, almost so that it scared him sometimes when he thought of the risk that she would fall straight down into one of life's pitfalls.

They had to wait a time before Henning and his family arrived. It hadn't been easy for them to get out there; the place was so full of people who were on the move. They had a little stroller with them for their son, two-year-old Lars-Olov. Four-year-old Ann-Charlotte held her mother's hand.

Erik had been to Henning's home a few times and met Barbro, but that was a long time ago now. She had grown a little paler and more delicate. But the smile was still there and still gave her color and life. He liked talking with her; she was unafraid and assured. Now he attended to her and let Berit attend to Henning. Or perhaps she attended mostly to the little boy, she was so crazy about children. She should be a children's nurse or a teacher. Instead she insisted on trying to get into the College of Arts, Crafts, and Design.

They made their way through the crowds of people for a while, stepping into some of the shops; the children got balloons. But there were so many people everywhere and it was hard to get through with the children. Instead, they took the adjacent route across the heights; from there Erik could point out everything that had been accomplished during the most recent years.

Henning tried to listen but felt a little bewildered by the new situation. He did not understand the reason for their being invited over now after so many years. What could have happened?

It wasn't until he met Joseph Schönlank at his father's home that he realized the connection; he had met Joseph before, out at Elisabet's place in the country.

Irene was also bewildered. She had been crying but hoped it wouldn't show, she had tried to get rid of the traces and Lena declared that nothing was noticeable. Lena had calmed her, Lena was kind and understanding. But more stubborn than she had believed; as far as Joseph was concerned she had gone her own way, been outright inconsiderate. Wouldn't she have relinquished Joseph if she had been as attached to Irene as Irene was to her?

But that was asking too much and it really wasn't Lena's fault that things had turned out as they had. Unfortunate circumstances. And Erik, Erik who had gotten Lena that confounded job. He could have avoided it, he with so many connections.

She felt the anger rising up inside her but tried to control herself.

Now they were coming, Lena said as she passed by the window.

Irene looked out quickly. She saw Erik at the side of a young woman, naturally! And Berit laughing and talking with a young man. That was typical, too; Berit found it way too easy to become acquainted with everybody, especially guys. But, of course, this was her half-brother. And the little children who were with them, Erik's grandchildren; he was actually a grandfather.

They had been married for over twenty years—and still sometimes he was like a stranger. Here he came with part of his life, a part she didn't know anything about. For a moment she felt a twinge of guilt; maybe it was her fault. And maybe it was right that his son finally was coming there.

She forced herself to be calm, walked smiling toward them.

All the tension that had existed before their meeting dissolved; so imperceptibly that one had to wonder if it had ever existed.

There was nothing to be afraid of. Henning seemed kind and decent. He did not remind her especially of Erik, seemed milder, calmer. There was no reason to feel out of sorts because he was there. No reason either to be jealous of Erik's past any longer, it was too long ago. She herself had had a lot male acquaintances before Erik. The fact that she didn't get pregnant before she got married was mostly luck.

And if she had had a child … then she certainly would have wanted Erik to accept it.

And Henning, who had been worried before meeting Irene, only found a perfectly ordinary middle-aged woman—plump, a little shrill—but not much more. It surprised him that his father could have given up his mother for this woman's sake.

He no longer felt any worry. But maybe something of estrangement. When he saw his father alone he felt in a completely different way that they were close with each other, that they were father and son. His father together with this Irene became something else; then his father was also changed into a stranger. Their tone of speaking with each other, their home—it was theirs but not his. He was only a guest, an outsider.

Then he found a completely different sense of belonging with his half-sisters and with Joseph. Regardless of whether they were relatives of his or not, they were the kind of people that he understood better. He had met Joseph before, sympathized with him. He had the opportunity to talk to Berit on the way there and they had had an immediate connection. Lena also felt familiar. If his father and Irene hadn't been there they could have had a lot of fun together.

Now it became a little more restrained, something of a show where Erik had the main role. He managed it well, no question about that.

It was dark outside now. The little children had fallen asleep on the sofa. Erik pulled the curtains aside on the wide windows.

And soon giant puffs of flame and smoke shot up; the fireworks had begun. Flowers grew, spread out and disappeared, shots boomed, stars rained down between the tall buildings that stood pale against the night sky. Vällingby was celebrating the inauguration of its center.

III

LEAPS

Years can be leaps, rapid transfers from one reality to another completely different. So quick that we don't have time to become accustomed, hardly notice what has happened. But instead, continue to live as before, in patterns that no longer apply. We follow the old tracks until we suddenly find the rails torn up and the abyss gaping. It's not until then, that we notice that the world we believed we lived in no longer exists.

Now the visionaries' farsightedness and the science fiction authors' fantasies have been transformed into everyday life and everyday existence at the same time as a lingering, more primitive time bubbles up to the surface by the light of day. On their television sets people could follow the path of the space rocket's journey around the earth—the earth where the human tribe still tried to plow the cracked, dry earth with wretched wooden plows. And skilled doctors found cures for previously unconquerable diseases—while people were hanged, tortured, and burned.

Fear and darkness grew faster than hope and light. The heritage of Nazism gained interest, people built new concentration camps and discovered new methods of torture. The French tortured Algerians in their attempts to crush the revolt in Algeria. In Hungary, a revolution broke out that was ruthlessly put an end to by Russian tanks and troops; the whole country was turned into one concentration camp. In America and the Soviet Union, German experts worked on nuclear weapons, and Egypt's new dictator, Nasser, granted asylum and jobs to experts of Jewish extermination.

Unrest broke out in more and more places. England and France took united action against Egypt when Nasser nationalized the Suez Canal. In Cuba, revolution broke out against the dictator, Batista; on Cypress opposition intensified between Greeks and Turks.

All these wars and upheavals were fought with conventional, often primitive weapons. At the same time, the major powers' arsenals of nuclear weapons grew, and more and more countries considered acquiring their own atom bombs. The conquering of outer space began. In October 1957, the Russians sent out their first sputnik in an orbit of the earth. After many failures, the Americans were able to launch their first Explorer; they were also building submarines armed with nuclear weapons that could travel under the polar ice.

The technological advances in Sweden were less sensational. A new airway to Japan went over the North Pole, and the right-wing leader, Hjalmarsson, came to election meetings by helicopter. The department of defense ordered remote control robots, and propaganda for Swedish production of atomic bombs for tactical use was promoted.

The development of social reforms progressed. National supplementary pensions were discussed. The fight over the shaping of social security led to new elections, which resulted in the coalition government being replaced by a social democratic government.

Increasing numbers of people bought television sets and a string of new popular heroes was born. Women continued to enter into new fields; now they could be police and clergy, too. Ration books for alcohol were abolished; the new feature, strong beer, was a large commercial success.

Standards rose, not least of all among the youth, who had become a sought-after labor force. Bands of leather-jacketed motorcyclists rumbled along the roadways. Masters of rock 'n' roll were greeted by flocks of screaming fans.

The city had also developed a new pace. It was still growing each year, had now reached over 800,000 inhabitants. But in contrast to before, most of them now lived in the suburbs. Far beyond the old tollgates.

The number of privately owned cars grew continually—gas rationing after the Suez crisis brought about only a temporary disruption. In ten years, the number of cars had doubled.

The construction of the subway had been forced through; many neighborhoods were torn down, makeshift streets climbed on rickety bridges high above chasms and tunnel holes. In February 1957, a connecting line was inaugurated; now the subway trains whooshed crosswise through the city and a new line was already being planned. The subway connected the many new suburbs with the inner city, and with each other; it also created a new life and new images of the city. From the underground stations with their giant ticket halls and their escalators, people made their way out in new pathways that created new thoroughfares and new areas in the city.

To make space for all the new, the old was torn down; even more of the once-mighty ridge, Brunkebergsåsen, disappeared. New traffic routes were opened and all of lower Norrmalm waited for its radical restructuring.

It was as if the city that Henning had grown up in and seen as his reality had suddenly been transformed to lies and stage sets, as if it was only a piece of drapery that hid the truth that no longer could be hidden.

It was night as he walked through the city; the spring nights had their air of unreality, the twilight dissolved all the hardness, shoreline and water were erased, all the contours were softened. The city slept, an innocent sleep. But now it felt like the innocence was only ignorance, as if sleeping was fleeing responsibility. Riddarfjärden Bay, still with a faint, rosy glow from the western sky—like a backwater, a deceitful idyll.

Had he avoided the knowledge, fled the responsibility, consciously made himself unaware? Yes, and no. There were certainly extenuating circumstances. A lot of work, responsibility for his family. Could an ordinary person achieve anything meaningful at all; weren't all attempts to do something just sham actions for the sake of a clean conscience? And wasn't it enough that someone took care of him or herself, was not a burden on anybody?

It did not feel that way now.

The knowledge of how things stood in the world had naturally not come to him all at once, it had grown slowly. The body of information existed, of course. But he had seen without really seeing, read without really understanding.

More than half of the world's people were starving. In some countries, close to half the number of children were affected before they had turned the age of one.

Yes, he had known it, read it—but not felt it before now. And one did not become aware of something before one felt it. It required both knowledge and feeling—knowledge without feeling was dead, feeling without knowledge only inebriation.

They had sat there and talked, some old friends from his discussion group. They didn't get together very often anymore; everyone was married and had kids. This evening they had talked about the countries people were beginning to call underdeveloped. Bertil had become even more involved in international relief work. Already, just after the war, he had traveled to Yugoslavia with a youth brigade to build a railroad, and then for several years, he had been abroad with Service Civil International, working in different countries.

His restlessness and enthusiasm had worn off on the others during the evening. And even though it was late, Henning had wanted to walk home through the city, hoping that his thoughts would become clearer along the way.

Had he been blind, he who not until now had seen the state of the world? Had he grown rigid, lost his feelings?

Maybe, to a certain extent, as people did. Throughout Barbro's illness he had had to devote more attention to his own family, he had likely occupied himself more with his children than fathers normally did. In that realm, within his own family, he must have given as much as he had of feeling and life. It was as if his energy would not have been able to accommodate more, as if he did not have the strength to perceive more.

Now he felt that it wasn't enough.

THE DREAM
OF PARADISE

The Klara neighborhood lay exposed in the afternoon sun's sharp light. Dilapidated old houses with cracks and crumbling plaster, storefronts where they already had time to have the liquidation sales and close. Everything was going to be gone soon, there was no reason to do anything more. A steam shovel pounded at collapsing walls, trucks filled with old building rubble, and bricks rolled away. Some journalists stood outside the Masonic Lodge W6, and talked with the coatroom attendant; inside the *Dagens Nyheter* newspaper across the street with the large windows, the presses rumbled.

Run-down, dilapidated. But still something of an idyll and a small-town street squeezed in beside the noisy traffic of Central Station and Tegelbacken. In a few years almost everything there would certainly be gone, the newspapers would move to Marieberg, the small shops would have to close forever. The big hole at Hötorget was only growing and eventually it would reach all the way over there, too. The Klara that had been the journalists', the freelancers', the bohemians', and the asocials' district, "the jungle," "the den of depravity," did not have a long period of grace left. It was difficult to defend, unthinkable to preserve—and still people would miss it, as one can miss a pair of worn out, shabby slippers: dirty, ragged, impossible to be seen in—but comfortable.

Henning had eaten his farewell lunch at W6 with some workmates; he was going to leave them and the newspaper. He had received an attractive offer that he had accepted. Higher salary, more independence. Mainly he had changed to get more regular work hours and evenings free.

He was going to turn thirty-five soon. He still could feel very young, untested—not least of all now when something new awaited. He had gone to the newspaper straight from his studies. He had stayed there for over twelve years.

It would be fun to try something new. He would be some kind of advertising man for a company and also publish a personnel newspaper and a newsletter for the company's customers.

He already felt like he missed a little bit the friendship that had existed, the work on a team, the planning. Maybe a little bit, too, the run-down district and the dark premises. He had seen his new workplace; it seemed coldly efficient.

Now he had a few hours when no special assignments were waiting for him. He decided to take the opportunity to go up to see Mormor and Emelie; it had been a while since the last time. And also there was something he wanted to ask Emelie about.

He walked across Vasabron and onto Stora Nygatan. He stopped and looked in the window of a second-hand bookshop, he had found a little publication there a few weeks ago. It was precisely this that he wanted to talk to Emelie about. It dealt with the neighborhood where he had grown up—*Retrospect of Fifteen Years of Mission Work in the White Hills in Stockholm*.

He had leafed through it and read a bit here and there in the little pamphlet, laughed a little at the sometimes unctuous tone. Yet he was captured by the many striking destinies that lay sprinkled in among the quotes from the Bible and the lines of prayer. Great adversity and deep poverty, homeless, drunken, and worn down people in "an ill-reputed place."

The fifteen years it was about were from 1876 to 1891. It ought to interest Emelie, who, so willingly, would recall anything old. She was born, of course, in 1870. So six years old when the mission station opened, over twenty when the description of it ended. It was her time it talked about, her childhood and youth. It seemed almost unbelievable that someone now alive had also lived then, in such a city at such a time.

He came out into the light at Kornhamnstorg, saw the green subway train shoot out across the new bridge toward Söder, the sun flashing on its windowpanes; like a giant, shiny larva, the train disappeared beneath the machinery of the locks. The row of cars glistening with chrome, rolled like beads in the lanes above it. The water of Riddarfjärden glittered. Everything appeared so light and new. And then, from Katarinavägen, he saw the whole city as if it were lying and basking in the sunshine, while some snub-nosed tugboats charged out toward the Baltic.

A beautiful picture, a picture of calm and happiness.

He had read in some magazine that a number of the small cottages on the hill at the end of Åsögatan were going to be fixed up and changed into a cultural preserve. The same plans were being made for the White Hills as well.

He took a turn up Åsögatan to look. Some of the wooden houses had been torn down almost completely and dark beams been replaced by shiny new ones. There were going to be very fine dwellings here, he understood that.

Old slums were in the process of becoming cultural preserves. Houses that poor human wreckage had frozen and starved in would be transformed into sought after idylls.

When Elsa Borg and her Bible ladies came to open their mission station, they had been welcomed by some printed verses from the Bible. One of them went:

The desert and the wasteland shall be made a paradise.

But that such a promise could be fulfilled up there in the hills must have truly seemed like an impossibility, even to the Bible ladies. A utopia that no one could really dare to believe in anyway. And now it was almost there.

Certainly one could be impatient, think that it took a long time. Still, it was a question of a total transformation, and it had happened during one person's lifetime. Emelie had been there for it. Suddenly he understood better why she returned to the past so often. It was undeniably something remarkable she had been part of.

Exactly how things had been at the mission station she no longer knew. But Emelie had surely seen the Bible ladies and also heard of their "porridge suppers." And the home for "fallen girls" that they opened in the old manor house that was still there at the bottom of the slope below the church. And the orphanage that had also been part of the mission's work.

Some of those fallen girls had, as a matter of fact, been at a yard party and kicked up a terrible ruckus. The yard had been located approximately where Renstiernasgatan now ran, blasted into the White Hills. Emelie had been there with her mother and her sister, Gertrud. And Thumbs and Matilda and Rudolf had also been there. She had danced with Rudolf. That was before he had begun to keep company with Gertrud.

Now they were all dead; there was no one left of them who had been there at that party, no one else but herself.

The party had ended, by the way, with an enormous accident; a rock blaster had committed suicide. He had almost killed his daughter, too. But she had been saved and then lived as a boarder at Emelie's mother's house. It was she who had painted the picture of Henning's mother's father that was hanging in the other room. Her name had been Gullpippi; she had emigrated to America later. They had not heard anything from her for many years now. She was surely dead, she, too.

Emelie had been young and danced. Henning had always thought of her as very old, almost as if she was born old. In recent years she had grown so little, shrunken. But when she talked about the past it was as if she healed and her eyes shone.

"Were things hard?" he asked. Like it said in the book.

Certainly things had been hard. When she thought about how things had been for her parents, she felt most of all like crying. How they had been worn down, how her father had died. He wasn't older when he died than Henning was now—but still a worn-out old man.

And how her mother had worked to keep them clean and whole and scrape enough together for food. How upset her mother had been when she had been forced to give up August.

Of course, it had been hard. Still, Emelie was grateful that she had gotten to live then, still she remembered so much that was beautiful and fun. She got to see how times got better and people did not have to have it so bad anymore, she had gotten to witness, too, how everything worked out for her closest kin.

He told her about the cottages out on Åsöberget, how nice they were in the process of becoming. Now they were beginning to work on the cottage she had been born in.

Yes, she knew. This time of year she and Jenny could get out and walk a little sometimes. They had walked to the park bench and sat there a while and watched the men working.

He didn't stay very long, did not have time to wait until his mother arrived. She looked in on them practically every day. Maj was alone now, ever since John had died two years ago.

On the streetcar home, he sat and thought about what Emelie had told him about circumstances before. And about all the people in other countries who were still starving and suffering.

There were connections there, there was also maybe some kind of hope. At one time, people had been starving in these small cottages that had now become cultural preserves. At one time, they had built mission stations here and opened homes for poverty-stricken people of all kinds. At that time, the city's outskirts had been seen as a wasteland and hardly anyone dared dream of it being transformed into a paradise.

Poverty could therefore be overcome. It had not even required any enormous sacrifices. What was required was actually another vision, that one exchange mercy and charity for justice. When justice had been brought to bear, the general prosperity had also increased. There was hardly anyone who was worse off; instead, all were better off.

Naturally he didn't know if what was applicable here was

applicable to the world at large. Still, it felt as if he had also received a mysterious communication to put on his wall, a promise.

THE
DARK WAVE

Emelie sat on her hard kitchen chair at the window in her kitchen, as she normally did. She was happiest that way. When she was out sometimes, kind people wanted to offer a place on soft chairs and sofas. She always had to explain that she sat best on a completely ordinary, hard chair. She only strained herself and had a hard time getting up if she sat on something too soft.

These days she sat mostly and thought, looked out a little from time to time. Before, she had read a lot, but since her eyes had gotten worse it ended up not being much more than the larger headlines in the newspaper. Sometimes Jenny read out loud to her from the newspaper, but Emelie was not especially eager for her to do that. She felt like she did not understand very much of what Jenny read; it was much harder to understand when one didn't see it oneself in print. Jenny pronounced many words in a different way, too. It wasn't so good to know that Jenny meant Nev-y-ork when she said, Nyu-yawrk.

For that reason it ended up that Emelie usually just sat and thought. And basically her thoughts always dealt with the past. She saw people who had once lived as if in a haze, houses and streets that had changed or disappeared, events that she had taken part in.

There was no real order to those images in her memory. They overlapped, were displaced. Sometimes she was not even really sure if what she imagined she remembered really had happened. She remembered Olof almost always as he looked in the painting that Gullpippi had done; he stood there in the yard at Nytorget and looked out from behind a bush. Every time she saw him she grew a little scared; he was so thin and so pale and in his gaze was both defiance and suffering.

Then the image would change, the green leaves disappear, now she saw Olof lying between the hospital's white sheets. Not the adult Olof that she had seen in the hospital in reality, but still the boy. The white sheets and the green leaves flowed into each other.

August was in a more secure dream. She always thought of him as old. When he sat there in the kitchen, when he stood on Norrmalmstorg and lifted his hat when they were going to the exhibition; that was in 1930, that one.

And Gertrud, who was sledding down Bondegatsbacken and tipped over and got so snowy. She stood up and brushed herself off and fell again. "I have such slippery boots!" she shouted, sounding just like the men from the Dihlström workhouse.

Maybe Emelie was dreaming sometimes. It happened that she nodded off as she was sitting there on the chair, her head sunken down. But then she would wake up and look around wonderingly; she might find that twilight had fallen without her noticing it. And Jenny would be standing there and saying, "Now we'll turn on the light. Otherwise you will sit there and fall asleep."

"Of course not," Emelie would answer then. "I'm not going to fall asleep before I've gone to bed."

She had felt a little ill for a period. They had had some unusually warm days and it became so stuffy in the small apartment. She was a little tired, too, but that happened, of course, when one grew old. Gunnar had talked about Emelie and Jenny coming out to his place for a few weeks so they could go outside more easily. But Emelie had wanted to wait until she felt better.

That feeling ill … it was just there. She couldn't really recall eating anything that had disagreed with her. It wasn't really like ordinary feeling ill either, it stretched from her stomach up to her head. Like a darkness that was inside her, a dark water, surges that swelled up. She forced them down, wondered if she should maybe try and take a powder. But she couldn't make up her mind to, didn't really want to. Maybe it was best to just sit still, wait for the wave to go back down.

Maybe she was nodding off, maybe she was dreaming. She found herself suddenly standing at the window in the house on Nytorget. It was she herself and yet not herself, a girl. She stood and looked out on the dark street. It was both dark and light; it was a winter evening with weak light but white snow. There was a platform wagon coming behind a horse, coming so slowly, so heavily.

And she heard Washer-Johanna crying and stammering out: "Take care of Olof, take care of Olof, take care of...."

"But Olof is dead," she answered. "He was so sick, I couldn't do anything. I wasn't allowed to do anything, he didn't want it."

And then she saw that her mother was lying in her coffin, right next to her. White, unmoving, almost a stranger.

"Mama, Mama!" she called.

And she felt how the wave shot up, that she couldn't hold it down any longer, that it overwhelmingly rose up and pulled her with it, that she disappeared in the darkness.

A little liquid ran from her open mouth; she fell from the chair.

Jenny, who was sitting at the table in the other room and pasting in old theater reviews, heard the thud and looked up, wondered what it was. She called out a question. When she didn't get a response, she took off her glasses and placed them on the table on the clipping, got up, and went out to the kitchen.

First she only saw the empty chair and thought that maybe Emelie had gone out to the bathroom and not heard her call. But then she saw the body that was lying on the floor, partially hidden by the table. She hurried over.

She must be alive, she was breathing, she wasn't dead.

But also anything that resembled death was something that would scare Jenny so that she would almost be panic-stricken. And now she was alone here with Emelie.

She didn't know how she did it, but got hold of her glasses and managed to dial the number to Maj's office.

Maj had taken the lid off the kitchen sofa, tried to lift Emelie up and place her on the bed that was under the lid. Emelie was probably paralyzed, a little crooked in her face. May she not lie and suffer too long, let it go fast.

When the doctor arrived, Maj received his confirmation—it was a stroke. And not much to be done about it. They could not send her to a regular hospital, in which case it would be a nursing home. If they didn't want to pay for a private care home, that was. The best thing would be if the patient could stay at home, if someone could take care of her. There was nothing to be done, as he said. It would probably not be very long, maybe it would be a question of only a few days.

Maj would arrange so she could take time off. That much she could do at any rate; Emelie would not have to die away from home.

Right after the doctor left Gunnar arrived. He stood silently at her bedside, stroking Emelie's hand. Tears came to his eyes, slid down his cheeks. He didn't try to hide them, nor dry them away.

Maj and Gunnar took turns at the bedside; in between Maj had to go in and look after Jenny, who sat apathetically in her room.

Suddenly Gunnar made a gesture like he was calling to Maj. She walked over to the kitchen sofa, saw that Emelie's one eye was open, that she was looking at them. As if she was trying to smile, say something. But her mouth didn't really want to, had lost the ability to move according to her wishes. But her eye was certainly glittering.

It was as if she was trying to lift her hand. But then it fell down on the blanket, her eye closed, it was as if she sank back, as if her head and body were being pulled down. A tremble, and then only stillness.

"It's over," Gunnar said. "She got to die peacefully."

Outside it was night now, pale blue summer night. The empty wooden chair stood as it usually did in front of the window, the eyeglasses that no one would use anymore lay folded on the kitchen table.

GATHERING, SCATTERING

They had a lot to be thankful for, those who gathered out at the Skogs Churchyard. But no one other than the minister spoke. As if none of them were capable of stepping forward; the words that they wanted to say could not be said here. It was probably more proper to remain quiet now, in any case; Emelie had never liked thank you speeches.

While the organ roared its recessional, they walked slowly out of the chapel, stopping in small groups on the open space outside. Unsure, as if abandoned.

No one had planned any general reception afterward. It was Emelie who had been the gatherer, it was mainly at her home that they had gotten together. Now, when she was no longer there, there wasn't anyone who could hold them together either. Some of them who were there now would probably never come again to any family gatherings. Not Karl Henrik and his son, not Erik. It was Emelie they had had the connection with, it was for her that they had paid their visit.

Erik had arrived late, almost too late. He'd had to sneak in after the other ones had sat down. Now he went over and said hello to Jenny and Maj. It had been a long time since they had seen each other. Maj had lost her husband since the last time.

Jenny seemed to barely notice him; she was still shaking with sobs. But Maj appeared calm, and when she responded to his greeting she did it as if it were an old friend she was seeing. He almost felt touched: kind, decent Maj, how he had liked her once upon a time. And he had always admired her strength; she was never as strong as just at the moment when strength was needed most.

The cars were waiting—but none of them for Erik; he hadn't come with the others, instead had taken a taxi out. He saw how Jenny and Maj went with Gunnar and his wife; they had room for the minister, too. And Henning and his wife had apparently gone with Allan. Erik looked around, a little lost. It was embarrassing to walk away completely alone. But there were Bengt and his Britta. They were alone in their car; he could hop in there. And Bengt wondered if Erik didn't want to go along with them and get a cup of coffee. Even if coffee was not exactly what he felt like, he accepted the invitation. Bengt was the only one of the siblings that he got together with, even if years might go by between their seeing each other.

To think that it should take a funeral for them to see each other....

Already, the day after Emelie's death, Jenny had moved to Maj's. She couldn't imagine staying in the old apartment where everything reminded her of Emelie—and of death. She didn't even want to return to pack her belongings. Now she sat like a refugee, huddled up in Maj's rocking chair, giving a start every time there was an unexpected noise.

There was plenty of room at Maj's now; Jenny got a room that she could have as her own. And Maj tried in various ways to distract her. She put a radio in her room, asked Elisabet to come by as often as she could.

Maj tried to organize the old abandoned home. It was she and Gunnar who had taken this task upon themselves. It seemed natural that those two would do it. They worked well together. They almost felt like siblings though they were only cousins; both of them had grown up at Emelie's and lived there together for many years.

Gunnar was the one who first came to Emelie, only six years old. Then Jenny had come and stayed as long as Emelie had lived, and had both of her daughters there. Then Bärta's children, Erik and Bengt, Tyra and Beda. Henning had not lived at Emelie's, it is true, but he had gone there every day. And Allan, Stig, and Gun had also come regularly to get food and care.

Among them all, Gunnar and Maj had been closest, now that Jenny could not be there. Maj was the one who knew where everything was, she had often helped Emelie and her mother, especially these latest years.

Maj was going to first and most importantly try and take care of Jenny's possessions; that was maybe the hardest task since Jenny had saved so much. Maj took most of it, emptied wardrobes and cupboards. Jenny herself would get to choose what should be thrown away. Theater posters and old clothes, paper garlands, and pages torn out of magazines. It was lucky there was plenty of space at home.

Gunnar's task was significantly easier; Emelie had prepared everything. Almost everything she owned but had not used daily, was neatly wrapped in packages with information about the contents on it.

Old dress. To be thrown away. Old hats. To be thrown away. Some old forks. Can be thrown away.

He picked up the packages and soon found that the somewhat varying designations were completely decisive. If it only said to be thrown away—then there wasn't much else to do, it was the type of thing that could hardly be of use. But if it said can be thrown away, that meant that Emelie had hesitated, and then the package contained the kind of thing that pretty definitely should be saved.

Like the old forks with their black shafts with brass rivets. And the bar of soap and pass card from the 1897 exhibition. He had the same bar of soap himself at home, had received it from Emelie during the year of the exhibition. So this one Maj should take care of.

What was this little packet? *An old handkerchief. Can be thrown away.*

That could be.... He unfolded the brown paper and found another wrapping within.

The writing on the inside paper had faded, almost disappeared. He held the little package close to the table lamp to see what was written there. Someone had printed in a childish hand:

Gift from My Father on My Birthday 1878

It must have been Emelie herself who wrote that once. 1878—eight years old, eighty years ago.

Carefully he unwrapped the package. A thin, almost falling apart little piece of cloth with embroidery. Forget-me-not. An E.

He showed Maj. Maj recalled that she had seen that little handker-chief once before. And that Emelie had said it was the only thing she had left of her father, their grandfather. He had died only a year later. It was from him that Maj's Henning had gotten his name.

"Maybe I could have that in exchange for something," Maj said.

"You take it," said Gunnar.

Gunnar's book was written on one package. It contained *Society's Enemies* by Leon Larson. And now he remembered. It was a little book he had once gotten so angry over that he had wanted to burn it up. A "revealing document" it had been called but, he didn't think it had revealed any truth, and instead consisted only of slander. It was surely before the big strike that he had received it. From his father, August. It must have been because it was a gift from August that Emelie had been so insistent that he not burn it up. The remarkable thing was that August had given it to Gunnar before he knew that he was Gunnar's father. And here Emelie had saved it all these years, let it lie here and wait for him.

He would take it and read it when he had the opportunity. But it was not very likely that he would become especially indignant this time.

Maj made coffee and they took a break from their work. They had managed to clear out a lot of Emilie and Jenny's things. He had helped Maj take down Jenny's mirror, the one that had hung in the old Panoptikon once upon a time. They had also lifted down and wrapped up the portrait of Olof.

Maj brought out Emelie's savings book and showed it to Gunnar. Once, after August's death, Emelie had inherited five thousand kro-nor. Much of that money had gone to repay old debts, it had also cost quite a lot to bring home everything that had landed in the pawnshop during all those difficult years. But some of it had remained in the sav-ings book, the money that Emelie had set aside for her funeral. Over the years that had subsequently followed, the sum had grown; interest upon interest and some small deposits. Now there was a good as five thousand kronor again.

That was so typical of Emelie, they thought: her life had gone full circle. The gift she had received was still there after she was gone. She had always been able to help. Often she did it to such a degree that there was hardly anything left for herself.

But the money she had received from August, it as there now. With the money the first and most important thing was to pay the funeral expenses. Of course, Gunnar would have liked to cover those costs, but he knew that Emelie wanted to do it herself. He remembered the old envelope she would put small amounts of money into—though she was often forced to take them out again. As far back as he could remember she had saved for her funeral.

She had always had an easy time of giving but a hard one of receiving. The big sister who would always make sure that the little ones got things first, who waited until she saw that there was something left. Who was given the responsibility at one time and felt it so keenly that she almost eradicated her own wishes and interests.

It was Emelie's wish that Jenny should have what there was. The money that was left, the few possessions. The kitchen sofa, the table and the chairs in the kitchen. The bureau that had once been Lotten's. And also a little bureau that was standing out in the hall; Emelie had received it from Thumbs when she moved to Fjällgatan in 1894. That was it in the way of furniture; the rest was already Jenny's from before.

While they worked, it was as if the old familiar apartment became more and more unfamiliar to them.

Emelie, Jenny, and Elisabet had moved here thirty years ago. Gunnar and Maj had been there and helped out with the moving too. Maj remembered that she had had Henning with her; he was only five then, and she had had stewed rhubarb purée for him, which he sat and shoveled down here at the kitchen table. Then he would sit still. Everything here had seemed exciting and new, and Elisabet had been so delighted that there was an indoor toilet; they had an outhouse in the courtyard where they had lived before.

Now it was pretty old-fashioned. Dilapidated, too; there had not been major repairs done to it. The pictures that were taken down left dark stains behind on the wallpaper.

To move everything, expose all the flaws—it almost felt like dishonoring the memories. Carrying out Emelie's old clothes to the trash barrel in the courtyard—and the wrapping paper she had written on—it was like lacking respect. But it had to be done; Emelie herself had wanted it to be thrown away.

In some ways it was almost liberating for the apartment to begin to feel so alien. Its soul had moved. The only thing left was a dead shell that would soon be filled with new life, new destinies, new people with their moments of happiness and their tragedies.

Here was where they had gathered. Who would bring them together now?

Maj felt her part in the responsibility; it was with her that Jenny was going to live and Jenny was the last of her generation. Jenny did not have such an easy time of bringing people together; now it depended on Maj herself.

Only Jenny left. Otherwise everyone was gone. Henning's and Lotten's children, Thumbs's sons. Even in the next generation they had begun to slip away. Tyra had died first, David, too, a few years ago. Then John. And the ones who were left were beginning to grow old, Maj herself sixty in a few years.

Their work took four evenings and every evening they finished up by bringing home some suitcases with fragile things for Jenny. Practically all the small things were Jenny's, the glass animals, the little pots and bowls, the photographs in frames.

And Jenny cried and said that she didn't want to see all those things again, but Maj knew when she came back from the office the next day Jenny would have placed them out on shelves and tables in her room.

Finally the truck arrived with the furniture. The old home was empty. As if an era and a world had been eradicated. Only a few traces, some things, had been saved, placed in a new environment.

And out in the churchyard an urn with ashes was lowered into a hole.

ONWARD

Someone dies. The closest kin stand shaken, bewildered, thrown out of their daily routine. Life can feel meaningless, only ends in death, yields only losses.

But death in this civilized culture forces action. One is obliged to observe the many formalities, the trivialities; one is forced to continue onward. And then everyday life slowly returns, even if a lot of it has become different, a lot also stays the same as before. The pain after the loss begins to smart again sometimes, but the wound has still begun to heal. The scar will always be there but, like the memory, it will eventually lose its fiery red hue, become muted, turn gray.

For those who were the oldest it felt the hardest. They had known Emelie the longest and been closest to her. And besides, it felt like they themselves had been placed on the outermost line; if everything progressed as it should, they were next in line. It was like aging quickly, being yanked closer to the end.

Jenny felt it that way. She had tried to tell herself that she in fact wasn't so old. Eleven years younger than Emelie in any case. But now she was the oldest, the last in that generation.

Jenny had exercised, been on stage, remained active. But a lot had been different after that accident when she had broken her leg. Ever since then she had not had any engagements, now she didn't look for any either. Now she was seventy-seven and could not do otherwise than acknowledge that she had grown old. And Emelie's death had dealt her a blow, released that fear of death that she had been able to hide before, sometimes almost forget.

Gunnar also felt older, old. He was a retired pensioner now, seventy soon. His son was in charge of the firm, even if Gunnar still took on some of the work. This time of year in the summer he took quite a lot of time off, he had actually intended to work at home in the garden. Though it didn't end up being that much work, he didn't have the strength for it in the same way as before. He would grow short of breath, had to sit down. When the gooseberries grew ripe he liked to pull the lawn chair over to the bushes. He had sat like this together with Emelie a few summers earlier. And the bushes on Fjällgatan—no other berries yet had ever tasted like that. Could those bushes have been some superior kind?

He thought he could see Emelie's slender hand reaching out. He remembered so well how she had sat here beside him. When he closed his eyes he could almost feel her close by.

He had always felt Emelie's closeness as a shield. When he was a boy she had really been his shield against the world around him and his foster father. But he had felt the same sense of safeness with her when she had grown old and infirm and it had been he, if anything, that could help and protect her.

Now there was no shield anymore. Now he himself stood on the outer line. He remembered that he had thought his father, August Bodin, had gotten to live a long time. It did not seem so now, only seventy-two. In a few years he would be as old as August had been when he died.

As long as Emelie had been alive he had still felt young beside her, always something of a boy. Now he was old.

Henning had always seen Emelie as someone who had lived a long time and surely couldn't have many years left. He had accepted what had happened: that's how things go, few got any older. But it was a pity about Mormor who was so alone now.

Right now Henning was also having a rather difficult period of adjustment to go through. His duties at the new workplace were completely different from the ones he had earlier. He was beginning to wonder if he hadn't made a mistake when he changed jobs, if he was really suited for the new one. Everything had such a commercial tone there. Cautious words were out of place. Unusual words were considered incomprehensible. Everything had to be smoothed over.

"Write something damned good now," his boss said.

"Such as?"

"Well, I don't exactly know what … but it should be damned good."

He tried, even though it somehow felt like spitting on himself and his journalistic ambitions. Several suggestions, the glossy words in new combinations.

"I said, goddamit, that it should be really damned good. And now you come up with this!"

He returned to his desk, sat and chewed over the words that felt more and more slimy and tasteless.

During lunch break he fled the office. Walked across Hötorget where a temporary market hall had been erected in place of the one that had been torn down. There was practically nothing remaining of the College of Arts and Crafts, only gravel. But the first of the five tall buildings had been fully erected. At its side the Concert Hall had shrunk to a doghouse.

With violent force the new grew out of the gravel; right now it felt like he himself was stuck and could not go along up. He longed to go back to the old-fashioned editing offices, to his old job and his friends there. The shiny, new tall buildings reminded him of the advertising slogans he was going through agonies over, each one just as soullessly polished, just as aggressively boastful.

The building would perhaps be better when it was put to use and once one got accustomed to it. Just as the job might actually feel better once he really had gotten into it. It was always difficult to change. One had to force oneself onward, grow accustomed. He had gotten higher pay, of course, better hours. So he had to stick it out.

That decision he had to test many times. Steel his will, get tougher.

Most of all he would have liked to escape. Not go back to his old job in any case, that would have been too humiliating; they had given him a party at the magazine, congratulated him on the new job.

He wondered sometimes if he should try and talk to his father,

maybe he with his many connections might have an idea. But that
went against the grain for him; he had gotten the work at the magazine through his father once, now he ought to be able to take care of
himself. Be able to stay where he was at least until he managed to find
something else himself.

Until now he had always been able to feel appreciated or at least
acknowledged. He was not sloppy, tried always to carry out a job
decently. He also felt that he knew his profession reasonably well.

But what he knew was not enough here. There was something he
was lacking that was needed. Here it wasn't about writing, it was
about playing with words, building houses of cards with them. Many
variations on the same theme.

He had a hard time being able to stand up to his new boss, also. At
the magazine there had been a team, collaboration. One of them had
been the editor-in-chief. But not a dictator. When Henning was writing for the magazine, he had written for those who would read it, and
not for the editor-in-chief.

Here he found that he thought more about his boss's reaction than
about the readers. If he had written so that it was acceptable to the
readers, he would not have had it approved. It was his boss he had to
write for, not for anyone else.

The boss was one of those types who obliterated his surroundings;
there wasn't room for any independent people in his vicinity. The
heads of the small departments sat there and devoted most of their
time figuring out how to please him. They had maybe arrived there
with ideas and suggestions, but they had never been able to imple-
ment them. The boss only believed in his own abilities.

Those department heads, stifled and care-worn through the years,
took it out by criticizing each other and their subordinates. They
whispered and tattled, but crept cautiously together and kept quiet
when the dangerous boss approached. They stood outside his door
and waited, with their suggestions and their gossip.

Their boss considered them idiots and treated them accordingly.

He was clever, a genius in his way. Otherwise the company would not have been able to exist. He did the work of ten, was everywhere, drew a few lines across the papers of his underlings and scrawled on them the solutions in the margins: "That way, that's how it should be. Get going now!"

Henning was the young one and the new one among those whose title was department head. They older ones saw him as a threat; who knew what someone who was young and new could come up with, if he didn't just outright succeed with the trick of getting in good with the boss.

The main thing was to win over the new person, make him harmless, get him to become one of them. One of the castrated and castigated.

For this reason they criticized everything he did. Amongst themselves, in the presence of the boss, directly to him.

Henning, who was used to succeeding. Now he failed continually; nothing he did met any approval. First he became nervous and then desperate. Since no one was satisfied with anything, he could leave them anything at all; it was still just as crazy.

But it wasn't that simple. The boss called him in and criticized him more and more roughly.

More and more Henning felt that he was a total failure. Despite the good salary and the regular work hours.

He was the one who could only make mistakes. He was incapable, impossible, the one everyone picked on.

So short was the step between success and failure. As accidental as which side one landed on. In the wrong situation every person could become worthless.

Of course, he had his family and his personal happiness, but it was difficult to be happy during his free time if he was one big failure during his work time.

He looked at those who should be called his friends, his workmates. The many regular employees probably got by the best there, as if the boss's violence and domination didn't extend all the way down to them. They took care of their jobs and despised their superiors.

With the department heads it was different. They all seemed to be broken. They had been so pleased over their promotions, their little power and increased salaries, that they hadn't been able to pull themselves away in time.

If he stayed, he would become one of them. They would certainly become a little more decent and a little less aggressive if they found that he was harmless, then he would be brought into the circle. And destroyed.

Yet he couldn't say that the boss was a scoundrel. Indeed he swore and yelled sometimes, but he could be quite decent, too, really meant well, paid well. It was only that he had to dominate, that he couldn't believe in any judgment other than his own. He had built up the company, he had succeeded. He had visions, knew how everything should be, how words should be formed. It was visions but not any work plans; to be able to carry out the drafts one had to be a visionary oneself, and in addition have exactly the same visions.

Henning had perceived his inability quite quickly. He could not carry out what was demanded, he was neither a visionary nor a medium.

That was how he saw the situation. Maybe he exaggerated, maybe it wasn't really that way, maybe his colleagues were not so completely broken as he believed, maybe the boss not really so domineering, maybe he himself did not fail as utterly as he believed.

But it felt that way; that was his truth.

Therefore he had to get away from there soon. He could not let what had happened knock him down totally. He had to try and shake the criticism off of himself, laugh at it, make himself indifferent to it. He began to have a hard time falling asleep in the evenings; he lay and went over and over everything that had happened.

He was not standing up well under the pressure. Tried but failed.

He had to get away, had to find something else. Not backward—forward.

He answered some advertisements of positions available. But what he could get seemed impossible to take. He would have to try and wait a little longer, see if something better showed up.

He continued to get on poorly, continued to fail.

While summer turned to fall and fall to winter.

A DAY
IN MAY

The spring sun shone and warmed him when Erik came out of his building in Vällingby and sat in the car. He rolled down the window and sat with his eyes half closed in the warmth of the sun. It felt like summer was near. He thought about going on some group tour to Yugoslavia, swim for a couple weeks in the Mediterranean, relax. He would have preferred to take Berit with him—but it would probably be Irene.

In spite of the winter being full of work, he felt in a good mood, in shape. He had always liked working and there was nothing so fun as when the hard work yielded results. And it had. The drawn-out struggle over supplementary pensions was finally settled.

He was not a member of parliament, of course, had not directly participated in the decisive battle. But during the course of several years he had worked to prepare what had now occurred. He had given countless talks in political and union clubs, egged on the canvassers to attempt new tries. For sure, he had had his little part in the victory of last year's extra election. And it was that that had created the conditions for the final victory.

A few days ago the decisive vote had been taken in the second chamber. The government's proposal had passed with 115 votes against 114. Thanks to one person abstaining from the vote, a member of the Liberal Party, who was a machinist.

Erik smiled to himself in the sunshine; it was an outcome that he liked. Dramatic, irritating to the opposition. A piece of the workers movement's solidarity might still exist even in a Liberal Party member. Enough to be effective in the decisive moment. Otherwise, he had always distrusted the nonconformists. But in a situation such as this one they were good to have—they had extra sensitive consciences.

He started the engine, which caught immediately, whirring softly. He looked a little impatiently over at the door: wasn't Berit coming soon? There she was now, running. Hat and gloves in hand, coat unbuttoned. And she would comb her hair once she sat down in the car. Sloppy!

She did that as the car rolled along in the traffic on Bergslagsvägen. Erik actually liked driving this way best, where speed was limited. Just fast enough. It suited him; he had calmed down with the years. And it was fun to sit here with Berit beside him; it could be for any length of time.

He still felt the same pleasant satisfaction. Everything would work out if one only took it prudently. He lived quite peacefully now, despite the pressured pace of work. Despite the conferences and meetings. Routine meant a lot, one learned to handle life. Before, he had rushed around, now he swam calmly.

Things were good at home, too. Lena had moved out, gotten married, had her first child. That was good, it suited Lena. Irene seemed to be a little happier than before. Berit was still free and single and lived at home. That was also good; it was nice to see her every day, have her beside him in the car. It was just as well that she didn't have a steady beau. He was probably a little jealous; Berit had always been his girl. He thought that there was hardly any guy good enough for her.

Though Irene irritated him a little. She kept on expanding. She still looked good, a pretty face. But it was as if the beauty she had had was in the process of drowning in all her flesh.

He preferred not to be seen out with Irene anymore. In truth she should have a job, get out, move a little. It was embarrassing to have a woman who stayed at home like some kind of damned house pet. But she had stopped working when she was expecting Lena. It was much too late to do anything about it now.

He erased Irene from his thoughts; she only bothered him. Berit sat and hummed to herself, looking like the kid she, in fact, was not any longer.

Berit was too daring, too open, too unsuspecting. She needed someone who guarded and warned her. But one couldn't do that. She wanted to live her own life, would not be stopped. Twenty-three soon, by then there isn't much one can say.

"You can get a ride home with me if you want," he said in any case. "I will be staying at the office pretty late, so just give me a ring."

"Just go if I haven't called by eleven," she answered. No promises then, no assurance. He usually had a hard time falling asleep before he heard her come in. He did not like to think about what she could be up to then.

He dropped her off at Kungsgatan. She had no steady job. He had given her every possible suggestion, but she did not like conventional regular work. She had wanted to go to the College of Arts and Crafts, but had not gotten in. She had been a film extra, had been in a costume atelier for a while. Knew photographers and was a model for fashion photography sometimes.

Not really good, slightly dangerous circles. But he hoped and wanted to believe that Berit in some way was indestructible. So genuine, so secure in the midst of insecurity. No normally constituted person could have the heart to do her any harm; one saw right away how much of the child there was left in her.

So he assuaged his worries.

And today the sun was shining, everything seemed so full of hope.

In the distance her coat shone like a clear red signal, then she disappeared into the crowd. And he put the car in first and pulled away slowly from the edge of the curb, into the grinding morning traffic.

It was Wednesday, and that was when he always met with the director of the company that his company worked with. Before, he had always taken the opportunity to say hello to Lena, but she was taking some time off, since her son had been born. So he usually talked to Elisabet instead.

After what had happened that night several years ago after the company party, they had barely spoken to each other. He readily acknowledged that she had a right to be angry with him; needless to say he had

ot be more than a few years away from fifty now.
Yet she still looked so fresh and young. Just as slender, as well dressed
and well groomed. Jenny's daughter kept her figure, like Jenny herself.

"Just as beautiful as ever," he said even though he knew that
Elisabet didn't like that tone.

She pretended not to hear. "I can say hello from Lena and Joseph,"
he said. "I was there yesterday. The boy is such a good baby."

The reminder that he was a grandfather subdued him a bit.
Though even so, despite not wanting to do it, he had to compare
Elisabet with Irene. Unbelievable how people could evolve differently.
Irene's youth had drowned, Elisabet's had been preserved. The man
who got to go out with Elisabet truly did not have to be ashamed of
her company. He wondered if her skin was still just as smooth and
fine.

"He's probably waiting for you," Elisabet said, and sat down in her
office chair.

Her legs glistened in the light from the window. He sighed invol-
untarily—and left.

It was jewelry that was being photographed today. Nothing of great
value, otherwise they would have chosen another model. These were
more simple items, intended for young girls with limited resources.
And as such Berit would fit in.

She had put on a white dress, and the photographer took some pictures—with necklaces and earrings. They had worked together several
times before; he knew how she should be photographed and she knew
how he wanted things. An assistant helped with a spotlight and the
cords; everything went routinely.

"I think we will take some with bare shoulders, too," he said.

"Okay."

She stood up, pulled down the zipper in back and pulled the dress off to her waist. She sat down again, pushed down the shoulder strap of her bra.

"It's just as well you take that off," he said.

She obeyed. He straightened the necklace, fastened it. Passed his hand across her breasts.

"Your tits are really pretty," he said. "You haven't changed your mind? I would actually love to take a few nude studies."

She shook her head.

"No," she said. "Not because it makes any difference to me … but you know. Papa would flip out if he found out."

"It's not likely he will."

"But if."

He kept quiet and photographed.

"You can get dressed again," he said. "It's done."

He sounded maybe a little sulky, thought she was a pain. She, who could behave so freely, suddenly beginning to give him an argument. But her papa was, of course, a city councilor, and was perhaps afraid that the voters would not like it if it came out that his daughter was showing her breasts.

"You're not a kid either," he said. "You have to be able to do what you want anyway."

"Yes, that's what I'm doing. I don't want to needlessly make him upset."

"The old bastard ought to be proud instead. It's really not everyone who looks good enough to show them off."

She got the money she was to be paid and walked out into the sunshine.

Berit liked to walk around town, sit on the stairs of the Concert Hall a while or outside the Royal Dramatic Theater. She met some people she knew and talked with them, bought a few small things: stockings, lipstick.

Fluttering along, like a butterfly. It was then she was happy. Papa had wanted her to sit in an office, chained down from morning till night. No matter how much she wanted to humor him, she could not imagine such a life. It would be like going willingly to jail.

And now she fluttered around. She sat down among the flowers beside Berns Hotel and drank a glass of juice, was up in NK department store and looked at a bikini swimming suit, sat and talked with two Italians on a bench in Kungsträdgården. She had never seen them before and would probably never see them again either. That was precisely why it was fun to talk to them.

When she left them, she decided to take a walk out toward Djurgården; one should do it on a weekday like this. Alongside Djurgårdsbron a car rolled up beside her and someone called her name. At first she didn't recognize the person driving, and then she remembered that they had met in a gang of people somewhere. He was some kind of advertising man, his name was Roffe if she recalled rightly. The girl beside him was called Tuttie; they were probably engaged. The guy who was sitting in the backseat she had met now and then; he sketched for an advertising firm and painted a little, too.

They were on their way to Djurgårdsbrunn Restaurant and asked if she wanted to follow along. She hopped into the back seat where Ville, the artist, threw his arms around her and kissed her. She laughed and patted his shaggy cheek.

They ate, Ruffe treated. Company entertainment, he and Ville had carried out some jobs together. They drank a lot, too, grew tipsy. They came up with the idea that they should drive out and look at the dog cemetery beside Lidingöbro. It was the right thing to do in the spring. Though in fact it was at its absolute best at dusk, completely unbelievably magnificent at that time.

Rays of sun penetrated through the large oak tree tops, crosses and stones stood half hidden in the brush. The atmosphere in the overgrown cemetery, the light intoxication, everything gave a feeling of unreality. Existence seemed to dissolve. Everything took on billowing soft contours, a world to flutter in.

They stopped in front of some big smooth slabs where rows of names stood, dark shadowed, carved into the shining stones.

"I have always dreamt of screwing a beautiful girl on a gravestone," Ville said. "On a spring day just like today."

"Ick, what a macabre fantasy you have," whined Tuttie.

"She would get a really cold bottom," said Berit.

"You can put my coat underneath," said Ville.

She laughed and continued on, in among the trees. He followed, caught up with her, grabbed her from behind and pressed her against himself.

"Can you come along up to the atelier for a bit?"

She went along, though truthfully she did not know why.

What he called an atelier was only a narrow and scruffy room in a house being torn down in Klara. The naked windows were gray with dirt; the coating gave a better, more subdued light, he said. Everywhere lay paints, brushes, and pencils; canvasses and frames stood stacked against the walls. The only pieces of furniture were a table and some chairs.

She hung up her red coat on a nail, looked around. This was certainly not the right place to go in a white dress. She pulled down her zipper and he helped her off with it. He pulled off his own clothes himself, threw them over a pile of canvasses, stood naked and hairy and looked hungrily at her while she continued to undress. She did it routinely and calmly, as if it were a photo shoot.

"But where?" she asked. "Where can we be?"

He pulled out a roll of frame backing paper that stood in a corner, threw it on the floor, rolled it out.

"On the gravestone, of course."

He took a black pastel crayon, drew something that looked like one of the slabs they had stood in front of. LOYAL, HONEST. And two small fat crosses.

"It's crazy," she said but laughed. Ville looked so silly where he sat on his haunches and drew, a hairy ape.

He stood up and came toward her, took hold of her buttocks and lifted her up. His tangled beard tickled her breasts as he carried her over to the paper he had spread on the floor.

"It's as I said," she said. "Cold. Bring the coat here!"

He just grunted, got on top of her.

The evening sun shone through the dirty window.

Afterward he absolutely wanted to go to the old tavern, Freden.

But they hadn't had time to do much more than eat before he remembered that he had to get going. He had promised his wife to take care of the kids. Berit recalled that she must have heard sometime that he was married.

"This wasn't really good, this thing," he said now. "I'm always ashamed afterward. For her sake—and the kids. It never would have happened if it hadn't been for that damned cemetery. I always get just as horny when I go there, can't understand why."

"Pardon me," he said. "You can't help this. You have been really great and nice in every way. It's just that bit about my being married. Don't you have anyone you think you might have betrayed just now?"

"LOYAL," she said. "HONEST."

"It probably feels good to be free," he said.

"Maybe it does."

"You're not mad? About anything?"

She shook her head again.

"But now I have to dash, I did promise. Stay sitting, you still have something in your glass."

He left and she thought that it was strange how indifferent she felt toward him now. It had been so the whole time except for just then, on the floor. Then he had meant something for a short while. It wasn't lust, only the closeness, not feeling so lonesome.

As a matter of fact, there wasn't really any person she was really attached to. Well, Papa. He would not have liked this, not been able to understand her. In some way he was so innocent, didn't understand anything. Had never understood, would probably never understand. It was so shameful to deceive him. But she had to—for the sake of his innocence.

A short time ago, she had nodded to someone who was sitting a few tables away from her. It was Henning, her half-brother. They had only met a few times but she liked him, he was easy to talk to. And she needed someone to talk to now; if she sat alone any longer she would begin to bawl. It felt impossible to go home right now.

She took her glass and went over to Henning's table. He was alone, had been at a meeting and taken the opportunity to eat out afterward.

Although they knew each other so slightly, she felt, anyways, that it was like meeting a friend.

Henning told her about his new job and his unhappiness there. That was something that she understood and could feel; she thought that he should quit immediately, whether or not he had something new. And she told him about all the jobs she herself had not had success with, and the photographing and walk-on parts that she was working with now.

On this day it was as if she continually said and did things without knowing why. As if she was lacking a shield, could not keep on the usual mask. She told him things that she had never spoken of to any person before. About how unhappy and anxious she felt at times. About what she had gone through and had to hide. At home they had believed that she was on vacation and having a good time—but she had undergone an abortion. It had been difficult, she had believed she would die, suspected that she would never be able to have children. That part with children did not mean so much to her, she didn't want any children. But to then get attached to someone felt like a deception. It was, of course, dumb, but that was how it felt; she could not get attached to anyone any longer. As if a piece of her was dead.

She was indifferent to most if it now. There were no longer any demands, no future to save anything for. Just the present.

Though Papa wasn't to know anything; for his sake maybe she might wish that things were different. He would not be able to understand. He would just become upset if he found out.

Eventually she went and called her father.

Erik arrived in the car, happy that she had called and would go home with him. Now he would be able to sleep calmly tonight, everything was as it should be.

She was waiting on the street, climbed in, and sat down beside him. The car rolled along the quays, silent in the evening, and up onto Tranebergsbron. He asked her how things had gone, had she had a lot to do, and she answered that there had been a lot but that she had had time to get out in the sunshine a little, too. That was good, he said, you should take the opportunity, take advantage of the springtime.

When she had gotten undressed she went into the bathroom and saw that it was as she had feared. Ville's chalk pastel had rubbed off onto her. Now it looked like she had a cross on one buttock. She managed to get the black mark off with a towel. There were black smudges on the towel instead.

Ville and his ideas! LOYAL and HONEST. Was he so crazy or was it only that he pretended to be that way to show he was an artist. Something sick about it, not fun anymore.

Now Ville was sitting and watching his children. And Henning was home with his kids and Barbro. That was maybe why people got married, to avoid being alone.

The light was on in her father's study. She entered in her nightgown, curled up in the old armchair he had there. From habit, a photography habit, she loosened the fabric a little from her body so that her "headlights" wouldn't show through her nightgown.

Her father pushed his newspaper aside, smiled at her.

"Give me a proper whiskey and soda," she asked him. "I fell like I'm having trouble falling asleep tonight."

"Spring sun, air," he said. "But can that be good for you? Whiskey and soda I mean."

"I'm not a child anymore," she said. "Try to get used to it."

"We'll each have one then," he said and got up "But only one—and that goes for both of us."

They sat and talked about nothing. And she felt how calm and drowsiness came to her.

"Thanks," she said. "Thanks for understanding."

She kissed him on the cheek, left.

She went past the bathroom, took the smudged towel and threw it in the dirty laundry.

"LOYAL and HONEST!"

Thank you, she thought. Thank you, God, that he doesn't understand anything.

NEAR THE SEA
OF TRANQUILITY

Indeed welfare grew; many people had it better than they had ever had before. Whether they were also happier was a personal question.

They got a car, a summer place, a television set; waited in queues to get a bigger apartment. The old members of the proletariat had been almost without possessions; their grandchildren amassed things in piles. Naturally there were exceptions, people who for some reason had landed on the side and had not been able to follow along with prosperity's upward wave. But they were forgotten almost; barely counted.

Elisabet and Lennart were among those who had become participants in the improvements. Even if Elisabet could still point out the many injustices and the many needs that they had not been able to meet, more had still happened than they had dared hope.

A few years ago they had been able to change apartments after many years waiting in the housing queue. They had moved from a one-room and a kitchen, to a three-room in Vällingby. When they had received the offer, Elisabet had been a little dubious at first, not primarily because of the high rent—but because Erik lived in Vällingby. She looked up his address in the telephone book and looked at the map and saw that there was quite a distance between the buildings in question. And, of course, they couldn't refrain from taking the opportunity when it finally arrived.

It had happened a couple of times that she had seen Erik out there, once together with a large, heavy woman. It was probably his wife. He did not look particularly happy when he came along with her, more like he was ashamed. Elisabet almost felt sorry for him.

Another important change had occurred one year earlier—Lennart had finally changed jobs. The printer's he had been at all those years had been forced to move from the Klara neighborhood because of the demolition, and with that he had gotten a more difficult commute to work. Then Joseph had moved to another printer's and a foreman's job had become available there. Joseph had encouraged Lennart to apply and recommended him. To his surprise, Lennart had gotten the position.

Once Lennart had gotten over the relocation difficulties, he had found himself well situated and was happier there more than he had ever been before. He felt that he could handle the duties, also felt the good will that he met with. From the beginning they had thought that he would be in charge of the hand setting, but now they preferred to have him in the orders department. They discovered that they had made a find.

Not only the responsibility and the pleasure he took in his work increased, but also the salary. Everything made him more assured, calmer. Soon he grew a little broader, too, was not so boyishly gangly any longer.

Some of the new assurance also had to do with his private life.

For a long time he had been very vulnerable, fragile. Elisabet's dissatisfaction and criticism had been hard on him, made him desperate and upset. But as the years had passed, his hide had become tougher and gradually he didn't feel the pokes in the same manner. He got used to it, didn't expect anything else.

He knew: it was to become numb, become coarsened, it meant that the love he had once felt no longer existed. She had rubbed it out.

Of course, he still liked her, also thought that there was hardly anyone as beautiful as she was. Deep inside, the memory and dream of love was still left. Memory and dream. But hardly life and reality any longer.

When they had moved and he had gone through all his old papers, he had found some notes that once had meant a lot to him. Some lines he had written during the years of unemployment when he had sat entire days at the city library. He had forgotten them afterward, not thought of them for many years.

We are never so defenseless against suffering as when we love.

It was Freud who had said it. He had, according to the notes, also said that happiness "is, by its nature, only possible as an episodic phenomenon."

He had especially been fixed on that first sentence, the one about suffering. It could almost stand as a motto above all his years with Elisabet. He had loved her as much as anyone can love someone. Only her and no one else. And for this reason he had been so defenseless when she had attacked him. Then he had huddled up. Huddled into his "dusty bundles" and hidden himself and his despair there.

For a time, a few years, much had been different. At the same time as he had experienced the worst he had also been the happiest. When she had told him about herself and Erik. Of course, he had been unhappy, jealous, felt betrayed. But she had never been so soft and friendly as then, he felt that her regret was genuine. And her love—as if it were manifested in the child she gave birth to. She had been very afraid of giving birth, believed that she would never be able to go through such pain. For this reason it was an enormous gift he received from her when she gave him this child. A token of love, an offering of reconciliation.

They had certainly experienced some unusually happy years then. Happy, though paid for dearly. But gradually most of it had reverted to the old ways. The natural conditions?

Not that his existence became unbearable; she was not that difficult. But if he had let it all get to him in the same way as before, then he would probably not have had the energy to go on. And that was his fault, at least as much as hers. He had been too sensitive. Because he loved her far too much?

He believed she did not want to hurt him. It was pretty certain that she didn't understand how much she did hurt him. It was only her way of being. That incomprehensible bitterness that was inside her and had to come out.

Jenny had once, jokingly, told about how Elisabet used to shut herself in the bathroom as a girl when she got in a bad mood. Emelie and Jenny had to stand and plead and knock on the door without being let in. When Elisabet was displeased with something, she would punish the people around her, whether they were the reason for her displeasure or not. She had to have an outlet for what she felt and then it would wash over those who stood closest. But those who loved and were defenseless felt personally afflicted by hate, stuck with pins, cut with knives. And suffered.

He had suffered. Until he did not have the strength to feel anymore. Until he found protection by killing his love.

He could stroke her and kiss her. But not love her like before.

This way he grew calm, this way he attained an assurance unknown to him before. He did not go around in constant anxiety anymore. When she dug in he would parry with a few lame words and sidestep the situation. That was enough, that was good. She could say what she wanted to let out, calm down. And he would barely notice what she had said, not been injured by it. It could be that simple. As a matter of fact, it was difficult to understand why he hadn't come up with that method earlier.

He had seen Erik out there, nodded to him. Meeting him wasn't a worry.

Naturally he wouldn't like it if some new affair ever occurred between Elisabet and Erik. For the sake of tranquility, and for his daughter. And also, maybe because he thought that he wouldn't have the strength for the rekindling of love that her regret, in such a case, would give rise to. He did not want to suffer anymore, did not want to love anymore. Things were good as they were.

Overall there was no reason at all for worry; it was out of the question that Elisabet might grow interested in Erik again.

But he felt very alone at home. Elisabet monopolized their daughter, Monika, so completely. It was, of course, natural, mother and daughter. They had so many interests in common, clothes and such.

His evasive manner and his silence resulted in his ending up a little on the outside. He accepted it.

It was when he got together with Joseph that he opened up, grew lively and talkative. He liked both Joseph and Lena a lot, preferred it when they went along out to the country.

Otherwise it had gotten so empty out there since John had died. He had also like John a lot, they had had a fine time when they had rowed out and fished together. They had sat mostly quiet out there in the inlet, had been able to be silent very well together. It had been like an escape, from all the small gnawing words.

Was there in fact anything finer than silence?

They had been at Joseph and Lena's one evening. Lena's sister Berit had come there totally unexpectedly.

As so often happened, they had talked about the summer cottage. And suddenly Berit had said that it would be so fun to be able to come along with them there.

"Of course, do that," Lennart had answered.

He usually did not answer so quickly, not decide anything. But in the company of Joseph he was different, less cautious. And then, it was also that he thought politeness required such a response. And Elisabet had just remained quiet.

She had become quite huffy, though she managed to control herself until they got home. There wasn't enough space in the cottage; they didn't know Berit, Maj might grow upset that they dragged yet one more of Erik's daughters out there; there wasn't enough space in the car either. Besides, the girl didn't seem at all as nice and good as Lena.

It didn't look like there was anything wrong with her, he thought. In any case maybe it wouldn't happen; a young girl surely had a lot of diversions to choose between.

But Berit came one Saturday, in Henning's car.

In the evening they gathered at Maj's. Joseph and Lena and their little boy, Elisabet and Lennart with Monika. Berit came together with Henning and Barbro and their children, she was going to sleep over at their place.

Maj's cottage was not so big, but still the nicest one to gather in. There was a big open fireplace there and it was cozy; the cottage had sort of been worn in and become pleasant in another way from the more newly built. Besides, it was best situated, close to the water and far from the pine trees.

Berit carried Lars-Olov on her shoulders when they came; the children adored her, she was so full of pranks.

They ate and drank coffee, sat and talked. The paraffin lamps and the fire cast a soft and friendly light. Berit had gotten hold of a large pillow and sat on the floor. She felt calmer and happier than she usually did, a quiet happiness. She felt comfortable—with the cottage, with the people who were there. Elisabet, maybe she was a little unsure of. But she liked Maj a lot; she was so calming, so friendly. And Barbro, they had laughed and joked with the children, become children themselves. Henning was good, he, too, a friend. Strangely enough she felt maybe most of a stranger with Joseph and Lena. She didn't really understand her sister and her love, that anyone could be delighted by Lena and that Lena could fall in love with Joseph. There was certainly nothing wrong with either of them—but she didn't comprehend them.

Yet maybe she liked Lennart best of all. She didn't know why, he was so silent, of course. But it was he who had said that she ought to come along. And also she felt safety in his presence. Maybe because he had happened to end up on the chair beside her. His trousered legs and heavy shoes beside the cushion she was sitting on.

Now he said something in any case. He was thinking of going out and fishing early the next morning, as he usually did. He wondered if anyone wanted to go along.

"Oh yes," she said. "That would be a lot of fun."

He looked at her a little quizzically. Actually he had thought that maybe Joseph or Henning would want to go with him. Though Henning was not so crazy about fishing and maybe Joseph didn't want to leave Lena.

"Can you manage to get up?" he asked. "Five o'clock."

"Of course, I'll do it."

He looked quickly over at Elisabet. She seemed completely uninterested.

"Let's plan on it then," he said.

Poor Lennart, Elisabet thought, now he will have to drag along that Berit and not get to be alone like he would really prefer. He never should have asked. She's only a kid, really, a persistent kid.

They didn't stay so late, because of the children. Lennart always stayed behind and helped dry while Maj did the dishes. But she didn't have to do the dishes that evening; Berit took care of it. Maj only had to put them away.

"Good help today," she said. "Thank you, that was kind of you. Will you find your way alright in the darkness?"

"I'll go with her," Lennart said.

The August evening was dark but warm, the dim lights from the cottage they had left did not reach far. As if the woods advanced closer, the path disappeared. A juniper shrub stood beside the way, looking like a man standing guard. Berit jumped back when she saw it.

"Can I hold your hand?" she asked. "So I don't fall in the darkness."

He reached out his hand and she took it. Her hand felt firm and warm but little, almost like a child's.

They walked through the tunnel of trees; he pushed aside some branches sticking out and thought how he should bring garden shears here and trim it a little; Maj had not had time for it. The girl came closer, her head against his shoulder when she swerved from the branches.

An unusual experience to walk like this in the dark with a girl. The feeling of kinship and fellowship that was there even though they knew each other so little.

"Look how the water's shining," she said.

"It's the moon."

"Let's go down!"

It was only a few steps across the tufts of lingonberry bushes. The trees came behind them, before them the open water, the sound of the gentle swells on the sand.

She let go of his hand, ran forward a few steps, squatted down and dipped her hand in the water.

"It's warm. Shouldn't we go in?"

"No," he said. "Wait until tomorrow. It's better."

"Will you wait for me if I take a quick dip?"

He wanted to make an objection but couldn't come up with anything. She took a few steps away from him, pulled off her dress. He turned his back to her, walked a little closer to the path. He heard her run out into the water, throw herself in. She gave a shriek; it was probably a little cold in any case.

Then it grew quiet. He waited but thought maybe it was best to see that nothing had happened and turned around. She was standing in the water beside the beach. White in the moonlight, as if shining. It wasn't until now that he really understood that she was no child but a woman. That maybe should have frightened him, but he felt rather that it made him glad to discover it. She gave him something just by being there, standing there.

"Do you have anything I can dry off on?"

"You can take my sweater."

"But it will get wet."

"It will have time to dry by tomorrow."

While he pulled off his sweater she came over to him and he felt a violent urge to embrace her, pull her to him. But he only placed the sweater across her shoulders, turning away while she got dressed.

"How shy you are!" she said. "But that's good. That's nice. You are nice."

They walked quietly up toward the cottage where she was spending the night. There was a light on in the kitchen where she was sleeping. He stopped a ways from the house; now she would find the way easily herself.

"You're not changing your mind?" he asked. "Shall I come at five o'clock?"

"That will be lovely."

"Bring your bathing suit with you if you want to swim."

She smiled.

They rowed out in the morning stillness; the sea lay smooth. He sat at the oars, she in the stern. The boat clung to the smooth surface, left a rippling stream behind. She let one hand dangle in the water.

"It feels chillier than yesterday evening," she said. "But I have my bathing suit on, underneath."

He rowed so they came past the point and were not visible from the beach. It was here he usually stayed. It felt somehow a little safer, too; he wasn't really sure about what she might get up to. When the sun grew warmer she took off her dress and sat in her bathing suit, laid his sweater behind her back and snuggled down so the light breeze wouldn't reach her. She laid and closed her eyes against the sun, while he sat and kept his eye on the float. And one on her at times. It was hard not to. He still felt disconcerted, unsure as to what he was in fact experiencing. There had only been one woman aside from his mother in his life, Elisabet. He had never had any thought that there would be anyone else, he was satisfied, it was enough. And now Berit lay there, so close. She had stood naked beside him last night. As if she was inviting him to just reach out his hand and take her. And he felt the desire to do it but still could not.

She looked up, looked at him.

"I like you a lot," she said. "I would like to have you."

"I'm married," he answered.

She smiled.

"Yes, I know that. That's fine, don't be afraid. I will satisfy myself with loving you from a distance."

Nothing more than that happened. During the day he didn't see her; she was with Barbro and Henning then. Later they ate together but then she sat beside Barbro. And when she went home it was in Henning's car, the one she had come in.

Nevertheless, it felt meaningful, like something decisive that never came to fruition but passed by very close.

Some weeks later, a bit into September, he took a few days off and stayed out in the cottage alone.

One evening he walked past Maj's cottage as he was taking a walk, continued on the path down to the beach. He stood where he had stood that night when Berit had bathed. Now no moon shone, it was windy and the waves rolled in. He thought he could hear her voice in the noise, how she had given a cry, come running across the sand. It felt as if he would be able to touch her naked body if he reached out his hand.

And as he stood there he got the idea that maybe she had come. Maybe she had heard from her sister that he would be out here alone, maybe she was sitting in the cottage and waiting now.

For a moment it felt like it was a certainty: she was there, she was waiting for him.

What should he do? Why should he say no if she said yes? Why shouldn't he be grateful and accept? If—if she wanted to give, if she was there.

Then he would come to her, he knew it now.

He began to run, wanted to come back to the cottage, to the decisive moment.

It lay dark and silent between the trees, as he had left it. There didn't seem to be anyone there. He went into the little bedroom and looked; had he really left the door slightly ajar? Maybe she lay on the bed, waiting.

But there was no one there either.

Though nothing had happened he knew that something nonetheless had happened. For the first time he had been completely prepared to betray Elisabet. He had longed to be able to do it, had half run to get to do it.

Before he would have been ashamed of it. Not now. Rather, he felt loss, pain. Too late, too old for her.

The one who loves cannot be unfaithful. He did not love anymore.

Not Elisabet. And not Berit either. But just now he felt great thankfulness toward Berit for what she had given him: the memory, the image, and the feeling. Thanks to her he still felt alive, as if he still owned the possibility to love once again. Had he already forgotten his suffering?

No. In fact he was probably only dreaming. An impossible dream.

He sat down on the cottage steps. Somewhere high above him, up there among the stars, was maybe a rocket on the way to the moon. He had the transistor radio beside him and heard it tell that *Lunik III* had landed beside the Sea of Tranquility. The Soviet Union had declared that they had no claims on the moon's territory.

And he thought of Berit in the moonlight, a dream he had dreamt, nothing more. He was calm again, near the Sea of Tranquility, alone in the silence.

OPPORTUNITIES

Through the television sets the world streamed into the homes. Intensively, tangibly. A complicated world, hard and cruel, filled with hate and suffering and seemingly irreconcilable antagonisms.

Machines guns rattled, people fleeing ran through the streets, revolting masses of people pushed forward, politicians and generals thundered out their realities.

Everything came so close. And seemed so insoluble, so impossible. And yet he wanted to believe in the opportunities.

Henning had had a difficult period.

He wondered if he wouldn't have given up without Barbro. She had made him believe in himself despite everything. Because she believed in him.

She gave him the strength to accomplish something on the side of his daily job. It began to feel more and more important to accomplish something else, like taking a deep breath before one dove.

He was writing again. At work it wasn't an issue of writing, only of stacking phrases on order. But at home he wrote. Nothing exceptional, but such that he still thought was worth spending time with. Small articles and discussion contributions about what concerned him, about the world's distress that had to be stopped, about the possibilities that had to be tried. He read a lot, combined what he read with what he knew. He sought his way, sought the possible.

It happened often during conversations with Barbro. And he thought about their first trip abroad, how they had discussed his articles, how much of her that was in what he wrote back then.

When she got sick, the conversation had been broken off, their working together couldn't function in the same way. She had not had the energy. But now it had been taken up again. And from the conversation came ideas and suggestions; he would disappear in to the typewriter a while and put down what had emerged. He would come back and read it aloud; the discussion would continue.

He got some of what he wrote published, was requested sometimes to come and talk at meetings of associations and to study groups. He was commissioned to write a study guide that would deal with conditions in poor countries and what could be done. He discovered how much material was missing, translated some smaller works and got a publisher to issue them.

It was such work that sustained him, gave him the means to endure. It also led to something he had not counted on. The publisher that had brought out his translations offered him a position.

When he quit his job he found that maybe he wasn't such a complete failure as he had believed. He was offered a higher salary to stay, more than the publisher would pay. But he left.

With him, he brought something that he knew he would keep: the awareness of how short the step was between failing and succeeding, the knowledge of how he himself in another situation than that day's could be the failure, the one who did not grasp anything nor was capable of it. After such an experience it was harder to judge, easier to understand.

Often he had to think of Olle, Gun's husband.

They didn't meet very often but once in a while it happened and it would be at Allan's home. It was Allan who tried to keep the siblings together and also maintain contact with Henning. The last time Lilian and her boys had been there. Per was "inside," Lilian said, for receiving stolen goods. That he was picked up by the police came as a shock both to Lilian and to himself; he had gotten by so many years now. How should he be able to keep track of whether what he was doing business with was stolen or not?

While Lilian had been there, Olle had had the sense to keep quiet. But as soon as she and her boys had disappeared, he had gotten going. He wanted stiffer punishments, someone like Per should never be let out again and instead be kept in forced labor for life. And Per's rascals for sons, already ruined, one could certainly see that. The kids should be spanked.

All that talk that people should help…. Only garbage.

Now he had turned to Henning, had apparently read something Henning had written.

Like those underdeveloped countries. People there had to learn to take care of themselves. They became only lazy and apathetic otherwise. You could see it already in this country, everyone who took sick days for no reason at all, all the drunkards who just lived on welfare. As long as people got what they needed without working, they would, of course, not make any effort.

Before, maybe there hadn't been any jobs. But now that there were, that was not an excuse. Now each and every one that really tried could get work and earn his bread himself. If it was so that someone didn't want to work, then he could just starve. It was criminal to take tax money and fatten up all these asocial, work-shy individuals.

Olle was bitter. A heavy job. Three children to support. He had toiled since he was a boy and could not, despite everything, really keep up in the race for the standard of living. They had bought a summer cottage but they had no car.

Gun kept quiet, maybe she was suffering. Her parents, Per, so many of her closest kin belonged to the ones Olle was condemning.

He ought to take sick leave himself instead of grumbling over those who did, Henning thought. It was a benefit he had to pay for and not some "poor allowance." But Olle did not see it that way.

Allan had tried to get them to talk about something else. He talked about the vacation trip he and Daggan and the kids had taken, a group tour to Rimini in Italy. It was actually cheaper than taking a vacation in Sweden. And so many fantastic things they got to experience. Daggan had to show the gold ring she had bought in San Marino. Unbelievably cheap.

Olle listened sulkily. They hadn't been able to afford any trips. In any case he had no desire to travel abroad and be jostled around with people when he couldn't comprehend what they were saying. First and foremost he would take care of the water issue and bring in electricity out at the cottage.

Allan's family didn't have any summer place. They traveled instead. Olle thought it was throwing away money. If you put it into a cottage then it was still there.

Just constantly wandering around. So typical of Allan.

He was a little afraid of Gun's relatives. Her father had never had a proper job in his whole life. Per let Lilian support him and dabbled apparently in stolen goods as well. Allan was surely a little backward though he did work. And Henning wrote in magazines and had such strange ideas. If Gun had had any of that in her he had succeeded in taking it out of her.

"Me and my siblings turned out to be real people," he often said. "We had to learn to mind our manners. There was no one to take us to Italy so we could get to swim in the Mediterranean. If we could get out to Källtorpssjön to swim that was plenty good. That had to be good enough for us. That can be good enough for our kids, too."

Olle saw without seeing, Henning thought. He sat faithfully in front of his TV, but still had not discovered that Sweden lay in the world. He thought you could close it out, draw protective boundaries around it, drew as many as he could around himself. Swedes should take care of their own and not worry about other countries; Stockholmers had no reason to concern themselves with the problems of those who lived in less populated areas; those who lived in Hökarängen could not give a hang about what happened in Bagarmossen.

Within all these boundaries Olle sat in a corner with his back to those around him. In his corner was everything that meant anything: his family, his job, his cottage. His back was the corner's defense; it was strong, it carried burdens and sustained blows. It protected and concealed, kept both the world and the sun away.

He gladly complained that everything happened "behind his back." But how could anything happen before his eyes when he always turned his back?

Maybe Olle and many with him were frightened by the multitude of opportunities. The constant necessity of choosing created anxiety, maybe in the end paralysis.

A big city in a welfare society in a technological world. That meant numerous opportunities. Good and bad.

In an isolated place the opportunities were few. They could have the right combination so they suited one person very well, providing happiness, comfort. They could suit another person in the same place less well, in which case it was often intolerable.

In harder times the opportunities had been fewer even in the city. As recently as during the years of unemployment in the thirties, they had been so few that many people had been forced to make choices that they knew they would regret all their lives.

Now it was teeming with opportunities of every kind. From studying and education, to amusements and entertainment. Stores weighed down with goods, daily newspapers and weekly magazines rolling out in never-ceasing streams, movie houses and theaters, radio and television enticing with their programs. Museums, libraries, and churches stood open and waiting, the new school welcomed all classes of society.

Naturally there were still shortages, areas where the resources were not enough for the increased demand or where perhaps people had been unsuccessful with their planning. The most difficult was the housing problem. The opportunities for the person who remained without housing seemed almost non-existent.

Some of the opportunities required specific conditions: aptitude, knowledge. Practically all cost something: money, work, time.

But the entire time, every day, people had to choose. And in a way that had never been before, people were responsible for their choices. Before, they could blame an accident on circumstances, oppositions, shortages. Now people could only blame themselves.

People might feel rushed. It was a question of having time for the most possible, get the most opportunities for the money. Be a good consumer, show proof of familiarity with goods. Is the fabric wrinkle-free? Is this really culture? Isn't the pork five öre cheaper across the street?

There were so many opportunities that tempted and offered, the packaging grew ever shinier and more dazzling, the ways to make advertisements for each thing more and more artful.

Choosing wrong was easily done, correcting the mistake could be considerably more difficult. Henning knew this from his own and dearly paid for experience.

Sometimes he could understand Olle who turned his back on everything. Though choose he had to do nevertheless: the corner, the dark, the narrowness.

Henning had chosen to be engaged even if his engagement was limited, he also had his family and his work. He joined a committee that supported Danilo Dolci's work in Sicily and participated in the planning of what would be undertaken from the Swedish side.

One evening when he had been to a meeting and come home, he found Berit sitting on the sofa beside Barbro. She had dropped by completely unexpectedly. She had been feeling down, needed to talk to someone. And so it happened to be Barbro.

Olle had maybe been scared by the number of opportunities, had withdrawn, turned his back. Berit had reacted the opposite way. Been attracted, tried to be able to test as many as possible. A little here, a little there. She had some vague dreams about the College of Arts and Design or maybe theater school. But there were demands made there and she didn't have enough knowledge or ability, nor a real desire to try and achieve what was required. There was so much else; she didn't want to forsake one thing for another. As long as the children had been up she had played with them, joked and laughed. Later, once they had fallen asleep, she had cried. When Henning arrived she had calmed down a little.

They sat curled up on the sofa, the fair Barbro and the dark Berit. Only the floor lamp was lit; it cast a soft and friendly circle of light around them. He stood in the door and looked at them, felt that he liked them both a lot.

Berit asked if she could spend the night, she could sleep anywhere: on the sofa, on the floor. She was afraid to leave, afraid of ending up in insecurity and despair again. It felt so safe here.

Of course, she could stay.

She was given a pillow and a couple of blankets and curled up on the sofa. The floor lamp got to stay on; she preferred to have it that way. The kids found her there the next morning and shrieked with joy, she cavorted with them so that they were almost late for school.

Both children went to school, the boy had begun in the fall. Now they were going to have winter vacation and Barbro and Henning had also taken the chance to take a week off from their jobs. They intended to travel out to their summerhouse. Though they were going to be in Maj's cottage, which was sturdier and kept the heat in better.

Barbro wondered if Henning had anything against Berit going along. Only one evening in peace and quiet could not help much, but maybe a week could.

It was a calm and lovely week. No neighbors were in the cottages next door; they stood closed and silent. The inlet was covered in ice and snow.

They sat in front of the fire in the evenings, talking low while the children slept in the next room. Berit talked about her time growing up, about her home, was especially willing to talk about her father. Henning felt like he got to know his father in a wholly different way from before. In some way it felt like Erik, his and Berit's father, was present. And when Berit talked, Henning could remember things that he had previously forgotten, glimpses of his childhood, from the time when he had still lived together with his father. It wasn't until now that he felt how he had missed him for many years, that something had been missing.

It showed that that week had done Berit good. She grew calmer, more even-humored. They took cross-country ski excursions, all five, helped make food together afterward.

On such days life was simple. It required so little, gave so much.

Henning filled the woodchip basket with wood, carried it in. The children lay on their stomachs on the floor and leafed through old Donald Duck comic books. In the narrow kitchen, Barbro and Berit stood side by side and took care of the dishes. They were about the same height, both slender, quick movements. One fair and one dark.

BEFORE A
NEW AUDIENCE

Jenny was listless, sad, and tired. She sat and sorted a little apatheti-cally through her papers; everything seemed so meaningless now. Before, Emelie had always been close by, to tell things to. Even if she had never been particularly interested in the theater world, she had lis-tened anyway. Now Jenny had to wait until Maj came home. And by then she had usually forgotten what she had meant to tell her.

So everything that Jenny had saved through the years just lay there, hardly entertained her anymore. It mostly just reminded her that she had failed. Now she had to admit that she had never become any-thing. She had not broken through, did not belong to those that would be remembered. It was possible that she had succeeded in entertaining some people once upon a time, surely people had had a good laugh at her sometimes. But now everyone had forgotten her. And those who set the tone, the critics, had basically always been indifferent, or outright nasty.

She thought about Olof. He had wanted so much, had had such big plans. But felt like he had failed, he, too. He had not been able to deal with that, he had cleaned out everything he had done, burned it up. Not left anything behind.

Maybe he had done the right thing, he had destroyed his work rather than letting time and oblivion do it. Though many times she had thought that it would have been really nice to still have that painting he had done of her just when they were getting to know each other.

The Söder girl, the hooligan girl in a flame red dress.

It would have been fun to have it. But her old newspaper clippings? Where it maybe stated "among the rest, Jenny Fält was noticed." That was nothing to save, no survivor could get any joy out of that. Nor she herself either. She ought to be, wanted to be as strong as Olof.

She stuffed all the clippings that lay on the table in a large bag, which she carried out and threw down the trash chute. She heard how it bounced in somewhere far below. It cut into her, she knew that she had acted too quickly again, that she already regretted it.

When Maj came home from the office Jenny was sitting in the dark and crying. But Maj went very resolutely down to the trash room and found the bag. It was a little smeared with things, but the clippings were fine. So now they stayed in any case. Jenny didn't know anymore if she was happy about it or not. In some way it felt like a new failure; her big decision had just become a small theatrical gesture.

She had muddled things up again, only caused problems for Maj. And had to admit that she was causing more and more muddles with the years. Forgetful, too. Now Maj had to worry that Jenny would forget to light the flame under the coffee pot once she had turned on the gas, or that she would forget the electric iron—she had done that once. Or lock herself out; that had also happened.

If she went out and took a walk sometimes it happened that she suddenly didn't know where she was. They were building everywhere, too, buildings she had once recognized could be gone. She would have to ask directions to find her way home. It had also happened that she would suddenly think that she still lived on Erstagatan and would not remember how things really were until she was standing there outside the door. Then it was terribly hard to get home again.

She preferred not to tell Maj about her misadventures; Maj would only get worried, maybe ask Jenny to stay inside. She wanted to get out, as long as she could. Her leg had really gotten better again at any rate.

At the same time as she was forgetting more and more, she remembered so much. Now that there wasn't so much new happening to her, she was glad to go back to her memories. She had indeed taken part in a lot in her life. She had been part of a theater troupe that had traveled through the countryside, and she had participated in the first filmmaking attempts. When she thought about those events she realized that she must be old.

Henning would ask about her experiences when he came over. Maybe he only did it to cheer he up. She probably exaggerated sometimes; the main thing was that her stories be funny. When he laughed she had to laugh too and then everything felt much better.

All Mormor's pranks and stories! Of course, he asked for them to cheer her up. But it was fun to listen too and get to know what things had been like. A lot sounded almost unbelievable now, a lot she probably expanded on. He remembered from when he was a child, how she would seemingly sacrifice anything for a joke, an effect. She never spared herself, gave herself totally.

Actually, her stories really might interest many people. Not in writing, then most of it disappeared. People should hear her herself, her tone of voice.

Over lunch he met with one of his old colleagues from the magazine editorship, Rune Stark. Rune was on the radio these days. They talked about suggestions and ideas and Henning mentioned his grandmother, her varied experiences and her gift for recounting. Rune became interested, thought that it ought to be something to make a radio program out of. And Henning agreed.

Rune wanted to come by and talk a little to Jenny first, wanted to sound her out. He called her up himself. He was welcome to come, Jenny said, but shouldn't have any hopes. She was just a little insignificant actress, and her life and experiences could hardly interest people.

Her voice was a little flat on the telephone; she sounded old and tired. She loosened up maybe when she talked with her close family. Maybe Henning, like so many others, had overrated a close relative's abilities.

He came without any great expectations and Jenny brought out the tray with coffee. The conversation began a little haltingly; he didn't really know how he should deal with her and she didn't think that she had anything of value to come with. But after a while things loosened up, then he barely needed to ask her anything at all. The memories and stories came pouring out. When she performed together with "Little Caruso," Max Hansen, at "The Happy Salmon" on Nytorget. And Ernst Rolf, "the happy man from Dalarna," he was called back then, of course, she had worked together with him, though it was before he became a ladies man. And when she filmed on Mosebacke's Terrace with Calle Barcklind, outside in a ball gown in the middle of winter…. Why? Because of the light, obviously; it didn't work to film indoors in those days.

"This will definitely be a good program," he said. They were going to record this at her home so she would not be inhibited by any unfamiliar and dreary milieu. She would just talk freely, exactly as she had done now. Not be afraid of losing the thread or of telling the same story two times; that didn't matter; those things they could cut out. They would record everything on a tape and produce it later. He would begin with a little introduction and then interject with a question now and then if he thought that something should be explained further. Or to remind her of something that she should include.

When Maj came home that evening Jenny was full of zeal. Now she sat and read through the clippings, and came across new things that should be included. Now it was really fortunate that Maj had found the bag, otherwise Jenny never would have remembered everything.

"You're not going to get too nervous, right?" Maj asked.

"Not at all!" It was just a question of sitting and telling stories; that was something each and every person could do. The big trick was surely what the editor would carry out afterward when he was going to cut out all the nonsense and make something sensible of the whole thing.

But when the recording van came and a cable was hoisted up and in through the window and some technicians bustled about in the apartment with a microphone and cords—then Jenny did not feel as sure any longer.

"Just take it easy," the editor, Stark, said. "It will definitely go well, believe me. We will just sit and talk a little first without recording, feel our way. But we will make sure that the equipment is ready first."

"We'll go ahead when I give you the signal," he said in a low voice to the soundman.

They sat and talked, as they had sat a few days earlier. She began cautiously and unsure now, too. But soon she forgot the microphone and only recounted things for the friendly editor Stark.

She talked about how she started, how she had done the Söder girl and sung "The Hooligan's Waltz" at small workers' variety shows.

"Sing it!" he said.

"I can't do that, can I?"

"Yes, try."

She hummed a little first, then she began to sway with her body, eyes half-closed, and sang:

> *A hooligan enters the Söder hall*
> *Ready to whirl and have a ball.*
> *All the girls feel so light and carefree*
> *A more stylish fellow they never did see.*

"That was Arthur Högstedt who wrote it," she said. "Arthur with the Hair, as we called him. He and Olof were good friends."

"Olof?"

"That was my husband. He died just a few years later. He painted, was an artist."

She grew silent, as if she lost the mood. She caught sight of the soundman, who was standing with the headphones over his ears, and asked: "That hasn't been on has it?"

"Yes. And it sounds great."

"But sing … I can't sing anymore."

"Everything will be decided when we cut," the editor said. "Take a little break now. Rest a while."

"Tell them to put on a new tape," he said. "So we avoid breaking off in the middle of something."

And she recounted some more. About the old theater barns where she had danced so far forward that the gaslights in the footlights had flickered and threatened to set fire to her long skirts, about Horse-Nisse and his cinematographic theater, about the filmmaking on Mosebacke's Terrace where they placed the camera on boards in the snow and placed strips of wood across the stage floor to keep the artists within range of the camera; the camera could not be turned. And "The Happy Salmon" where she had appeared as "The Genuine Stockholmer" and spoke a dialect that had to be incomprehensible for those who lived as close as north of Slussen.

"Fantastic," the editor said.

But that evening Jenny was nervous anyway, sure that the whole thing was a failure. For sure he would call the next day and say it was impossible to use.

She regretted what she had gotten involved in, she was much too old to take part in this kind of thing.

"You will have to be ashamed of me again," she told Maj.

"That will be for the first time if that's the case," Maj replied. "But I believe that it will be good indeed. Henning says that Stark is very capable; he probably doesn't make any bad programs."

"I hope he cuts out a lot of it," said Jenny "So that almost only he is left."

They came up from the radio magazine a couple of days later and took photographs of her. They got to borrow a couple of old photographs, too. A dreadful fuss, Jenny thought. It would surely end with a big crash.

The program aired on an evening in April. Luckily it aired in the evening so that Maj could be at home and comfort her. She didn't dare think about how it would feel to be completely alone and listen.

The editor, Stark, began. And then suddenly Jenny heard herself—and yet not herself. Her voice was different, she didn't recognize it. Darker. And what a terrible Stockholm dialect she spoke, it could really be heard that she was an old Söder-bird. But then she talked, of course, too, about how she was billed as the "Genuine Stockholm Girl" at the old Salmon; that part they hadn't cut.

Ashamed and proud. Red in the face from excitement. Now she was singing too! It didn't sound good. What would people say?

Maj said that it was both funny and good. She didn't have time to say more before the telephone rang. It was Henning; he thought that she had been brilliant. Then Gunnar rang and praised her. And then Erik who she hadn't seen since Emelie's funeral. He had thought of requesting a telephone queue, he said. And claimed that it had been a long time since he had had so much fun.

They were really kind. Too kind. But relatives and friends didn't really count. No matter how enthusiastic they were, they did not influence the public at large and the reviewers. But talk radio like this was surely not reviewed, she would probably be spared that.

She looked in the paper in the morning anyhow. And when she saw what was written she went out and bought the others as well.

She couldn't believe her eyes. They wrote. Many lines. They were kind, indeed, more than that.

When she had dashed around the countryside and the whole land, and performed in the theater, or when she had been part of making a film—then nobody cared about it. Sometimes she had received a line or two and thought of it as a success. But now, when she had just sat and talked—then! Then they talked about her "wonderful Stockholm dialect;" one called her "an original with a genuine gift for story-telling." "A program that absolutely must be aired as a repeat," wrote several.

A few days later the kind editor Stark sent her a whole bundle of carbon copies of excellent radio reviews from the press in the provinces. Around the whole country, in cities where she had never set foot, people had sat and listened.

She couldn't comprehend any of it.

Letters arrived, from old friends and from completely unknown people. Every single one was kind. One contained a book on spiritual edification; the letter writer urged Jenny to observe conduct more worthy of an old person who ought to be thinking of death.

She received flowers. From the director who had been there when she broke her leg and from an unknown person who claimed that he still laughed every time he remembered how she had fluttered about in Anderssonskans Kalle.

She was also paid. Incredibly much.

They called from a weekly magazine and wanted to come up and interview her. A young, learned gentleman also came from an institution at the university; he was occupied with studying Stockholm speech. He had discovered that she spoke an unusually genuine Stockholm dialect, he said.

Gradually, everything returned to normal again. But something had occurred nevertheless, something quite remarkable. And it gave back to her a whole lot of her good humor and zest for life. She had gotten full-time work, too, with pasting in all the new clippings. In this way her clippings collection had really gotten a happy ending.

So most things were pretty good. All of her relatives and friends had been so friendly and said so many kind things about the program.

All except for one. All except for the one who she perhaps most longed to receive a little praise from. Elisabet kept silent. Jenny did not dare ask if she had listened. Most likely she had indeed, though she didn't say anything.

Jenny suspected that it was probably the same as before when she had performed: Elisabet was ashamed of her. Elisabet was surely afraid her friends and colleagues would have listened, that they would know that Jenny was her mother. Elisabet would probably be happiest if Jenny sat quiet and still and did not get up to anything else.

Elisabet could rest easy; there would probably not be any more performances. Even if Jenny could still dream of a success that would be so great that even Elisabet would have to applaud. The radio performance, Jenny's life's biggest and more unexpected success, was apparently not enough. In which case there was probably no hope.

THE
ALIEN PEOPLE

The traffic thickened, the subway trains rolled out across the bridges and into the dark tunnels. The city—a piece of machinery where people and material moved forward on transport bands, where many small cogs would mesh at the right moment. The pace was hard, the demand for precision great.

The main thing was not to let go. To cope with stopwatches, time and motion study men, contracts, and restructuring.

Not everyone had the strength to keep up; some people maybe even preferred to stand on the sidelines. Some of those who refused to participate in society's daily life and work, built sort of a city within the city, a group who lived their own life. Street muggings, break-ins, and car thefts increased; drug trafficking and bootlegging became more common. People started to talk about the city as "mob run" and "gangster city." Many older people hardly dared go out on the streets; no woman could walk unaccosted in the center at night. Drunken gang members terrorized riders on the streetcars and subway, beggars threatened to hit people when they were denied money or cigarettes. Bellowing youths filled Kungsgatan with their big hot rods and crowded into Kungsträdgården in huge packs.

For an older generation they seemed to belong to an alien people who had occupied the city. People had a hard time understanding them. They had received better opportunities than any generation before them. But instead of being happy and grateful, they seemed to be filled with threats and defiance.

More and more young people got their own cars. Leather-jacketed motorcyclists were succeeded by the hot rodders in their cars. They came in big American cars from the end of the forties, often brightly colored, decorated with signs that showed which motorcycle gang the owner belonged to: "The Road Devils," "The Car Angels."

They put foxtails, the symbol of the hunt, up on their antennas and went off to pick up girls. They rolled along Kungsgatan, made raids to the drive-in snack bar by the Tennis Stadium or to Skarpnäcksfältet. In the summertime, caravans of them drove out to the countryside; sometimes with larger motor events as their goal.

Stories about the hot rodders and their wreaking havoc were numerous. Their big cars were seen as traveling bordellos; there was talk of "a motorized youth proletariat."

Still, most of them were pretty normal and pretty decent young people who found some excitement and adventure in their hot rodder life in what was otherwise a rather dull everyday life. Most of them attended to their jobs. And they didn't drink as much as people believed; if for no other reason than that big cars were expensive to operate and ate up every single öre they earned. "Sexual orgies" were not usually so much more advanced than their parents' had in their time.

In the criticism of the youth there may have sometimes been an element of envy. Their parents had never had such opportunities. They had been forced to take the job they could get, then the children had arrived and responsibility and they had not dared change jobs or misbehave. Young people quit when they grew tired, changed for something better, or complained. Anyone who was too old to dare do the same might find him or herself unjustly dealt with, and preferred to transform his or her lack of courage and opportunities into a sense of responsibility and a public spirit. What would the world actually look like if people could not endure their daily hell?

But the youth today did not care about bearing up. They had no sense of responsibility, no public spirit. They only demanded and didn't want to give anything.

All those idle loafers should be gathered up and sent to forced labor, many said. Keep them in such tough jobs that they didn't have the energy to get up to any foolishness in their free time.

Allan wanted to understand the hot rodder youths. Especially since his daughter, Stina, was a hot rodder broad.

That they were happy in their cars was something Allan could understand especially well. Most of them were definitely living in pretty cramped conditions at home with their parents. The majority lived in the new suburbs that were not especially fun; they needed to come into town and ride around on Kungsgatan for a while.

They lacked a place to be—but got it in the car. Small warm lairs to ride around in. As a boy Allan had dreamt of getting to lie snugly bedded down in a hot dog stand. Snow and cold outside but warm and cozy inside the stand with the glowing paraffin lamp and the smell of hot dogs. It was probably sort of like that for them, warm and comfortable inside their cars.

He wasn't worried about Stina. She was good and could take care of herself. Daggan had talked to her also, so Stina knew about life.

Stina stood in the doorway. Big and strong, she reminded him quite a lot of Daggan. Maybe she wasn't especially beautiful—but fun and genuine. Her scrub brush-like hair was pulled back in a ponytail at the nape of her neck. Beneath the shiny leather jacket she had on a heavy, gray sweater that pulled across her ample breasts. Her broad backside stretched out her tight, black, long pants.

She worked at the post office, sat and sorted receipt stubs. Maybe she could be having more fun, but she was one of those who accepted her situation such as it was rather easily.

That riding around with hot rodders thing had started about a year ago, when she was sixteen. She and her friend, who was named Annmari but was called "Lenten Bun," had begun to sit in a café where a whole lot of the guys with motors came. The girls had gone along now and then; usually it was the girls who paid for the movies and the coffee while the guys treated them to car rides.

Stina and Lenten Bun had their strategy: they always stayed together, wouldn't let themselves be separated. It was safest that way; they didn't know all the guys they rode around with and they wouldn't know what the guys would go for until afterward. If there were two of them, they could always handle things better, especially since Stina was as strong as a guy. A few times they had been tricked, of course— guys who had not been able to sleep with them had kicked them out of the car. One time they had to walk the whole way from Ågesta since they didn't even have money for the subway from Farsta.

Gradually, they had begun to go around steadily with two guys who also stuck together, Rooster and Lelle. Rooster, who was a red-head, was Stina's guy; it was he who owned the car, he had a job as a car mechanic. Lenten Bun and Lelle each had their jobs. Lenten Bun was an elevator girl in a department store; Lelle worked at a ware-house.

"I'm taking off now," said Stina.

"Bye," replied Allan. "If you feel like coffee you can come on up— Mom has been baking as you know."

"Then we'll probably come. Rooster is crazy about Mom's buns."

Allan laughed his enormous laugh.

Stina heard it echo behind her as she ran down the stairs. Dad! He was probably pretty crazy … like Mom usually said. But none of her pals had such a nice dad.

Lenten Bun lived in the same building, on the ground floor. The two girls stood at the window and waited until the car arrived. They saw how it whizzed around the corner and stopped at the door with a lurch; Rooster liked that little hard lurch. The car horn blasted.

The girls waved to show that they had heard, hurried out.

Rooster sat at the wheel, nearest the sidewalk, the window rolled down. The girls bent over, stuck their heads halfway in through the window. Asked if the boys were going to go for a spin, if they could go along. Things were clear and decided, but that little negotiation was part of the game. Then they hopped into the back seat. It usually started out that way, the boys in the front, the girls in the back. Later Stina would move forward to Rooster and Lelle back to Lenten Bun.

Rooster tore away so that the girls fell over in the back seat. Then things went a little more smoothly; they drove across the high bridge,

Skanstullbron, onto Götgatan, over the locks at Slussen, down toward the center. They took some of their usual loops along Sveavägen, Kungsgatan, and Stureplan. There were mostly hot rodders slowly riding around, stopping at the edges of sidewalks, trolling for girls who would climb in after they stood there and waggled their hips a minute just like Stina and Lenten Bun had done a short while ago. But Rooster and Lelle already had fixed their pick ups so they just drove a few loops as a matter of form.

Then they rolled out of the circuit, went up Sturegatan instead, past the Stadium, and over to the drive-in snack bar where they each ate a hot dog. Here they took the opportunity to change places before their tour went into Lill-jans Wood and past the spring, Ugglavikskällan. Soon Rooster let the car glide into the shadow under some trees, turned off the headlights and the motor, but left the parking lights on. The couples moved closer together in the semi-darkness.

Rooster placed his arm around Stina and she slid down a little, half-lying against him. She felt his rough hand come inside her sweater. She pulled his face down toward hers, kissed him. Though she knew he didn't really like it, maybe he considered it unmanly.

He got his other hand in there, too. And so they just sat there, pretty still and quiet. They felt the closeness, the warmth.

In the back seat it was livelier. Panting and snorting. But gradually it grew calmer there, too.

Stina opened her eyes, shook herself. "What time is it?" she asked.

"Almost nine."

"Mom has baked buns," Stina said. "Shall we go home and have some coffee?"

Rooster started the motor and turned on the headlights. They glided out of the shadow of the trees, picked up speed. In the back seat Lenten Bun sat up, pulled up her pants zipper that Lelle had managed to unzip.

While they drove home to Hammarbyhöjden Stina sat quietly. She had been gripped by a wish that she had tried to push away before because she found it disloyal, breaking from her and her gang's conventions. She wanted to be alone with Rooster. She wished that only she and Rooster would go out in the car, that Lenten Bun and Lelle would not be there. Of course, she and Lenten Bun were best friends and had promised each other to always stay together. And for Lenten Bun it was probably good that Stina was there when she got together with Lelle. Lenten Bun gave in more and Lelle wasn't at all as shy and unsure as Rooster.

It was different with Rooster. Stina felt, knew, that he wouldn't do anything with her that she herself didn't want. It was more that she had to help him keep on track a little.

Stina possessed the strength that a person needs to be able to be free. Naturally to a large part she followed the rules that applied, in society and in the gang. But she was not a slave to them, she dared break a convention that didn't suit her.

For that reason she lingered at Rooster's side while he rolled up the windows and locked the car; she said: "Let's go out alone on Sunday. Don't say anything to Lelle instead just meet me down at the kiosk at ten o'clock."

He looked a little worried but nodded.

Stina was probably a little worried herself, too, she had taken the initiative to something that could be decisive. Maybe she had betrayed Lenten Bun as well.

The time for their meeting was good; at that time Lenten Bun was surely not awake yet. A little shame-facedly Stina walked past Lenten Bun's door.

As soon as she saw the kiosk she saw the car, too; Rooster had come in plenty of time. He had taken down the hot rodder tail from his antenna, as if he wanted to show that he wasn't out hot rodding today.

She sat down beside him, placed a bag with a coffee thermos and a length of cardamom bread in it in the back seat.

"Where are we driving?" he asked.

"Out toward the country," she said.

He remembered that he had driven to Saltsjöbaden once and that from there you could get out to Erstavik pretty easily, down to the water.

They sat silently while he drove. Unused to being alone with each other. Maybe he was a little mad: going without Lelle and Lenten Bun! What kind of plans did Stina have?

He parked the car and they got out; he walked a little ways from her. She realized that it was actually the first time they had walked together more than a few steps to and from the car. She had hardly seen him walk before. The path was uneven and sloped steeply downward. When he tried to put his feet against it to not have to begin running, he looked so funny that she burst into laughter.

"You look funny when you walk," she said and took his hand, giving him a yank and making him run with her down the incline.

After they had followed the shoreline for a stretch, they climbed up onto a rocky embankment, finding themselves a comfortable sheltered spot. She pulled off her leather jacket and sat on it; he followed her example.

"Do you like me?" she asked.

"Of course."

"For real, I mean. Not just to go out hot rodding with, but so that we can stay together for a long time?"

He blushed, looked so lost and unsure that she almost felt sorry for him.

"Ye-e-s," he came out with. "I do actually."

"I thought that we had to know how things stand and we never can do that when Lelle and Lenten Bun are with us. Then we can't talk about these things."

He still looked just as unsure, as if he didn't know what the situation might now require of him. He cast his gaze down, looked at his chapped hands. When he looked up again he thought that Stina was smiling a smile that he had never seen on her before, in fact not on anyone else either. Although he couldn't get himself to even think the impossible word, he understood that it was a smile of love.

But he understood also that things would never again be able to really be like before. With the car, with his friends, with hot rodding, with Lelle and Lenten Bun. He maybe would miss something. But nothing was worth as much as what he had gained now. He felt that.

"We should take ourselves and go to the housing department one day this week," she said as they drove home. "It's just as well to put our names down, you probably have to wait up to ten years to get anything."

And then I'll go to that public health center and get a diaphragm fitted, she thought. But she didn't say that; that could be a surprise, almost like a present. Besides, it was best that she take Lenten Bun with her at the same time. Since now Lenten Bun would surely end up alone with Lelle sometimes, and alone she would not be able to resist him for even fifteen minutes.

IN THE
AUTUMN LIGHT

The sharp autumn light gave the city such clear contours; every detail emerged. Even if the leaves had not begun to wither yet, there was still a feeling of fall; the buildings stood a clear yellow, in the air was a hint of winter's ice.

Elisabet stood and waited on the sidewalk. She felt insecure and observed; she usually didn't. Insecurity was already there in her indecision between light and shadow, the warming but revealing sunlight or the chilling but protective shade. And the uncomfortable thought that she had just had: that her new fall coat seemed too youthful.

Her circumstances had become more complicated recently. The firm she worked for had merged with their sister company. It was rational and justified since they had so much to do with each other and their work tasks partly coincided. It was the question of the boss that had been a little sensitive and that had made things drag on for a while. They had waited until one of the two bosses had retired. That had been her boss. And that meant that it was Erik who had taken over in his place now.

She had wondered a lot as to what position she would have in the future. She had the best qualifications as far as head secretary went, she herself thought. But she had wondered if Erik—with the past in mind—maybe out of consideration would prefer to keep the secretary he had. He had chosen Elisabet. Whatever one could say about Erik, he wasn't afraid.

Elisabet had tried to put it into her head that she wasn't afraid either. What had happened between her and Erik lay so far in the past; there was no reason to think of it anymore. They ought to be able to work together just as well as any other people could.

Still, there was something left, always had been between them. A tension, an excitement. She tried to quash it. But she felt how she was attracted to him, that she could never be indifferent to him when he was in her vicinity. When he looked at her she felt his gaze so tangibly that she got pins and needles.

For long periods, most of the time, the tension had expressed itself in hate or feigned indifference. When they had not had so much to do with each other no problems had arisen. He had said a few joking, sometimes slightly risqué words. She had shunted it aside. Nothing more than that. Yet, anyone listening carefully would certainly have been able to feel some of the excitement. Lena had done so, interpreted it as animosity and tried to get them to be friends.

Friends or enemies, if they seldom met it didn't mean anything. When they worked together all day long everything would be different. Then animosity would be intolerable. And was just friendship equally impossible? Naturally not for people who were more or less disinterested in each other. But for those who continually felt the tension, the attraction?

For this reason she was afraid. For this reason she could feel bothered even by the sunlight, feel like it unmasked her. Wasn't everything she felt expressed in her face? Mustn't Erik and—and all the others—see it?

She took a few steps nearer the curb, to see if he wasn't coming soon and maybe also to show herself that she wasn't afraid of the light. At the same moment a big hot rodder growled past and she doubled quickly back again; they drove like idiots!

In general she disliked those hot rodders, dirty and unkempt, asocial loafers. It was from those kinds that she would hear that she drove like a hen. According to the rules she maybe should have let them drive past her that one time. But she didn't like to think that she had any reason to give way to such individuals. Those puppies had hardly turned eighteen before they sat at their own steering wheels; she herself had had to wait until she was over forty. One ought to make it more difficult for them, maybe forbid the resale of used cars or raise the drivers license age to thirty. There were too many cars on the streets; they could very well wait.

Erik was coming now; she stepped out into the light again. He had fetched his car in the garage a few blocks away. He had absolutely wanted her to go along and look at a location that the company had leased out in Farsta; the idea was that there would be warehouses and dispatch offices out there; the office would luckily get to remain in the city. She had her steno pad in her purse if there were to be something that had to be noted down.

He opened the car door; she sat down beside him. She felt him glance at her legs; the old thorns were still there. She pulled her coat down over her knees.

As they drove through town, across Vasabron and into the crowded Old Town, he talked about Lena who had started working again. She seemed so lively and happy, it was really fun to see. And then her little boy, what a chap! With Berit things were a little worse; she was having trouble with her nerves. He didn't understand why the girl had to be so tense and worried, why she couldn't just be happy, she didn't want for anything; he was prepared to help her in every way. As a little child she had been so plucky; he didn't understand what had happened to her.

And a regular job, that didn't work; she didn't want it. Sometimes he thought that the best thing would be if she found some nice and steady guy and got married. And had children; she liked children, had a way with kids. Before, he had thought that it would be sad when she got married. But now he wondered if it wouldn't be the best all the same.

Strange to sit here and talk this way with Erik, about his daughters and his worries. But it went along easily, felt natural. It was pleasant. If only the excitement had not been there. And what had happened once, that should be forgotten.

Still he continued talking.

When they came out onto Nynäsvägen, he drove to the side of the rode, stopped, rolled down the windows.

"We can sit in the sun and just enjoy it for a minute," he said. "We can allow ourselves a little pleasure."

Then it came out: "I want to ask your forgiveness for what happened once, that I behaved like such an unforgivable bastard. Maybe you ought to know that there was a whole lot of confusion at the bottom of it. Somehow you had attracted me all those years, though maybe it was unconscious on your part. I thought you were toying with me and wanted to get back at you. Because there was no hope, because it could never be we two. There was way too much in between, on both sides things that made it impossible."

"We won't talk about that anymore," she answered. "It must be forgotten now. It was my fault, too. It was probably like you said, I wanted to toy with you. I saw that you were a little interested, it must have flattered me."

She had hardly admitted that even to herself before, had tried to believe that what had happened had been one special evening's aberration that it had depended on the dance and the alcohol and the circumstances. But, of course, she had always noticed Erik's interest and toyed with it. Already that time they had moved to Erstagatan and she had stood on the ladder above his head and known so well that he saw what he saw. That time she hadn't been a kid, seventeen years old or so. Though admitting that she herself was interested—she had not done that, only thought that he was fresh and annoying.

"I have regretted that so often," he said. "But still thought that what happened was best, that it never grew into anything else. For everyone's sake. When I understood that it was you I wanted to have, by then it was too late. We sat where we sat, both of us."

"You shouldn't say that," she said.

"No," he said. "I really shouldn't." But he knew that said was said, that he had finally come out with what he had wanted to say for so long. And that it was inside her now. Despite everything it was important that she know it; it felt good to have said it.

He rolled up the windows, started the car.

Now it had been said. In truth she could have just as well said it herself: when I understood that it was you I wanted to have, by then it was too late. We sat where we sat, both of us.

Of course, she had liked Lennart a lot, still liked him. She had met him so early; he had really been the first one for her. And he had sort of represented the young girl's dream of love: always so fine, so considerate, so careful of her. He had overlooked her whims and her hot temper, had faithfully and kindly waited for many years till at last he had her. He had given her everything, and done it without demanding anything himself.

While she had been difficult, temperamental, dissatisfied with most everything. She had been difficult in bed, too. Not wanted to when he had, pretended to be asleep, seldom tried to really meet him halfway, as if she didn't want to make the effort, take the trouble. She had never been able to forget herself completely, almost lain there like an observer.

It wasn't until that time with Erik that she had really been able to understand herself and her relationship with Lennart. Why she was the way she was, what was wrong. And that what was wrong was irreparable

Lennart was too fine and too cool for her, what was required to melt her chill was a ruthless heat. He didn't have enough force, he did not manage to set her alight and get her to burn. What she missed in him was something that she had imagined she feared and never wanted to encounter, something that she thought of as disagreeable and dirty: sex.

It wasn't until with Erik at his place that she had encountered it. Brimstone, besottedness, fire—whatever one wanted to call it. The undeniable that couldn't be stopped, that finally transformed her from observer to participant.

Lennart almost asked her pardon, he was afraid of hurting her, didn't want to shock her, came to her in the dark.

Erik had not asked if it hurt or felt good. Maybe he was too egotistical to do that—but it had felt right, all of that was meaningless just then, impossible to answer. He probably had shocked her—though that wasn't the right word, since nothing at the time had seemed impossible to her or repugnant. And she remembered that he had turned on the lamp above the foot of the bed; that what had happened had happened in light.

No, she did not want to experience such a thing again, it was over, had happened so long ago. As Erik had said: too late. They sat where they sat. Had they missed their opportunities? He was a little over sixty, she would soon turn fifty. They shouldn't make fools of themselves, not risk anything when it was too late anyway.

He had his Irene, she had Lennart. They had their children. They had their calm, their security.

Though it was true her relationship to Lennart had changed during recent years. If anything happened now it would not mean that she was betraying him in the same way as before. Now there was not so much to betray any longer.

But that was her own fault.

Lennart had changed. He was not as warm and thoughtful as he had been before. Not that he was unfriendly, just uninterested, unengaged. She understood that he did not love her anymore, not like he had previously. Maybe he still liked her; they were used to each other. Things happened that way when one grew older, more tired. His new job apparently meant a lot to him, had given him a new confidence that also made him not as dependent on her as before.

For her part she was mostly interested in Monika; they stuck together like a couple of friends now; the girl would soon be grown, fifteen years old. For Monika's sake nothing should happen, things should just continue as they were: secure, calm.

Elisabet had accepted that she was no longer young, that love was something that belonged in the past. Now Erik had suddenly aroused something within her that ought to stay asleep. He had reminded her that at one time a long time ago, she had experienced something profound, a great joy that had then been yanked away.

He asked her suddenly: "How do you do it? How can you still look like a girl?"

She felt herself blushing. Maybe because it seemed like he could read her thoughts. But maybe still mostly from happiness—and shame at the same time. Joy meant, of course, that she was hoping, that what had died wasn't dead. The sunshine that streamed in through the window suddenly felt revealing; she turned her face away.

He said something, pointing. In front of them the construction scaffoldings were rising up around the new Farsta center.

"It will be real saccharine pornography," he said. "Harem castle and cake boxes, knight's fortress, and Italian piazza. Have you been in Italy, by the way?"

"No, not farther than Denmark."

"I would like to show you ... Venice. Naples. One can always dream. Here it is."

They walked around through the buildings. Erik had set up a meeting with the overseer, wanted to discuss a number of finishing details. He had brought drawings with him, spread them out on a workbench. In fact there wasn't a lot for Elisabet to do and she wondered why he had wanted her to come. Was it to say what he had said?

She placed herself by the window and looked out at the tall buildings that were being constructed on the heights above what would be the structure of the center. It felt good in the sunshine; the window stood slightly open. She felt how calm was beginning to return. But it was not the same calm that had been there before, but a new one: what is going to happen will happen.

Somewhere out there a motor was rumbling, it drowned out the voices behind her. It didn't disturb her, just the opposite. She loosened her coat a little, placed her face in the middle of the window opening and the sun, dozed a little.

Then she suddenly felt that someone had placed an arm around her and realized it was Erik. She said nothing, didn't move but looked up.

"Nice in the sun?"

She nodded. "Are you two done? Is there something I can do?"

He laughed and let his lips brush against her cheek. Coolly and lightly, but still she began to tremble a little confronted with the step from thought to reality.

"Everything done," he said. "But there is nothing you need to do. Other than eat lunch with me now."

BENEATH
THE SURFACE

They met at the office every day, he dictated and she wrote, organized his papers, kept track of his meetings. She was careful to be perfect; there shouldn't be anything to complain about. And he didn't complain either.

She found pleasure in subordinating herself, in being the one who wasn't seen. He was the director, she an almost nameless shadow. When she saw him at work like this close up, she had to admire him. He was quite hard at times—but she liked it. Here in the company those who were lazy and incapable did not grow old when he was in charge. People complained about many cooperative companies and said they were inefficient, but that wasn't the case here.

Efficient work, calm assurance, correct conduct. But the whole time there was a life beneath the surface, something that couldn't be seen but still existed. Something that was never really laid out or spoken, not declared. But that they still could never really get away from.

His words were inside her: *when I realized it was you I wanted to have ... I would like to show you Venice, Naples ... one can always dream.*

She herself had not said such things but he knew anyway. She had not pulled back when he had placed his arm around her, not recoiled from his kiss. When it concerned Elisabet such a thing meant something.

He knew that she was waiting for his initiative and that she was prepared to follow it. She knew that he knew.

And even if he could become eager at the thought that she was waiting for him, he didn't want to get carried away and do something dumb they both would regret. From the time he began working in the company it had been his principle to not mix together work and love. He had made one single departure from that rule, the time with her, a long time ago.

What they felt for each other should not destroy too much for others. Young people perhaps had to get divorced, couldn't put up with things. Old sensible people could live in another way. It wasn't at all certain that he and Elisabet would be able to live happily together if they got married, barely even believable. It surely suited them better to have an office rather than a home together.

But naturally there was something more than the office he wanted to have together with her. A party sometimes, a bed together. Something that made life into something more than work and routine.

He needed a cleansing bath sometimes, a rejuvenation treatment, a glass of water when his thirst became too great.

He felt a little refreshed every day already, from seeing her. It perked him up, put him in fine form. He grew stimulated, actually worked better; ideas were planting themselves in him like on a conveyor belt. The young girls in their short skirts irritated him if anything, made him think of his daughters. But seeing Elisabet reminded him of the possibilities waiting, that she was waiting.

He said it one day: "I am so happy that you are here. Just the thought of meeting you here makes me want to work. As soon as I catch sight of you I feel at least fifteen years younger."

"That was much too kindly said," she said. "But, of course, it's nice to hear it."

"And you?"

She turned away, looked out the window. She didn't think she could give the answer she had. And she didn't dare show her face.

"You know," he said. "I want to have you. Soon. I don't want to wait any longer."

She turned back around; now she dared look at him, now that he had said what she was waiting for.

"You have to go with me to Norrköping the day after tomorrow," he said quickly. "I really do need a secretary along with me."

She knew what it was concerning; it was a meeting with some

ombudsmen. She had just intended to book his hotel room and train ticket that afternoon.

"Then I'll get tickets for two," she said. "And another room."

She nodded and left. She was surprised that she could leave as if nothing had happened, though she had felt like fainting.

So it was decided. Was she insane? Prepared to sacrifice her calm ingrained life to satisfy the excitement that had gripped her. But she only felt a strong relief, a dizzying happiness.

He came forward so directly, so straight out. They hadn't even kissed each other, not said a word about love. But it felt right. And she was prepared. For everything, for what he wanted, when it suited him.

He had a lot of work with him and for the greater part of the trip they sat fully occupied in the first-class compartment. Together they planned the afternoon, went through all the questions that would be brought up.

The meeting should end at five-thirty, he calculated.

"Then we will finally get to be alone."

His hand quickly caressed her cheek, lifted her chin.

"Look happy," he said.

"Yes," she answered and tried to smile. "I am happy."

"Are you afraid?"

Then she smiled, for real.

"No," she said. "Not afraid of you. And not of being found out either. But maybe of all the newness. That I won't be able to, won't be good enough. That I am too old. That you will think you've made a mistake."

"That fear is more what I ought to feel," he responded. "I who am so much older. But I know we will have it good together."

The day had been filled with work; Erik had driven things at a pretty hard pace. Once again she had the opportunity to admire his abilities. He quickly got to the vital points, cutting out things that were of less importance, making the rest of the participants feel their share of the responsibility and like concentrating on doing effective work.

Elisabet had plenty to do; this little conference would be the source of a number of written communications in the near future. She had to wonder how Erik would have managed if he had been alone. She certainly was of help, she didn't have to feel that she was undertaking a pleasure outing at the expense of the firm.

Finally they were finished and left. The air felt especially fresh now after the many hours in the smoky workroom. They walked a few blocks, taking a detour to the hotel to get a little exercise.

When they went up in the elevator he said: "Now work has had its due. Now it's we who are going to get ours. First of all we can rest a while, wash off the work dust. I have no other suit with me—so you will have to satisfy yourself with seeing me like this at dinner."

He opened the door to her room, went in with her. He held her a little ways from him and looked at her.

"It's incredible," he said.

And she stayed standing there in the middle of the floor after he left her, as if she didn't really know what she should be doing. They were going to eat at 7:30 he had said.

She closed the curtains in front of the window, turned on the ceiling light. She slowly got undressed and looked at her body critically in the big mirror. Naturally she was no longer young. But she had taken care of herself, she could probably state that she was well preserved.

She herself always thought that she seemed so cool. Fair, pale, no voluptuous curves.

How could she, who was so cool, have come here? She didn't understand it herself. But now it was unavoidable; now she wanted to finally get there. To what it was going to be. And she wasn't afraid any longer; Erik's calm had almost made her calm. His way of working, of leading the negotiations, of taking the initiative, and reaching decisions. She only had to do like him, now, too.

She went into the bathroom, showered, and brushed her teeth, following the whole careful program she usually went through every morning. She would be as perfect as she could be when he came to her. She had brought with her extra underwear that she took out, maybe a little coquettish and not exactly appropriate for the time of year. But they weren't going out, had just reserved a table in the hotel's restaurant.

She took out the dress she had with her. Black, simple, not so low-cut, but sleeveless. Her light, tinted hair and her white arms were enhanced by the blackness of the fabric.

When he knocked on the door she was ready. She was pleased by his expression when he saw her.

"My God, girl," he said in the elevator on the way down. "You are more beautiful now than when you were eighteen. People must think you are my daughter."

She usually hardly drank anything and didn't want much now either. He was maybe more careful than he usually was, but encouraged her to keep him company. And so she drank a glass of wine and a little sherry with dessert.

They sat and listened to music, felt good. She saw his gaze and liked it, felt secure. He decided everything. And when he asked if they should go she felt like it was almost an order and answered: "yes, boss."

But in the elevator they stood silent; she felt his hand over her bare arm.

"I'm coming in two minutes," he said.

She closed the window that had been slightly open; it felt cold in the room now. The floor lamp was on as when she had left the room, but the chambermaid had apparently been in and taken off the bedspread.

When Erik came in Elisabet was sitting on the edge of the bed. She stood up and walked toward him and he pulled her immediately to him. He caressed her as she had never been caressed before; it wasn't caresses but something more, conquering and capturing her.

She lay and looked at him, how he placed his clothes on the chair where he had just placed hers, how he came naked across the floor.

But he was still vigorous, exercised and had massages; they joked about that at the office.

She disappeared almost completely in his embrace, she felt. Now he seemed so big and she herself was so little. But she wasn't cold with him, rather was warmed by his warmth. It was like he was all around her, there was enough of him everywhere. And she felt how every part of her body became warm and alive with him, she grew soft and the last of her tension and unease disappeared.

When he came to her she maybe grew a little afraid still, wondered how she was going to be able and capable of receiving him. But she neither wanted to nor could offer resistance. She just gave in, went along with it. And tried to come closer and closer. As if in her fear of losing him she couldn't come close enough. Until they lay there, still, beside each other, her head on his chest; she heard his heart heating hard against her ear.

"Like this," he said, "I hardly believed that I was able to any longer. It is because it was you; I became almost young again."

The same tone of voice as when he had done a successful business deal. And she was happy about it.

"Was it good?" he asked. "Was it good for you, too?"

She had to think; there wasn't a word for it.

"It was something much more," she said at last. "Something that I never experienced before. I felt freed from myself, I was filled by you, wanted to be wholly merged with you, be united. I feel completely wiped out now. But completely happy, too."

"Poor thing," he said. Now his caresses were almost putting her to sleep. And she was so worn out that she fell asleep, barely noticed when he left her.

He pulled the quilt over her, got dressed for safety's sake, turned out the lamp, and left.

On the train home the next morning he was filled with the desire to work again. She had to pull out notebooks and papers, go through the notes from the day before with him. He wanted to have the minutes and the memoranda, gave her enough assignments to last her the rest of the day once she got to the office.

"We are going to get a lot of satisfaction from this trip," he said. "There is going to be a completely different tempo in this district now. I think this is the right method, to just gather a few together but gnaw on them even harder. We'll continue doing it; there are more districts that can use an injection."

She tried to smile but didn't really have the energy.

This suited her fine, of course, she wanted to be with Erik. Without him life would be meaningless now. But with him it would be very complicated; she understood that. It wouldn't be easy to keep the secret. But they had to if they didn't want to lose what they had before. One relief was that Lena had stopped working at the office, she was expecting a child again.

Now the train was rolling across the railway bridge. Snow whirled above the waters of Riddarfjärden, came as if in puffs; sometimes one could hardly see the shorelines, sometimes the image cleared and buildings and towers emerged.

IV

USED UP
AND RENEWED

Humankind's earth—dirtied and plundered.

Seas and waterways transformed to cesspools. Air polluted by soot and exhaust gasses. The soil poisoned.

At the same time as the world's population was increasing at an ever-faster rate. In thirty years it would probably be doubled—while sources of raw materials were already beginning to dwindle and accessibility to food was diminishing.

But the rich people didn't save. Consumption rose, their garbage piles grew into mountains, their fields fertilized with fish that could feed the hungry.

Large numbers of people died from diseases for which there were cures. The large resources were not allocated to save lives but to kill, to perfect methods for making war with the aid of bacteria and infect whole populations with sickness.

Every day airplanes loaded with atomic weapons soared above the earth, ready to initiate the total destruction.

The world might seem used up, impossible to save.

In the shadow of this death threat, diseased and sickly sprouts germinated: reactionary mindsets, hate, and torture.

But also something else: a will to live, a striving for human worth, a wish to build a new and better world.

Everywhere those who had been oppressed for centuries were now demanding freedom and human rights. Many of them tried to speak for a fight without violence. Such as Luthuli in South Africa, Martin Luther King in the U.S.A. Others found that non-violence was met by even more brutal violence and therefore took up weapons themselves.

Perhaps the opportunities for renewal lay with those so long oppressed, with those who didn't want to give up. Who still had the strength to hope, who wanted to live and make life better.

In Sweden one could feel far away from the problem, almost imagine it didn't affect people there. What could such a little country do? Increase foreign aid some. Feel pride in being Swedish; Dag Hammerskjöld was appointed secretary general of the United Nations. When he died in a plane crash in the civil war-torn Congo, there was something of a national day of mourning.

The election at the beginning of the sixties gave the Social Democrats new gains; they were riding on the wave that the debate on a general retirement pension had stirred up. Expansion of the social welfare system continued; a national insurance law was passed as well as a law for four weeks vacation.

In the city there were, in its plan, oppositions as well between run down sections and renewal. In the middle of neighborhoods that had been long-time slums, new buildings rose up. Cheek by jowl with dilapidated buildings housing drug addicts' dens and various haunts of every kind, neon lights blazed above shiny glass and glazed tile. Dirty and lost youths in articles of clothing from discarded American uniforms hung about the subway station passageways, swigged beer, and scrawled on the blank walls. In the midst of welfare and masses of opportunities were desperation, degeneracy, and distress.

It was hard to understand one's world, one's city, oneself. Hard to find meaning, hard to hope.

THE BROTHERHOOD
OF THE OUTCASTS

The subway trains raced onward beneath the city; escalators ferried passengers to the large ticket halls and to the street level. Beneath Vasagatan, steady streams of people made their way between the railroad station and the subway station, past underground shops and stalls.

Some police came strolling along slowly, letting their gazes quickly travel over the clusters of longhaired and somewhat ragged youths. As soon as they had turned their backs, someone chugged a beer, let the bottle roll across the floor. In every nook and cranny lay empty bottles; the stairs up toward Klara Church had glass splinters on almost every step.

Hasse and Klasse had been sitting in a café in Central Station, beside Klaraberg's viaduct. Until they were driven away after a few hours.

They walked a block along Klarabergsgatan but ducked down into the subway passageways again. Under Drottninggatan and Sergels Torg. It was here their buddies usually hung out. They grabbed a bag of bananas out of an insufficiently guarded carrying bag, and placed themselves by one of the concrete pillars and ate, throwing the peels in a circle around themselves. They emerged in the daylight again at Hötorget. They sat down on the Concert Hall stairs a while, then they found some empty glasses to throw in the fountain. That always bothered someone.

They felt at home here, in the passageways of the subway stations and on the stairs. If only all the police would go to hell everything would be fine.

"Damn," said Hasse. "We have to get some cash."

He hadn't worked for some time now. It would be summer soon, too, not a convenient time to be working.

Klasse was still in school but took time off a lot.

Tosse would figure out the booze.

"Sure. But no booze without cash. He's stingy, that bastard."

The compulsion to get money drove them on. Toward home, up in the direction of Söder. Though they had sponged it off of Mom as much as they could. And Dad was out of the question, besides he was sitting in the clink again. But they were looking for the streets they knew best. Back streets, where there weren't so many people out on a weekday afternoon.

"We should do something really big," Klasse said. "A bank or something."

Yeah. Sometime. But not now. Now a little something would have to do. Hasse had figured out how to do it a long time ago. They would take someone safe, an old lady or old man standing alone in her or his shop.

Like that tobacconist they had thought about once before. But then some guy had come along.

They looked through the window; it seemed empty. Green light. They walked in, pretended it was the pornographic magazines they were interested in. But when the owner turned his back Hasse jumped him.

"I'll strangle you if you scream, you old devil!"

He got the man inside a little room within the shop and locked him in from the outside. During that time Klasse had taken what there was in the cash register. Not more than a hundred kronor; apparently the old guy had more in his wallet but it was safest to get lost before someone came. They scrambled together some packs of cigarettes and chocolate bars on the way out, grabbing one of the magazines they had been leafing through—there was a goddam unbelievable picture in one of them.

They heard the old man yelling and pounding from inside the cubbyhole. But they walked calmly, not until they had gone a ways did they begin to run.

"Nicely done. So damn easy."

Still a little shaken up, they sat down on a bench in "The Hole," the park on Ringvägen.

They hadn't tried this kind of thing before. Purse snatching and shoplifting, and borrowing cars. Bur never a real robbery. It was riskier, they might meet with resistance. There were even old ladies who might begin to fight.

But it had gone easily, much more easily than they would have believed. And no one had seen them.

"Let's go home and eat first," Hasse said. "Before we get the booze."

They walked through the park, blocked the way for a girl coming from the other direction. She tried to avoid them, but Hasse pinched her backside and Klasse gave her a shove so that she fell forward over a bush. If it had been dark they could have had a little more fun with her, but now it was best to take off before people came.

Lilian was waiting with the meal; she was used to waiting. When Per was home, the boys tried to come on time. They didn't dare do otherwise; when Per grew angry he would just start hitting them. Sometimes he wondered how long it would be before they beat him up instead. But maybe they were being careful, wanted to live at home in any case, get food and board for free.

They sat down at the kitchen table. She could hear that they were wound up and asked if something funny had happened. Just a broad who had gotten so mad when they pushed her around a little. Well, well, they were starting to grow up now.

Lilian wondered if they weren't going to be home that evening anyway, there was something good on TV. But they were going out, of course. As always she nagged a little: they shouldn't do anything dumb. Hasse had to think of his probation and Klasse had already been called in to the principle several times.

"Yeah, don't nag."

But they should look for jobs. In the fall. No hurry.

Always just as hopeless. They were cut out like their father. She herself had never had any dealings with the authorities.

She must have been too lenient, too. Because Per had been too hard handed. They couldn't be in the living room when he came home. And they had never received one öre from him.

There was nothing she could do any more. The boys had gotten beyond her, gotten habits she couldn't change. She could only ask them to think of the risks. Then they did as they pleased.

As soon as they had eaten they left. And Lilian cleared the table, did the dishes, tried to hide her worry beneath all the usual chores. Did not understand why she had married Per once upon a time, just think of how well she would be doing if she had stayed single.

As the boys were going down the stairs they met the girl who lived one flight up from them. She stopped, collected herself as if in defense.

"If you touch me I'll scream."

"Who the hell wants to touch you," Hasse said. "Not even with a pole."

They knew she would scream, she had done it before. They spat a cascade of swear words at her. Now she would tell on them again; her mom would come running.

But no one else had heard them. So they could say whatever they damn well pleased. Besides, they could retort that it was she instead who had said something so damned fresh. That thought amused them; they spent a long time figuring out what she could have said. There were two of them, two were worth more than one if there anything got talked about.

Tosse had arranged the booze he had promised. A whole bottle of aquavit for three people. They went up to the White Hills Park where they found a good and sufficiently dark corner.

Once they had emptied it they were probably pretty drunk, especially Tosse, who thought he should guzzle the most since he was the one who had gotten the bottle. Hasse wanted to get hold of a car, go out and drive, maybe pick up some broads. But Tosse wanted to go home and they let him go.

Down on Malmgårdsvägen they found a car that they could get into. Hasse was great at hot-wiring; it didn't take long before the engine started. At the last minute a guy came running. But they blew him off, of course; he didn't stand a chance.

"Damn, if I get confident when I have a little in me," Hasse said. They thundered along on Ringvägen, past the building where they lived. Now Mom would see them; she was probably choking on her coffee.

Beside Björns Trädgård Park they found a broad who was willing to hop in. Hasse knew her from before, she was never unavailable. But she wasn't especially good-looking either. She had to sit beside Hasse; Klasse was feeling rotten and curled up in the back seat where he soon fell asleep.

Hasse took Folkungagatan straight out, toward Danvikstull. He was close to ramming into the pillar that held up the railroad bridge over the street. There was a taxi behind it, it slowly pulled out, keeping its distance carefully.

He hadn't gotten farther than Nacka Church before he realized that he had the police after him; the taxi had apparently sounded the alarm.

Britt wanted out. But now he couldn't stop; now the main thing was to drive like nobody's business if they were going to get away. He managed to clear the tight roundabout at Ektorp, came out onto Skurubron, through the Björknäs, all quiet for the night; down a steep hill, continued on the road out across a field.

Now Klasse had woken up, sat up in the back seat and screamed: "He's gaining on us!"

On the curves just before Boo Church, Hasse couldn't hold the car on the road any longer. It touched a guardrail, got deflected out onto the wrong side of the road, slid on its side toward an oncoming car.

"Everything's going to hell," he yelled. "Duck, duck damn it."

Then the crash, the thunder of sheet metal against sheet metal. And someone who screamed in the sudden silence.

Hasse punched and kicked until he succeeded in getting the door open. He tried to shake Britt, take her with him. But she had blood all over her face, only fell over when he moved her. Where was Klasse? Had he already taken off? One of the backdoors stood open.

Now it was a question of saving himself. He ran a few steps, tried to get into the trees beside the road. But he had two policemen after him, felt that he was drunk and shaken up, would never make it. He kicked and tried to get loose but the police had a solid grip.

Afterward he found out: Britt was dead. They had driven Klasse to the hospital. And he himself was guilty of causing another's death, car theft, drinking while intoxicated, reckless speeding, attempting to flee the scene, resisting and assaulting the police. Maybe they could come up with still more. But there was the old probation sentence, too.

Of course, it was too bad about Britt. But what the hell could he have done? And she had gone with him, too, though she had seen he was sloshed and though she knew he neither had a driver's license nor a car.

The affair in the tobacconist's shop was cleared up at the same time. Hasse did not have the strength to deny it.

"It wasn't what we meant to do," he sniffed. "Everything just happened this way."

Of course, Lilian was upset. Still, she had to admit that it was a relief not to have the boys at home when Per was released this time. He was bitterer and more enraged than ever, completely impossible to talk to. It never would have worked with the boys at home.

Everything just grew worse and worse. She couldn't even have the TV on when Per was there. The only way to get away from everything for a while was to buy a few weekly magazines and hide in a corner and read about happy people. She herself couldn't dream if finding any happiness again.

Fate, it was hard on her. But it didn't work to fight it.

WHILE
SUMMER REMAINS

Erik sat in an outdoor reclining chair outside his summerhouse. The whiskey and soda cooled by the refrigerator bubbled in the glass beside him. The newspaper lay on the ground beside him and he had stuffed his glasses in his breast pocket. He didn't really feel like reading now, the world would have to wait. He sipped his whiskey and soda instead, stretched and enjoyed himself. He liked sitting here in the light shade, it felt friendly, soothing. Neither his eyes nor his skin got irritated and he did not have to be so warm.

He looked at Elisabet who had set up her chair in the sun. She was insatiable when it came to sun. Before, she had been afraid of the sun, afraid of sunburn, she had told him. But she had gotten used to it, trained her skin to tolerate it more. And, of course, she looked magnificent when her skin was tanned like that. Though it cost her a lot, too, she had to torture herself to get that color.

On a day like this it was good to be alive. In general things were good for him now, better than they had ever been before.

Everything had been resolved surprisingly easily. Better than they had dared hope. Of course, they had had a few complicated years. But they had gotten through them.

That first period with Elisabet. They had had a lot of fun together. But a lot had been difficult, too. He had grown out of the time and age when he might have found a certain pleasure in cheating and sneaking, when the tension had an intrinsic value and the forbidden a special attraction. Now he would rather acknowledge his actions and pay what the party cost. At least when it was a question of something real and serious.

As soon as he had realized that this thing with Elisabet was not quickly passing, but rather something unavoidable and final, he had begun to prepare what had to happen. Long before he and Elisabet had even spoken about the possibility of their getting married, he had made clear to Irene that he wanted a divorce and that his decision was irrevocable. He hadn't said that there was someone else, that would only provoke her, cause her to make difficulties. No, it was simply that what had been between them was over. And so he considered that the right thing for them to do was to get a divorce.

He had had to bribe her a little, of course. Promise her an apartment in town and good alimony. She had never been happy out there in Vällingby, had missed the city. Now she was getting her chance. And she had given in more easily than he had believed. She had probably grown tired of things, she, too; he had been really difficult at times. She probably didn't have any guy waiting in the wings now, was probably out of the game. If she got remarried she would lose her alimony.

Maybe he wouldn't have acted so quickly and definitively if Berit hadn't gotten married. And along with that there was no reason for him and Irene to stay together any longer. He would have moved out a long time ago if it hadn't been for Berit's sake. Even if he had never met Elisabet again.

A soon as Irene had gone along with the divorce he had exchanged his apartment in Vällingby for a smaller one in the city that she could take. He had lived at his summer place in the beginning. His commute was, of course, on the long side, forty kilometers into town. It was quite strenuous, especially in the winter when snow shoveling and such were added; he wasn't so young, of course, anymore. But there were people who had to go even farther to their jobs. And the house was good; he had not stinted when they had built and he had benefited from that now.

In that way, he and Elisabet had also gotten a place where they could meet undisturbed. The summer place had been their first common home even if she hadn't been able to be there so much at first.

Still, she had quickly transformed the house, made it into something new and different, taken away the memories of Irene.

Elisabet had been admirable during those difficult years, he thought. Brave. Not complained though she must have had a hard time, much worse than himself. The difficult period had been for almost four years. It was too much, too much.

But she had gotten through it, been prepared to give much more than she demanded.

He looked over at her, felt how grateful he was to her, would want to say it to her again. But she was sitting there with her eyes closed; it was a pity to disturb her now.

For Elisabet, extricating herself had taken longer. She had not wanted to divorce Lennart, for Monika's sake. But quite early on she had explained to him how things stood.

And Lennart had understood her, almost better than she understood herself. During all those years he had felt that she wasn't satisfied with him, not happy with him. It was hard to imagine that she had hurt Lennart so, that he had had to suffer so long. She had loved him. But never completely, never unconditionally. She had thought that he was the finest person she had met, might think it still. And still she had been lacking something.

Lennart had not presented any difficulties. He had accepted what had happened long before it really had happened. He had felt that she wasn't his anymore even if she wasn't anyone else's either. He had not even had anything against her staying as long as Monika lived at home. For the girl's sake, for the relatives, for those around them.

Then it had not taken more than a few years before Monika got married to an Englishman she had met during a summer course; she was living in England now. And then they had gotten divorced, then there was nothing that prevented them anymore. Still, it had been hard, maybe the divorce from Lennart was the hardest thing she had ever experienced.

It was just at the time when Jenny died.

Jenny had been doing poorly for a long time before she died, almost two years. It had been difficult for Maj; she had been obliged to take out an early retirement pension to stay at home and take care of her mother.

It had felt a little shameful to tell Maj about Erik. But Maj had been understanding. Though she had certainly felt sorry for Lennart; Elisabet understood that. But now Elisabet couldn't live with Lennart without hurting him; she had tormented him all those years. Even if he were to maybe miss her, he would indeed live more calmly and better without her.

A lot had been difficult. Still, the entangled situation was able to be sorted out more neatly and more considerately than she had dared believe. There was, in fact, only one person who openly and clearly voiced disapproval, contempt: Lena.

Lena was the one who stood closest to the shunted aside and abandoned party. She was with her mother a lot and she was married to Lennart's best friend, Joseph.

Elisabet had wanted to say to her: you can't understand us. You are so kind and loyal but so temperate. You can never land in the same situation as me. You can't hurt anyone like I can—against my will. And you can't love like this either.

But she had kept quiet, been receptive. And not told Erik about it, didn't want him to feel any bitterness toward Lena. She knew that Lena would not show her emotions in the same way in front of Erik, she forgave her father. He was a man, he was allowed to kick over the traces. Lena had insinuated that it wasn't the first time that her father had had affairs on the side. But the previous women had released him, not let it go so far. They had been sensible and understanding.

Lena believed everything ought to and could be patched up. She didn't understand that people's feelings could be so strong that this wouldn't work. She didn't know how much that could hurt—but how necessary it still could feel.

To get divorced was to tear something apart, a piece of oneself. Still, she could feel happy now, afterward. She had never been so calm before, so secure. Finally she had found the right one. It was late but at any rate not too late.

She looked over at Erik who was sitting in his reclining chair. The plaid over shirt hung over his light long pants, he had placed his glasses far down on his nose now.

She smiled and turned to the frying pan of the sun again. She wasn't insatiable as she had believed at times; she could be satisfied. And naturally she had it good, everything she could want. The dissatisfaction she had always felt before was gone.

Once the dissatisfaction was gone she had become loyal. She was loyal to Erik in a way that she had never been toward Lennart. And she wanted Erik to decide, to command her. He never forced her to do anything. And wouldn't need to either, she did as he wished anyway. She sometimes was surprised at her desire to obey. Maybe it was because she had been forced to decide for all those years; Lennart had always left all the decisions to her. Erik gave no orders, except for at the office, of course, but he led her. She felt like she walked holding his hand like a little girl with her father. It felt secure; she liked it. She wanted to follow his advice.

Such as when it came to the car. Erik stated that she couldn't drive, that she was entirely unfit. He had refused to ride with her and asked her to stop driving alone. At first it, perhaps, had felt a little bad to have to abstain, she who liked her car so much. But she had obeyed and gradually also thought he was right. Now she had not driven for several years and would probably never dare place herself behind a wheel again.

He knew what was best for her. And what he asked of her she wanted to give. And more.

He lowered the newspaper, looked over at her again. She had turned over, now she was lying with her backside facing him. Actually he would have liked to go over there and pat her a little, but in any case he picked up his whiskey and soda again.

Now she was probably lying there way too long, would get too burned. She didn't always think about it, he was allowed to think for her sometimes. He liked it, it was nice to think of her, watch over her.

"Don't sun yourself anymore," he said. "You will only pay for it tonight."

"You're right," she said. "Though no pain no gain."

"Come, let me look at you."

She got up, walked over to him, placed her hand in his.

"You are really totally gorgeous enough," he said.

She bent over and kissed him.

"Get dressed," he said. "Then we'll eat. The potatoes must have been done a long time ago. I'll look at them."

"What dress shall I wear?"

"The white one," he said. "Though it's only just us two—or maybe because."

She nodded and left, smiling because he had said that bit about the dress; she thought herself that the white one looked best on her when she was so suntanned.

He watched her go and once more marveled that she didn't grow old, but continued to be so smooth and soft, with such a youthful body. He himself was not as spry and athletic anymore, felt that he was beginning to grow older. It was a pity that he hadn't gotten a few more years together with her. But it probably wasn't until they had gotten older that they could get together for real, could be happy with each other. Earlier on they probably wouldn't have managed it successfully.

He got up, walked into the kitchen to take the potatoes off the stove and open the can with boiled ham. The strawberries were in their bowl on the kitchen counter. He set the table in the little eating nook by the kitchen; they usually ate there when they were alone. He had time to get everything done by the time Elisabet stood in the doorway.

"Dinner is served, Madame," he said and pulled out her chair from the table.

In a half year, at the end of the year, he would be retired.

And he would probably not get re-elected in the fall to the city council. He didn't believe so. He had moved down a place on the list at the nomination. Maybe a little unjustly, he had done quite a lot for the party. But in any case, he had not been as active during the most recent four-year term. That was because of this relationship with Elisabet, of course, because he had gotten something else that he had become absorbed in. If the election went as it should, he would still be re-elected, despite his moving down. But things were going worse this year; he felt it in the air. And he had always had a nose for such things.

Even if they retired him from the firm and he didn't get re-elected to the city council, he would still continue to work, not just go rest. He didn't feel that old. If he now, finally, after a life of service to the workers' movement, started his own company, then no one could readily blame him. They themselves had discarded him. He was tough, he wasn't finished yet. Least of all now when he had Elisabet. He had plans that they would carry out together.

In truth, it might be enjoyable to leave the company. He had been there since the beginning of the thirties, practically built up the whole operation. And however things were settled, there was certainly a lot of talk about the two of them; it could be pleasant for Elisabet to get away from there, too. There were too many who knew them too well, who also saw Irene and Lennart. And who now, afterward, could calculate one or another conference and meeting that he and Elisabet had gone to.

While they sat at the dinner table, Berit came out completely unexpectedly. In a car, that she was driving herself. Erik didn't like that; she was unquestionably one of those people who should not be driving; she drove exactly like Elisabet.

Things seemed to be working out for Berit. She had met a man who seemingly was the right one for her and now she seemed much calmer, almost happy. Although, one couldn't hope and believe too much; she was impulsive, she could tire of things.

Now, in any case, she had good news to tell; it showed all over her. She almost flew in, hugging them, hardly had time to sit down before she said it.

She was expecting a child.

But there was something else, too, that she felt she had to tell now even though it happened a long time ago.

Elisabet got up, thought she would slip away. But Berit said: "It doesn't matter if you hear it, I want you to hear it."

She talked about the abortion she had undergone, back then when Irene and Erik had thought she was on vacation. And that she had been sure she would never be able to have any children after that.

That was why she hadn't wanted to get married either. She had told Lars-Erik everything but he had still said the two were together. And now, she knew she was going to have a child. Wasn't it a miracle?

"And you never said anything," Erik said. "I would have done everything to help you."

"You would have just gotten upset," said Berit. "It's different when it's over. And now you understand why I'm so happy, so uncommonly happy. It's a miracle that has happened."

"And I didn't guess anything," said Erik. "I must have become deaf and blind pretty early. I thought you were so young at that time, only a child. And in fact you are really still that...."

"Listen to him," she said to Elisabet. "A middle-aged woman of thirty and he thinks I'm a child. Do you understand how it isn't easy?"

They laughed at him. And he laughed, too. Everything was fine now, Berit happy.

She would soon be on her way again; they were going on vacation with the car, start the following morning. She had just wanted to drive out and tell them.

He saw the car almost bounce out on the country rode and felt a pang of fear.

"Drive carefully!" he screamed after her.

But she was already on her way; only a little cloud of dust was left on the country road.

He picked up a bottle of wine and they sat in the living room and drank a few glasses. They didn't bother to turn on the lights, they watched the dusk slowly fall, lay its film across the field.

They talked about their daughters. Close kin who at times could become strangers, who one believed one knew everything about but maybe barely knew. About the pain one can feel when one understands one had not understood.

About their own childhood. The loneliness they had felt, the alienation. Elisabet talked about her father who she knew so little about. The feeling of belonging together with a stranger who was ever barely mentioned had sometimes made her feel like a stranger herself. She had thought it was Maj but not herself who was at home in their home. Maj was Emelie's brother's daughter, of course, Elisabet went around with the name Törnberg all by herself. They had certainly never treated her differently or worse than Maj; it wasn't Jenny or Emelie who had done anything wrong. Still she had been able to feel bitter toward Jenny at times, felt like her mother was to blame for Elisabet herself not fitting into her environment.

She might regret it now, she had not been kind to Jenny. She had had such a hard time accepting that people were laughing at her mother, thought that Jenny played the monkey, degraded herself. Like on that radio program. It wasn't until Erik had talked about how good Jenny had been that Elisabet had really understood that it was so. She had tried to say it to Jenny, too, thought it was so long after. Maybe too late, she wasn't sure her mother had understood.

"She must have understood," said Erik. "Without a doubt she did."

Their conversation floated out into the twilight, was muffled, disappeared.

A stranger who had found her way home at last. That was how she felt.

ALONE

Maj was quite alone now, since both John and Jenny were gone and she had stopped working. She was at Henning's sometimes, of course; she saw Elisabet and Erik quite seldom. Sometimes she went out to Gunnar and Hjordis's house, sometimes Beda dropped by. Funnily enough it was Allan and his family that she saw most often, next to Henning. Allan had always been so loyal.

Entire summers and far into the fall Maj was out at the cottage in the archipelago. She liked it there, took care of her flowers, could feel the memory, the presence of John. Almost everything that was there was his work. But Henning had gotten to take over the boat that he had. It was on land that Maj felt at home.

Sometimes, but not especially often, she saw Lennart out there. He wasn't out there very often and she understood that; everything in the cottage must be filled with memories of Elisabet.

But the times that Lennart was out there he would usually drop by Maj's. He always came just as it was beginning to grow dark—or did she just think that. That was how she saw him, a gray figure in the evening mist. She usually invited him for coffee; they would sit and talk a while and then he would go again, would disappear in the darkness between the trees. In the city she never heard from him.

"I was taking a walk," he would say. "And I was walking right past and thought I would look in."

About Elisabet he didn't say much. But the few words he could say were never bitter. He hoped that things were good for her, that she was satisfied.

As for himself, he was fully occupied with work, apparently had more and more say in things at the printer's. And he seemed to live pretty much without worries; Elisabet had not wanted to accept any alimony; he had no one other than himself to think of. He had never demanded especially much from life, had no expensive habits. Now he was in fact earning more than he really needed.

No one needed him; he could come out with that again sometimes. And then there was maybe something of bitterness nevertheless. Monika didn't need him, nor Elisabet either.

Although he had more time now that he was alone, he didn't read as much as before. Partly it may have been because of the nature of his work, now that he had so much to think about; he grew tired by the time evening arrived. But it was also as if he didn't have the same need for books and study any longer. As long as he had found life meaningful he had also had a reason to read and learn more about it. Now it was different. He had piled up a whole lot of his old notes and carried them up to the attic. Now he almost preferred to sit in front of the TV for a while than to read.

Indeed, he had lost something, Maj thought. His lost was maybe not mainly Elisabet; in some ways he lived perhaps more happily without her. But a *reason,* a cause to live for, something to work for.

It's true, he met with Joseph sometimes. For Joseph's sake he read this and that, to enrich their conversations.

Otherwise he was alone.

Maj herself still read a great deal; it was her chief pleasure. Whereas the TV set in her city apartment usually stood silent and dark. In the country she had a radio so she could listen to the news.

Despite her loneliness Maj did not feel unhappy. Possibly a little resigned, aware that she had her active time behind her, that most of those who had been closest to her were dead and that her own time certainly also had its limits. The difficult years when Jenny had been sick had left their mark, dampened her liveliness and made her feel old herself.

At Erik and Elisabet's house she maybe had felt it especially strongly. Elisabet seemed almost young still, almost too girlish in her short dress. And Erik exercised and got massages, seemed also to carry the years rather lightly. Maj had felt so much older than both of them; they had just begun a new life together, she had lived hers.

One fall evening, when Lennart had been out and seen to his cottage, he took the route out along the beach. He walked the few steps down to the water's edge, stood there a while and remembered that summer evening when Berit had gone in the water. And earlier summers when he had swum here with Elisabet; it was before so many cottages had sprung up close by; back then one had been more undisturbed, been able to swim without a bathing suit.

Elisabet, Berit. Rather faded memories now, memories of quickly disappearing happiness, of moments when he had lived. He hoped that things were good for Berit. Elisabet, too. And Monika. If one of them ever needed help sometime then ... but it would probably never happen.

He felt a little melancholy to think about them. The ones who had disappeared, those who didn't need him. Who had chosen others to live together with. He was glad that he and Elisabet had been able to part as friends.

Naturally, he was living more calmly now. When no one needed him he didn't have to be capable of anything anymore either, no one had any demands on him. He had said to Elisabet already a long time ago that he knew he was a lousy lover, that he understood she thought that. She had denied it. Out of kindness, maybe a little out of love, too. Still, it was surely so, had been proven so well by what had happened.

The insight that he didn't measure up to demands had inhibited him. That was surely why he hardly dared take hold of Berit, why he never would dare seek another woman's love.

He had run through the woods when he had imagined that Berit was waiting for him. But when he found that it only was a dream, a silly idea—hadn't he been rather relieved then, glad to avoid the test? Avoid failing once again.

He hadn't dared. Didn't want to dare. Avoided, it was over now. No one needed him and no one could demand anything. No one waited.

In the dream *she* could, someone, maybe Elisabet or maybe Berit or someone he didn't know, still come to him. That was enough. He was satisfied with the dream, didn't wish for reality anymore.

When he came back to his empty cottage, he lighted a fire in the fireplace, placed a pork chop to grill on the grating.

He set the alarm clock before he fell asleep; had to get up early to catch the first bus to work. He had important things he had to deal with as soon as he got there.

Even if he wasn't exactly needed anymore, it was good to live anyway. He had often been frightened by all the urgent and insistent voices in his life. Now he only had solitude; it demanded so little of him.

NEW SIGHTS

Every time Henning walked through town he thought he had better check up on things. It was unreliable, constantly trying to fool him, took the opportunity to carry out its transformation number in an unguarded moment.

Suddenly one day, he had discovered that one could see the Royal Dramatic Theater from Drottninggatan. Another day he had found that the old stable beside Tegelbacken had disappeared. But when he had been down at Kornhamnstorg not so long ago, he had succeeded in arriving at just the moment of transformation: they were in the process of towing away the floating fish market hall that had been there for many years.

Much disappeared and much came into existence. Now the brick colossus of the Technical Office Building of the City of Stockholm's was standing on the old junkyards beside Separator's factory at the Klara Lake canal. Gröna Lund amusement park had suddenly gotten a one hundred meter high lookout tower, and at Kaknäs they were building one even higher. A few months ago, the enormous Essingeleden motorway with its bridges spanning the waters of Lake Mälar, had been inaugurated.

As if giants were modeling the city, its whole topography was being transformed. More and more of the Brunkebergsåsen ridge disappeared; sometimes when he walked along Klarabergsgatan he amused himself with trying to remember all the small shops that had lined the old vanished street by the same name, which had climbed up there somewhere high above his head. The Pewter Foundry, the bakery, the old book auction house.... Now, of course, he had forgotten most of them.

It went so fast that one could hardly keep up. A lot that was new he had not seen, only read about. A ski lift that went up the hills formed by the demolition materials dumpsite, Högdalstoppen. Or

Märsta Center. A few days earlier they had dug the first spadefuls for the settlement out at Järvafältet by Tennsta. He didn't even know where that really was.

It felt like the first sign of aging: he couldn't keep up any longer.

Even his family was being transformed. The children were growing up, becoming independent, people with their own ideas and opinions. Ann-Charlotte was not a child any longer, but a little woman in a mini skirt keeping company with boys. Lars-Olov was fourteen; in him there was more of the child left. Both lived in a world that could feel quite alien to their parents. Op and pop and whatever it was called, a cacophony of glaring colors, disturbing shapes, jarring sounds.

And he who had believed that the youth who grew up in the new society would become more conservative than their parents had been. They surely couldn't have the same need to fight against social injustice, they did not have the same experiences of poverty and unemployment.

If that thought had bothered him before, he could instead be bothered by the opposite now, at least where Ann-Charlotte was concerned. And she didn't become more staid through the boy she was going out with; he was one of those young protestors who popped up everywhere with their placards and flyers.

Naturally, Henning could smile at himself: only his own nuance was good enough, it wasn't really good if the young went farther to the right or to the left, they should dutifully follow in his tracks. Even if he never had made any attempts to convince them, only wanted them to choose for themselves. But yet, choose what he wanted, his recipe?

He wasn't that difficult. But he could feel worried. Regarding his own choice, for the world's. He felt like one had such a narrow footbridge to balance on, it didn't allow for any wrong steps, neither to the right nor to the left. At least today that footbridge was his opportunity, his choice. A choice that sometimes could seem unacceptable and shocking, but that he found was the only one possible.

The person who isn't for is against. The moderate ones will be spat out. The rules were old but they seemed to be hardening now. They yelled and hit to drive people into the fold, to get them to accept even what couldn't be accepted. People were hardest toward those that were close to, but not completely for something. They were the most dangerous, with their doubting they could entice other doubters away, who had already been successfully brought into the fold.

On one side were the forces that were sometimes called "the free world," "the democracies." But that were also called capitalist states and colonial nations, oppressors and extortionists. The western world, defender of freedom against suppressors of free opinion and terrorist regimes. But the freedom one claimed to be defending all too often was a freedom at others' expense. Freedom to dominate and extort, freedom for others to starve and suffer. Freedom to own in the midst of the dispossessed, freedom to profit from the hunger of others.

On the other side, those who could call themselves "the revolutionary masses," "the people." The poor and the oppressed, who at last broke their shackles and vanquished their old rulers. The Eastern Block, freedom's defender against extorters and colonialists. But also iron hard dictators where deviating opinions were severely punished. Where they built their walls, enclosed people like in prisons, and shot down those who tried to escape.

The one or the other freedom, the one or the other unjustness. There was nothing else to choose between. And when one chose, one had to take the whole package, the bad with the good.

Didn't there have to be a third possibility? A possibility that wasn't impossible?

People talked about "the third world" and were usually referring to the new, small and poor countries that, despite all the pressures, had managed to keep themselves outside the two big blocks. Also, for the private individual there has to be a third possibility, a route that was accessible. Today perhaps it was narrow like a plank, like the line dancer's line. But perhaps eventually it would be able to be transformed into a real route.

Since he believed in that route, he hoped that his children would not get stuck in the fold, that they would not feel obligated to do so. He did not want to choose for them, the choice was theirs. But he hoped.

What he wanted was both freedom of opinion and social equalizing, neither the dictatorship of the proletariat nor the capitalist extorters. What he was looking for was really a democratic socialism.

If you reversed the words it became a social democracy. He had voted for them this year, too, but not with any great enthusiasm. He thought they had the possibility but not taken advantage of it; with the help of the map they ought to be able to find the third route, point out to where it led. It didn't seem as if they wanted to or dared to, and now they were crouching down more than ever after the slam they had gotten in the election.

A vision: that they would rise up, pull out the map that they certainly must have somewhere in their baggage, show the way. Dare to lead the way instead of limping behind. Speak for the third possibility, collect the unfettered people and states, begin working with transforming the United Nations into what it had to become: a power factor, a world government.

He had no blueprint, no comprehensive plan. Only a vision. Of course, he liked youthful engagement. It was important that they reacted, wanted to take part, were moved. But youth could scare him somewhat, and then he thought he saw a sort of inhumanity, being bound to dogmas, a disdain for suffering if it didn't specifically affect the people they themselves were crusading for.

He understood those who considered that violence could be necessary in the struggle for liberation, but not those who gave violence an intrinsic value and romanticized it. He understood those who wanted to give all the support they could to the side they sympathized with, but not that they simultaneously sabotaged humanitarian aid activities whose aim was to save victims without taking note of dividing lines and boundaries.

He could never forget the barricade across a street on the outskirts of a town; he had seen it the first time he had traveled out in Europe. The destitution and hunger on one side of the barricade, the abundance on the other. That was the way they wanted to have things again. A bleeding and screaming child on the wrong side of the barricade could not be helped; that was helping the enemy.

It was apparent that the man from Samaria was a traitor or at least a misguided fool. He should have looked for the party label before he helped.

In engagement there was also hate. It was maybe natural. But if hate was allowed to color and permeate negotiations, that which was clear and clean disappeared; it poisoned those who were engaged. Then they destroyed more than they built up, damaged more than they helped.

That engagement was what he feared.

Maybe he didn't have to be so worried for his daughter after all. Right now she was full of enthusiasm when she came home, had heard of something completely new, a new movement. The idea had come from Holland; they called themselves "Provos."

He had read something about it in the newspapers, youth who put on "street theater" at Hötorget, played dead, wanted to show what could happen if an atom bomb fell.

Ann-Charlotte had brought a copy of their magazine home with her. There was so much freshness and stubborn joy in it. He had to smile when he read it, but also acknowledge that there was a whole lot worth thinking about.

The parks shall be filled with fruit trees and berry bushes.

Free 25-öre pieces for the use of toilets.

Free trips on the subway, streetcars, and city busses.

Larger cities shall have at least one square where youth may play guitar barefoot without "friends of law and order (= dull conventionality)" being allowed to call for the police.

If he had been young and accepted by them, then he would have wanted to take part. He felt like he recognized a lot of the spirit and ideas from the discussion group his own gang had once had. There, they, too, had wanted to turn most things upside down, call things into question, generate change.

Nonetheless he said, of course: "Yes, yes, it really sounds interesting. But you do have school to think of, too."

Even if sometimes he might be made uneasy, more often he had to feel delight, marvel at how healthy and wholesome these youth still seemed to be. Despite all the attempts to poison them, all the risks, not least of all the risk to grow apathetic. They devoured books, they were interested in theater and art, they read politics, they lived as well. The soft cotton wadding did no seem to have stifled them, on the contrary, they were more sensitive and sharper than his own generation had been. They were not as caught up thinking about themselves and their own problems, but were able to engage in others' problems, in the world's problems.

They were eager, ready to help. They sought out tasks, jumped at opportunities to act. It was something to feel pleased about. But naturally also maybe dangerous; in their zeal they could be all too easily drawn in, become easy prey for those who had the ability to compel a frame of mind, those who shouted the loudest.

Sometimes he thought he sensed a game beneath the surface, speculation, an attempt to exploit people's suffering for one's own purposes. People talked about Vietnam, but thought about their own political party's successes.

He hoped that the young enthusiasts would not be fooled, come to find out that they had been used.

But he recognized, too, that he himself and his generation had done all too little, not given the young any visions worth working for, any assignments possible to take on. Maybe because they had been too insecure themselves.

He would have liked to talk about the possibilities of the third route, about the necessity of not getting stuck in the fold. Speak without forcing, without enticing and deceiving. But in such a way that they would understand, guess the vision that he could not really make out clearly. So that they would try to create a better world that he hoped for but could not sketch out, since his gaze was not capable of piercing through the mist.

He hoped that they would be able to see farther, reach farther. That they would find the way even if he would not be able to take himself across the footbridge.

MAY FIRST

It was a strange spring. At first it looked like it intended to begin already in February; all of March was also mild. In April there wasn't much sun but it was still relatively warm. But then, when spring really should have arrived, on Walpurgis Eve, it snowed.

Maj had considered traveling out to the country, but then it didn't happen and she could be happy about it now; there wasn't any pleasure in sitting snowed in at the cottage.

Now that she was alone it sometimes happened that she tried to remind herself of various things that Emelie and Jenny had told her. But what she remembered was not more than fragments, remnants.

Emelie had once told her about one first of May. Apparently the first that had been celebrated as a day of demonstration, maybe ten years before the turn of the century. The demonstration procession along Karlavägen then, too, the "Esplanade" Emelie had called it. They had demonstrated for an eight-hour workday, though it had taken many years afterward for the demand to be made reality.

What Maj remembered most, because she remembered Emelie's solemn, almost prophetic tone when she pronounced the words, was that one of the speakers said that that day would thenceforth always be considered the workers' spring day, dawning and full of promise.

The words captivated her, engaged her. A spring day, dawning and full of promise.

When young, Maj had often walked in the demonstration parades together with Erik. Then she hadn't made it to them anymore. John had wanted to go out to the country when he had a day off, so they were usually at the cottage on Walpurgis Eve and on the first of May. She had continued doing that since as well.

Henning called, asked if she wanted to go with him and see the demonstration parade. The meeting place would be held at the Stadium this year, too, it would probably hardly ever be at Gärdet anymore. Then Maj could sit while they listened to the speakers.

He picked her up in his car; Lars-Olov was with him. Barbro had a cold and had stayed home. Ann-Charlotte was out with her boyfriend. The weather was still unpredictable, pretty gray, sometimes a rain shower. They got out there in good time, and Henning managed to find both parking on Valhallavägen and a seat under a roof at the Stadium.

Finally the demonstrators arrived. The banners billowed in through the entrances of the Stadium. In the lead was the Swedish Trade Union Confederation chairman, Arne Geijer, and beside him Hjalmar Mehr and then Axel Höjer who had just come home from Vietnam and brought greetings from Ho Chi Minh. Tage Ehrlander was in Malmö this year. A small dark boy was walking there, too, son of one of the leaders of Southwest Africa's liberation struggle.

Streamers, placards, worded banners. First the domestic political speakers about work, security, and development, more power to the people and less to big finance. Then the veterans who spoke about raising the standards of living for public pensioners and wished for "bread and freedom for the whole world." Then the professional division with the whole array of standards at the fore. There they demanded full employment and increased construction, diminished income gaps and increased equality.

It was an impressive procession and also a beautiful spectacle, Maj thought; the red banners, the music, the masses of people.

Maj had brought a pair of binoculars with her, let them sweep across the texts and the demonstrators. She grew excited and pointed: there was Gunnar! He had taken his hat in his hand, he was holding it up just now, and his hair shone white when it fluttered in the wind. He resembled his father, August Bodin, a lot now. Gunnar walked in the parade every year despite the fact that he had owned his own company for a long time. He was turning seventy-eight this year, but still walked on foot. Otherwise many of the older people rode on truck beds behind the "old guard's" slogans.

Now the international divisions arrived. First a float with a globe on it and then the enormous banner and flags from all the countries of the world. Here they were demanding increased resources to the U.N. and solidarity with the poor. Spaniards, South Africans, and Greeks demanded liberation for their people. And time after time it was about Vietnam: Stop the War, Bombs Do Not Create Peace.

The large international element, the strong protest against the U.S.A. and President Lyndon Johnson and against the war—that was something new, Maj thought. They had not been so internationally aware once upon a time, according to what she could remember.

A lot of it was also better directed than it had been before, with several features aimed directly at the onlookers. Like the young woman dressed in white who stood bound to a float as a symbol of Greece in fetters.

But gradually the parade changed character. There were more and more FNL, Front for National Liberation, flags; the streamers had texts that were surely not authorized by the organizers of the demonstration. They arrived with a feeling of threat in the air. Those who were now marching screamed in perfect time:

USA – murderer
USA – murderer
Arm the FNL
Arm the FNL

And another spoken chorus shouted:

Tage and Geijer
Lyndon's lackeys
Tage and Geijer
Lyndon's lackeys

Many had obviously mainly come to demonstrate against the

demonstration. While Geijer was speaking they shouted over him, time after time:

Lyndon's lackeys
Lyndon's lackeys

He had a hard time making himself heard. They booed at him. The demonstrators ran out onto the field and placed the FNL flag among the array of standards. A Saigon sympathizer tried to run around the open area with the South Vietnamese flag, but was caught up with by opponents and beaten down. Suddenly a man rushed out onto the grassy field and kicked the American flag out of the massed standards. The Provo youths raised their placards:

Demonstrate Without Permission!
Zero Taxation Now!
Fuck!

Some were only driven out; others had to go with the police. Geijer managed to finish his speech with great trouble; when a representative for the Greek resistance movement was going to give his address, the cries still rang out:

Tage and Geijer
Lyndon's lackeys

Flags and leaflets flew through the air. Hjalmar Mehr appealed to the disrupters to at least allow the invited guests to speak in peace. Were those who were speaking in favor of liberation for the people of Greece and Southwest Africa to be insulted?

Then it grew quieter for a while, but there was still something of a rumbling, threatening feeling remaining.

Maj felt shaken up when she left. Unsure, had met moods that she did not recognize. Certainly she had read about the unrest and riots and smashed embassy windows, but now it had become tangible. It reminded her of her youth, all the "hunger marches" during the First World War, the fracases at Gustav Adolf's Square, Erik with a saber wound and a bandaged head.

Were they on the way back to the bad old days? Back to harsh oppositions, to violence and desperation? Why, now that there was no hunger and destitution? Yes there was, out in the world. Now it was not only a question of their own country. It was a question of the world.

Outside the Stadium they met Gunnar. He got a ride with them in their car and came home to Henning's for a while. He no longer drove, thought he was too old.

Gunnar was also a little shaken by what had happened, angry, too—so typical of the Communists, they weren't capable of organizing their own demonstrations but they could ruin others', that's what they could do.

Maj remembered how Erik had sometimes bragged a long time ago, when he was part of Kilbom's party, about how his party achieved coups against the Social Democrats. Gradually, Erik became a Social Democrat himself, a bit of a bigwig. Now, for the most part, he was out of politics since he had had to leave the city council. He had not been there at the Stadium today; he and Elisabet were in France now; they traveled quite a bit.

Maj's memory of moods resembling the one she had just witnessed, came from the years of the First World War and the early twenties. Gunnar's could go further back. He had lived through the Young Socialists' golden years, had been with them himself, if only on the fringes.

That was from around 1905 and on for a few years. There was a lot then that reminded him of the circumstances today. Scuffling between demonstrators and police, coups of varying types. Back then they had posted atheist proclamations on church doors and, in the presence of the king, taken up the cry of "Long Live the Republic." That was what Kalle Palm, the master's son, had done when Sankt Eriksbron was being inaugurated. Back then, they talked a lot about bombs; Gunnar had met the poet Leon Larson, had had a lot to do with him just before it was revealed that bomb making was going on at home in Larson's apartment. Then it turned bloody serious, too. The Amaltea affair when a strikebreaker was killed by an explosion, the mail robbery in Skåne, the gunning down of a general in Kungsträdgården.

Of course, those who had joined the Young Socialists had been intensely involved. They hated the Socialist Democrats, thought that their reform-minded calm represented the most serious obstacle for the thing the Young Socialists were working for. The Young Socialists had spoken in favor of violence and revolution: the workers should join the sharp shooters movement and take charge of the weapons and point them in the right direction. At the same time, many of them had been conscientious objectors, spoken against fratricide.

They aroused a great commotion, great alarm. The "preservers of society" raged and demanded strict countermeasures. The vocal powers of the young followers of Hinke Bergegren had been so strong that people had believed they represented a mighty wave.

But they had never been so many, had never really been able to have any significance. The wave was, despite everything, only a ripple, movement on the surface. The acts of violence that had been unleashed by the heated propaganda had frightened the Young Socialists themselves as well; during the great strike they had kept quiet, been paralyzed.

Many who had been pulled in by the preaching, had abandoned the movement when they lived through the results, the desperate actions. Gunnar himself was one of them; he had gone to the Social Democrats that he had so despised earlier on. He had experienced the fire of enthusiasm but been burned by it; disappointed, he had left the camp of the rebellion's instigators.

He saw many similarities with today's situation. Now the young revolutionaries were smashing windowpanes, organizing spontaneous demonstrations, and getting into fights with the police, and achieved their coups, such as today at the Stadium. The whole thing could have happened before. He hoped that the day's young protestors would not go as far as his comrades had gone, but would refrain from bombs and murder. Maybe they were wiser, they had gotten to study and learn more than his generation.

They were so audible and so visible today, too. They could appear to be so many, almost a whole generation. But maybe there weren't any more of them than the Young Socialists had once been. Maybe not a wave but just a ripple. Something that would soon be gone. Many would certainly tire when they received their knocks and blows. And they would grow older, calming down. One day they would maybe sit where Erik had sat, in the city council for the Social Democrats. Or like Gunnar himself now, almost astonished at what he had once taken part in.

FRIENDS
AND ENEMIES

Joseph Schönlank had had a dream: to sometime be able to return to
Israel.

He had not been born there, had never been there. Still it would be
like coming home.

The birth of Israel had meant that all the Jewish refugees of the
world at last had gotten a homeland. For centuries they had lacked
their own land. Some had succeeded in putting down roots in the
countries where they had settled, others had remained rootless
strangers, having a home in a land that only existed in their dreams.

To create Israel, to place it on the map and in the world of reality
had become a necessity.

"The world will be freed through our liberty," the founder of
Zionism, Theodor Herzl, had said. Liberty could only come through
their own work. Long before the state of Israel had come into existence, the first colonists to return home had begun to transform the
marshlands and deserts into fertile lands.

Joseph had eagerly followed what had been happening, felt his
involvement. Right from its very birth, the new state had been threatened. Herzl had dreamed that Jews and Arabs would work peacefully
side by side and build the country together. He had hoped that the
activity of the Jews would be catching and give that whole part of the
world a new and richer life. It had not turned out that way; instead
hate and antagonisms had been sharpened. Now the Arab neighbor-
ing countries were calling for the destruction of Israel. Forty-five million Arabs stood against a little over two million Israelis.

The moment was at hand to show solidarity. To travel home and
join together with his people.

He wanted to go, he should have gone. If he hadn't had Lena and the children. He couldn't leave Lena now, not force her to leave her country for an insecure future in a little war camp. It may have been wrong for him to have gotten married at one time. Maybe he should have been single, prepared, all set to pull out. As things stood now he had double loyalties.

Israel's neighbors had united in a war pact, blocked the sea routes, demanded removal of the U.N. forces that were guarding the Israeli-Egyptian border.

Then the war had come.

"In Israel, in order to be a realist you must believe in miracles," David Ben-Gurion had said.

Joseph had been reading a lot these days, had been looking for comfort. Mostly in Herzl. Time after time he returned to the words:

The world will be freed through our liberty.

Yes, every people's liberty freed the world and every people's imprisonment weighed on all. Israel had to remain free. But the Arabs, even the Arabs in Israel, had to have their freedom as well. By working together they could transform their world, as Herzl had said. As enemies they could only destroy each other, weigh each other down with their shackles.

In Stockholm, a demonstration for Israel was being prepared. The people who had been interned in Hitler's concentration camps were encouraged to participate and put on the yellow stars they had been forced to wear in the camps.

Naturally Joseph wanted to take part. But if felt hard, almost unbearable to once again wear the stars of the camps. In the name of solidarity he put it on.

On the day of the demonstration the situation had completely changed; the conflict practically over. From the beginning, Israel had had the advantage, driven the Arabs to flight. Losses had been great, especially for the Egyptians and the Jordanians.

Sentiment in favor of Israel had been strong those days. But Joseph felt the absence of many. Those who he thought he felt solidarity with, who were called radicals. He thought they should have spoken out for a small people's right to survive, that they should have exhorted Jews and Arabs to work together instead of making war. But they saw Israel as a state in the rich world and the Arab states as exploited under-developed countries.

Instead he found new sympathizers who almost scared him, people who normally he would place in the opposite camp.

He felt like the land of his dreams had been transformed to a pawn that people pushed away or pulled back in, all according to the game.

But Lennart was with him, and perhaps more strongly than ever he felt the value of their friendship.

To Lennart he quoted Herzl:

"All people must have a home... Then people will come to love each other more and understand each other better."

Indeed, everyone must have a home, a homeland. The Arabs, too. The Jews, too.

A few days later Lena moved out to their country house with the children. Joseph didn't travel out there every day. The commutes became quite long since he didn't drive a car. Instead, he ended up meeting Lennart more often than usual.

They would eat together at a grill bar, then liked to go sit some-where at an outdoor café and drink coffee. They had time to talk about a lot that they didn't usually get to talk about. Maybe also get into areas that they otherwise usually avoided, their private lives.

Lennart did not blame Elisabet for anything. And he was contented now, things were good, he lived more calmly than before. That was what he wanted to say.

Joseph nodded. He understood. He had always maybe thought that Lennart and Elisabet were a mismatched couple.

Joseph started talking about Irene, Lena's mother. Irene was bitter, talked a lot about how Erik had betrayed her, how Elisabet had captured him. Irene saw Erik as a possession she had lost. Maybe she didn't think that his value was so great but it bothered her to be robbed. Irene neither could nor wanted to understand.

And Lena was loyal, she always had been. He felt that she had to side with Irene, help her—and help her hate as well, if she wanted to. For them, Elisabet would always have to remain the guilty party and Erik the victim. To say anything else would be to inconvenience Irene, confirm that she wasn't good enough.

Lennart sensed that Lena might also view Joseph as her possession. And that Joseph was willing to let her own him because she was his friend, so loyal. But that also meant, too, that if something happened, something similar to what had happened to him and Elisabet, then she could become Joseph's enemy.

It felt good to be away from all of that now, the whole game of love and hate, power and dependency. The person who was alone could go his or her own way and on the way one could maybe have the companionship of a friend.

Gradually, the difficult days passed on, the closest threat had been avoided. Joseph grew calmer; those days were over when his loyalty to Israel seemed to tug and pull at him every day.

He could once again feel at home in the homeland he had chosen, in the city where he had settled. The evening walks with Lennart had helped him feel more of a connection with the city. He gotten to know it better, observed things that he had never noticed before.

During his first years there, he had had difficulties with the language and thought that a lot of things felt alien and strange. Now he spoke perfectly, there was almost no accent left. The time when he had lived in other countries and cities felt so distant, as if it had been someone other than himself who had lived through it. It was here that he was at home now, he had his family, his work, his friends.

The anxiety of the refugee began to make way for the calm of the resident. The anxiety had come back when he had felt himself threatened once more; now the calm could flow back in.

One evening as they walked together in the White Hills, they found that throngs of people were making their way into the park, expectant, as if they were anticipating something fun. Joseph and Lennart followed them, walking between the community gardens on one side and the row of small wooden houses on the other.

There was going to be a show in the open-air theater below the old white music pavilion. Several thousand people had gathered, seating themselves on rows of wooden benches or on the grass.

Lennart told him how it used to be. When he was a boy the park had been a spot for outings for the people around there. They had come there with picnic baskets and blankets and lain there whole Sundays. Sometimes an orchestra played in the little white pavilion. It was on such an evening that he had met Elisabet here.

Now the spotlights were turned on. Carl Anton, the singer, arrived, walking from his house on Mejtensgränd with his guitar under his arm, jumped up on the stage, began to sing. Then Monika Nielsen and Åker Grönberg sang. The entire audience lived the music with them, following every word and tone of voice. It was seldom one encountered such an atmosphere, such a response.

Carl Anton sang:

> Do you see the lamp is lighted
> Over our yard and our lane.
> Lighting up scenes of the still evening
> Lighting up the cat that slunk
> Through a hole in our fence
> Lighting up outhouses and lilacs....

It was the small town within the big city, the quiet life in an old outlying quarter. Something to take in.

With the many people enjoying themselves together in the lovely summer evening under the treetops, Joseph felt fellowship. It felt like being among friends. He had probably never felt so at home here in the city as this evening. It was such a friendly atmosphere; they were laughing together, being delighted. They dared let go of some of their stiffness and shyness in the protective twilight, they dared take part.

His friends suddenly seemed to be many more than he had imagined, their friendliness more widespread than he had dared believe.

They walked toward home through calm and evening-quiet neighborhoods.

The city was his wife's city and his children's city, so it was also his. Their boy was eight now, their girl six. They were born there; they would live there. They would not have to become refugees and foreigners.

H-DAY

Five o'clock on Sunday morning, September third, Sweden was going to switch to right-hand traffic.

Preparations had gone on for several years. New buses had been ordered, streets had become one-way, old traffic islands had been torn up and new ones set in. Signals and signs, temporarily covered with black plastic, had been put out.

Many feared that day, many were irritated about the changeover that waited. Everywhere it was the subject of conversations; television, radio and newspapers gave steady reminders.

One evening at Allan's home, the question came up for discussion again. Olle expected that it would be pure slaughter; old people would be mown down, people would die like flies.

He considered the traffic switch an encroachment by the authorities. A number of years ago there had been a popular vote taken concerning the question, and an overwhelming majority had wanted to keep the old way. Now the changeover was being carried out anyway, against the people's will.

Everything had to be accommodated for the small group of motorists who wanted to travel around in different countries without having to think. Why not forbid car traffic across borders instead? Then someone would avoid driving to his or her death just because Sweden had left-hand traffic.

What ordinary people thought they didn't give a damn about. There was an upper echelon that they made a fuss about and a bottom echelon that they coddled. But the ones who worked hard for low pay and never applied for assistance, they were taken advantage of, their voices were not heard.

It was typical that they intended to take away the streetcars. The streetcars could usually get through on the streets while the buses got stuck among all the private cars. Old people didn't dare go down on the subway stations' escalators and they were also afraid of the careening buses; they wanted to have the streetcars stay. But the streetcars got in the way of the cars, if you please. It didn't matter if the old people had to sit shut in their rooms, or if ordinary workers had longer commuting times. The main thing was that the motorists were happy.

Henning didn't say very much, he listened. As always, when Olle talked there was something beneath the words that could give Henning a feeling of guilt. Something that he had to try and figure out, explain to himself.

He couldn't get away from it. Sweden was still, in many people's opinion, a class society. It was natural if Olle was bitter.

At one time the boundaries between the classes had been sharper, harder to force through. If someone was born in one group it was as good as impossible to get oneself into another. Some had, of course, succeeded in doing so; around them sayings had been spun; they had become "kings:" "Newspaper king," "Söder king" or "aquavit king," who had started their journey with "two empty hands."

The pattern had changed. Now schools were open to all. In theory the opportunities were equal, in practice, of course, children from homes where people could test them on their English or correct their math homework had an easier time than others.

People competed. And some came first and some came last and most landed in the middle. The competition was democratic; everybody had to take part. Specially trained and disabled side by side. The prizes naturally depended on placement. The top job with the top salary to the top men, dirty and boring bottom jobs with bottom salaries to those who came last. Could it be set up more fairly?

The fight, the competition affected children already. To be sure, as they put it, all educational paths were equally good, vocational school compared with high school, for example. But so far neither children nor their parents had learned to see it that way. This one passes at this level, that one a notch higher, the first one has to stay below. The scale was simple and clear: graded by points. Competition was iron hard; one was sifted out or was chosen. The point scale became a ranking scale.

Consciousness of the scale was always there.

Then one landed in different groups, lived under various conditions. Henning earned perhaps double what Olle did. And someone like Claes Bodin, in his day, earned easily several times as much as Henning.

There lay something in what Olle would usually say: even though he was related to relatives of the Bodins, and even though they lived in the same city, it was completely inconceivable they would ever meet on the same level, as equals and of equal worth. For Claes, tables were set up at the finest restaurants even if they were fully booked—if Olle himself wanted to go to a restaurant on a Saturday, they would almost sniff his throat first before they would let him in as a favor. Claes was surely a welcome customer in the fine specialty shops, while Olle would have to be jostled at counters and at the cashier in the self-service stores. Claes sat in his big boss room and gave orders, Olle stood among roaring machines, rushed by contracts and time clocks. Claes calculated how many he should fire or hire to achieve the best economic result. Olle went around feeling anxious that he one day would be "laid off."

That was how Olle could see it, black-white. And, of course, there were differences, there was no real equality.

One tried to weigh it all, lessen the differences. Progressive taxation cut off some of the salary peaks, but became more and more unpopular when inflation drove more and more groups into the threads of the tax screws. With subventions and allowances one could fill out some of the deepest holes.

Still, it seemed as if the divisions were growing. There was a right-minded way of thinking that drove these developments. Those with high salaries saw themselves unfairly treated if their incomes did not grow percentage wise as much as those with low salaries. If the low salary groups received three percent, then the high salary groups must also have it. And still see themselves as victims of injustice; they had to pay a percentage-wise higher tax on their increase since they found themselves higher up in the tax screw's whorls.

There were certainly not many—not any?—who starved in present day Sweden. But there were many who felt unfairly treated and pursued. When the standards of those around went up, one's own lacks were more noticeable. And those who were paid worst, also had the heaviest and hardest jobs and were often the ones who were threatened first when there began to be talk of structural reorganization, relocations, and cutbacks.

It wasn't so hard to understand that Olle was tired and bitter, that he opposed everything that he saw as new concessions to a privileged group. For Olle it was much more important to get a few more kronor in his pay envelope than to get the traffic moved to the other side of the street. For him the right-hand traffic changeover was just as useless an escapade as space travel must be for poor people in underdeveloped countries. An amusement for the upper class, both of the nation and the world.

Henning was for the traffic changeover; it fit into his view of the world—it was a measure to facilitate connections, attain a greater unity and community.

And now that the change had been decided and would soon arrive, it seemed as if the youth at any rate were looking forward to it. Maybe because they, in a way different from older people, were used to looking at the world as a whole, as theirs.

Stina and her fiancé, "Rooster," were going to go out and drive around in Europe next summer when Rooster had practiced the right-hand driving enough. And Olle's Bertil, who worked at a gas station, was going to get his driver's license now, had had thought it was better to wait with it until he could start driving on the right immediately.

Lilian and her youngest son, Klas, were also there at Allan's. The older son, Hans, or Hasse, was in jail, of course. Like his father. But Klas had come home from reform school now. He belonged to the mod set, or whatever it was called these days, long hair. He stayed with his mother, didn't seem interested in his cousins of his own age. They weren't part of his gang, had another style.

In his gaze, in his manner and clothing, there was disdain for those who fit in, "the average Svenssons." He smiled scornfully when Olle spoke, lighted a cigarette and blew out the smoke in the face of whoever was sitting closest.

Lilian had seated herself beside Barbro and was talking animatedly. Barbro nodded seriously.

On the way home, Henning found out what it was all about: Lilian had asked Barbro to be Klas's probation guardian. Barbro had had this kind of assignment before. Klas wanted so badly to avoid having someone from the committee, and Barbro had promised to try. She was conscious that the task was difficult, maybe hopeless. Even though the boy could be really nice, when his brother came home he would surely go along with him on everything. If anything genuine was going to happen, it would have to happen through Hans, together with Hans.

The changeover wasn't going to happen until Sunday morning, but already on Saturday morning all the private traffic in the inner city ceased. But streetcars, buses, and taxicabs were in motion on the streets, and many work vehicles that were out to set up new signs and cover the old ones. A lot was very confusing now. The new signs and directions were not yet valid, the people were supposed to still drive like before, even if the arrows pointed in the opposite direction.

Barbro and Henning stayed in with Lars-Olov that evening, watched the big Hyland program on TV. But Ann-Charlotte wanted to experience the historic moment out in the city. Gösta came and picked her up. He was in his last year of the same school as she was.

They strolled down toward the city center. On Söder, where Ann-Charlotte's family had moved back a few years earlier, the streets were quite empty of people, as if paralyzed when all the regular traffic had disappeared. A few streetcars were still running; their light blue sheen seemed more melancholy than usual now.

In the center, and especially around Kungsgatan, there was another atmosphere—something of a carnival in the air. Many had brought out their bicycles; bicycling was permitted. Some girls even came riding on horses.

But mainly the city belonged to the pedestrians. They were streaming everywhere, occupying streets and driving lanes. They stood in clusters and looked at the acrobatic installers who were putting up signs on the new gate-like support structures.

The city was waiting, the atmosphere was expectant. The usual aggressiveness had disappeared. People were out to enjoy themselves and not to make a disturbance.

Gösta went on a streetcar with Ann-Charlotte, a number seven on its way out toward Djurgården. It was probably one of the last cars, in any case they should take their last ride now. They traveled out with it—and then back into the city again. There were many who had come up with the same idea; the streetcar filled up, no one wanted to get off. Some had screwdrivers with them and began to unscrew signs and other details. At Djurgårsbron there were crowds of people and they shouted hurrahs and sang "Long may she live" in honor of the old car.

They went along all the way to Enskede, to the streetcar graveyard at Blåsut. At one-thirty the power would be cut in the electric cables.

They took the subway back in to the center, saw the barriers that closed off all the bridges into the city. Out in the country private motorists would be able to drive at six o'clock on Sunday morning, but in the city the halt would be until three o'clock in the afternoon.

And so, finally it was five o'clock on Sunday morning, when traffic stood still for a moment and then slowly began to function following new patterns. It was as if all the cars with permission to drive had gathered on Kungsgatan; they were surrounded by a mad dash of pedestrians when they went to drive over to the opposite side of the street, then came slowly into place. Someone turned up the radio loudspeaker; people heard the "H-general" Skiöld's voice: "Now

Sweden has right-hand traffic."

The big change had been carried out. But still, assiduous workers and military men were in the process of moving posts and painting white lines on the streets.

Ann-Charlotte and Gösta went back home toward Söder. There wasn't any regular traffic now. The city appeared peaceful; it was early Sunday morning, quite warm, beautiful.

GRAVESIDE SPEECH FOR RUTAN

Fifty-five-year-old Rut Berg died on a November day in one of the city hospitals, where she had been transferred from Katarina Police Station. She was one of the women who usually hung out with the drunken gang in the park beside Folkungagatan.

No one other than the minister spoke at the burial, no one followed her to the grave. But in a tenement building on Ringvägen, something was held that nevertheless might still resemble a graveside speech. The one who spoke was her cousin and former pimp, several times convicted, Per Berg. The only listener was Per's wife, Lilian.

"Rutan," he said. "Rutan, she was Negro Village. You can't say Negro Village without thinking of Rutan. She could be so damned good. She let the police and everyone from every damned committee know what she thought of them. What they were worth. She didn't want to go to the trouble of pissing on them even. They didn't understand anything; no one who hasn't lived in Negro Village can understand anything. She always said that. Not even everyone who has lived there. A lot of them didn't belong there, wanted to get away. Not fine enough, of course. But some of us were at home there, and even though they have torn down and burned down all of Negro Village, we are still actually still there anyway. We took it with us, Rutan said. We had it in us, all the way up to our throats. But if there was anyone who talked shit about Negro Village—then we'd beat them up right away. For that's who we were.

"As a matter of fact, Rutan was the only really genuine person in all of Negro Village. You could depend on her, she would fix it. 'You, Rutan,' someone would say, 'fix fifty smackers for me, okay?' 'Okay,' Rutan would say then, 'bring a couple of johns here and then we can split the pot.' She would go along with everything. You could go over there with two or three guys who would have to sit in the kitchen and wait like in some damned doctor's reception room. And she would take each one in his turn and give them their treatment so they would come out wiped out and red in the face with bliss.

"Rutan was a whore and she admitted it, she was proud of it. But you others went around with your noses in the air and talked shit about her. You were in fact bigger whores than she was. It was all of you who were the real whores."

"All of you?," Lilian said, though she knew his answer and wanted to avoid it. "Which you? It wasn't me in any case."

"You! You who were almost the worst of all of them. And everyone in all of Negro Village sure knew it. You and your damned old man! We would stand outside your door and listen, the whole gang of guys. We had it all figured out, what was really going on."

"And if that was really so," she said. "So what? He was for sure the only person who cared about me, the only one who has ever cared about me."

"The only one who cared," he imitated. "About your backside you mean, of course. It was really what he cared about. There wasn't an ass more worn out than yours in all of Negro Village. And then he would sleep with you—it's not worth your denying it."

"No," she said. "He didn't."

"You're talking bullshit...."

"Maybe he needed someone to hit to get back at everything," Lilian said. "Poor and sick like he was all his life. So if he liked to hit so let him do it. And Mama he didn't dare say boo to. She was much stronger, in any case. She would never have let him hit her."

"But you—you allowed it."

"Allowed! What could I do? But no matter what, he was a person who cared about me. I could feel at least that I mattered to someone. That's more than I do now. Now not one person would miss me if I were dead. You would never say anything kind about me—like you said about Rutan."

"I can't talk about you and Rutan on the same day."

"There's no one who cares about me anymore," she said. "Not one person, since Papa died."

"Cares about you! Who the hell cares about us? And who do we care about?"

"You ought to care a little more about what the boys do anyway. Not just drive them out."

"Ha! Talking bullshit."

"So things turn out the way they turn out."

"Turn out how then?"

"With the boys. They'll end up like you, get to sit in jail half their lives. Sometimes I think it's Negro Village's fault. It's infected them, too."

"Negro Village," he said. "That was living."

"You believed everything people said about me there," Lilian said. "All the evil slander about Papa. He wasn't at all as bad as people said, he could be really kind, too. I—I didn't believe what people said about you. Otherwise I would have never asked you to move in here."

"What did people say?"

"That you went around bragging about stuff you had never really done. Only bluster. That in fact you were a weakling, a jerk. That Rutan treated you like a jerk, too. It wasn't you who drove her, like you make it sound now. It was she who bullied you and threw a fiver at you sometimes. You only dared to tackle the old and the weak— and Rutan wasn't weak, not at that time anyway."

"I see, that was what you and your friends said. Well anyhow I've broken you for sure."

"Yes, because I was weak. I should have gotten myself away from you. But that doesn't mean anything anymore. Now the only important thing is to try and help the boys. So you don't succeed in making them become like you."

"I'll sure as hell show you."

"There's nothing you have to show that I haven't seen before. I know all about you now."

"I'll show you who decides!" he screamed. "Why have you brought that upper class bitch in here? If she comes one more time I'll kick her out."

"I have asked Barbro to help Klasse," she said. "She is kind and good and can take him the right way."

"I don't give a damn about how she can take him. I don't want to see that person here anymore."

"You know yourself what you've said about the guardians they assign. So it's still better for Klas to have someone like Barbro. It's for his sake."

"I don't want anything to do with those relatives, I don't want anything to thank them for. Besides, what can someone like that understand? She hasn't seen Negro Village, not even on a postcard."

No, he would have had someone like Rutan as guardian, of course.

"Yes, indeed, that would have been something. But Rutan, she's dead now. I wasn't more than seventeen when she and I began to hang out together, just like Klasse is now. Rutan must have been about twenty-five. It was she who taught me both the one thing and the other. I could have gone to a worse school."

"So you're so pleased with the result."

"That things happened the way they happened was nothing Rutan could have helped. She was unlucky."

"You can call it that. But do you really want Klas to have to live the same kind of life that you live?"

"He can live the best fucking way he wants. But that Barbro doesn't stick her foot in here anymore, that much you know. You cut her off if you don't want to have more of the lash than your father ever gave you."

He had taken off and Lilian sat there alone, feeling the total hopelessness of it all.

What Per had said—about Rutan and about herself and her father didn't matter so much to her, most of it she had heard many times before. Whatever he said was all the same to her.

The only thing that meant anything was what he did. Not with her, that was basically all the same to her now, too. But with the boys and most of all the youngest, Klas.

She had pretty much given up hope on Hans, even if she really didn't want to admit it.

Klas could maybe be saved. She had seen Barbro as an opportunity, been pleased at how Klas had been influenced. Barbro was good. But an opportunity that Per would not agree to.

What Per said usually did not mean so much; he could threaten but seldom had the energy to do more than that. Except for when it was something he absolutely got into his head. Then there wasn't a chance to talk around him or to try and sneak past him. Then he became like a leech, held on tight, never gave up.

Lilian knew that she would be obliged to say no to Barbro's help now. And go up to the committee and ask them to assign someone else. If it was one of the ones Klas had had before or someone like that, then everything was ruined.

"We have it with us," Rutan had said about Negro Village.

Lilian could agree with her about that. She felt like she had been in flight from Negro Village her whole life. But she had never managed to get away from it and now she knew why.

They carried Negro Village inside themselves, always carried it with them.

The poison from Negro Village, from all the slum shacks of the city and tenement buildings on the outskirts. Consumption, filth, crime, alcoholism, resignation.

The strong could deal with it; the weak were poisoned.

The gang of youths had stood at her door and listened when she got a beating, taken pleasure in her humiliation. She had seen them, could still see them. When she met someone she recognized from Negro Village she knew: you know, you remember, you think about it now. The humiliation was still there, the poison still at work.

It had been as bad as they thought—or even worse. She had been totally deserted, sacrificed. Her mother had known about it, allowed it—maybe to avoid it herself. Her siblings had known about it, they had fled from home as soon as they could, never wanted to have anything to do with her. Per knew about it, he hardly wanted to touch her.

Everyone knew. But she would still never confess it, least of all to Per.

Negro Village destroyed Papa, she thought. It wasn't his fault, he could be kind, too. It destroyed Mama, destroyed me, destroyed Per. Now it's destroying Hans and Klas even though it doesn't exist anymore.

The strong had escaped. Even Allan and Gun. But both she and Per came from weakness. Per's parents, Yellow David who had certainly not had a real job in his whole life, and his Tyra who drank to keep up with him, though she had to scrub and toil for the whole family. Her own parents. They all belonged to those who had Negro Village up to their throats, drowned in it. At one time Lilian may have dared believe that she had succeeded in escaping. But then she had met Per and then everything had all come back again, as if they had created a new and private Negro Village.

It probably wouldn't work to help Hans any longer. But Klas had to get away, away from Negro Village.

A HAND,
A FRIEND

Suddenly it was spring; snowdrops and crocuses were blooming on south-facing slopes, small green leaves were budding on recently bare bushes.

That spring arrived with much hope, but also with new fear and bewilderment. President Johnson had declared that the U.S.A. wanted to enter peace negotiations with Vietnam. At the same time he had announced that he would refrain from running in the upcoming presidential election. The American presidential candidates who had spoken in favor of peace, Eugene McCarthy and Robert Kennedy, had attained noticeable success in their campaigning. In Czechoslovakia a revolutionary democratization process had been begun, and it looked like several of the eastern states were on their way toward greater freedom and increased independence from Moscow. Much could be interpreted as hopeful signs, promises.

But then Martin Luther King, the non-violence advocate among the American blacks, was assassinated. The event unleashed a wave of embitterment and violence across the entire U.S.A.

A torchlight procession and a memorial service were organized in Stockholm. They walked from Kungsträdgården to Storkyrkan; the torches were extinguished outside the church, while people sang "We shall overcome," the song about the dream that had to become reality, friendship's victory.

> *We'll walk hand in hand, we'll walk hand in hand*
> *we'll walk hand in hand some day.*
> *O—oh deep in my heart, I do believe*
> *We'll walk hand in hand some day.*

Ann-Charlotte had walked in the torchlight procession together with her classmate, Inger. Gösta was going to take his high school examination soon and had to stay in and study more than usual. He had gotten behind in his studies, had devoted the larger part of his time to demonstrating and spreading the word; now he had to cram.

Ann-Charlotte had been caught up in the mood, in the song, in the words. She believed that King had acted rightly when he tried to avoid violence, believed in silent opposition as opposed to Gösta, who spoke in favor of "black power" and the necessity of violence.

Gösta and his views had changed, she thought. They had hardened, had taken on a sort of inhumanness. He had grown bitterer; there was so much he hated. In this regard he would become different from her, too, somehow more brutal.

When she met up with him a few days after the torchlight procession, he said that she had allowed herself to be taken in by the mood. There was no reason to mourn King. Just the opposite, what had happened proved how wrong King had been, that his dream was only a dream and that such dreams stood in the way of the process of change. Violence was the only possibility. With the help of violence they could create a new Vietnam right in the middle of the U.S.A. The violence of the counterrevolutionaries could only be met with the violence of the revolutionaries, as Mao had said. The blacks had to meet the white imperialist terror with revolt. Those who tried to prevent it must be removed.

For once she had stood her ground, not given in to Gösta's attacks. The situation had been otherwise for a long time: she would yield for his sake and for the sake of their solidarity. This time she couldn't do it.

So they had parted on bad terms.

Now she was sitting in the car on Easter Eve, on her way out to the country, sulking a little to herself, not knowing if she regretted it or not.

Even if the weather was beautiful and spring was in the air, it was a pretty gloomy Easter now. After that thing with Gösta.

Otherwise there were going to be a lot of people out in the cottages over Easter.

Henning had asked Allan if he and his family felt like coming out there, too. Barbro had talked to Lilian and asked if it might not be fun for Klas to come. He was still in the city, but the committee had arranged a farm where they would take care of him and give him work. Lilian had dared accept for Klas's sake since Per was in the hospital and didn't need to know anything.

Allan's family came in their own car. Or rather in two cars actually, since Stina and her fiancé drove on their own. Maj went with Allan.

Klas got a ride with Henning, sat in the backseat together with Ann-Charlotte and Lars-Olov. The car wasn't very big and it was maybe a little tight, especially for Ann-Charlotte who sat between the two boys.

She looked a little cautiously at Klas from time to time. She was possibly a bit afraid of him. She knew that Mama was his probation guardian and why.

He was probably rough, she thought. Though he didn't look that way. One could hardly believe that he had been involved in so much, had been at reform school. He seemed insecure, childish. They were exactly the same age, eighteen this year.

He had hardly said a word the whole way. He was probably sulking because he had to go. It was Mama who had been so anxious that he not hang around town during Easter weekend. Even if Ann-Charlotte had no desire to talk, she felt like she had to say something anyway, be a little friendly.

She looked ahead, looked at her bare legs. She had put on short socks today, calf-length and white. She tried to pull down her mini skirt a little, though she knew it was useless, it rode up again as soon as she moved.

She asked him if he was in school and he answered that he had finished last spring. She had one year left. He thought that was a lot, he was glad that he had gotten out of it. He had never liked studying.

He mostly partied, he said.

Then he began to laugh, seemed to loosen up a little. He pulled out a crumpled pack of cigarettes and offered her one. But she didn't want any, in any case not now when her parents were present.

They were almost there now, turned onto the narrow and bumpy road that led down to the cottages. The car gave a jolt; Klas seemed to lose his balance and placed a hand on her bare leg. He did it clumsily; she noticed that it was intentional. She would probably have to watch out for him. Maybe it wasn't worth trying to be friendly.

It was on the afternoon of Easter Eve they arrived out there, and that evening they ate together in Maj's cottage.

Ann-Charlotte helped with dinner and the dishes. Often she tried to sneak out of doing the chores, today it was as if she was trying to sneak to them. Stina disappeared as soon as she could with her fiancé, Rooster. Lars-Olov usually had a lot of fun together with Tage, though there were quite a few years between them; they had gotten the boat in the water now. So it was only Klas and her left of the young people, and she really would have preferred to avoid him.

He mainly sat and leafed through a magazine the whole evening.

On Easter Day the weather was not perhaps as beautiful, but it was still quite warm in the air and it wasn't raining. Barbro and Henning were working beside their cottage, Maj and Daggan were raking leaves, and Allan was replacing some rotting boards on Maj's porch.

Lars-Olov and Tage were burning branches. When Henning saw them, he got to thinking about how he and Allan had created an equally unmatched pair once. Now, too, it seemed like it was the younger one who decided things, who enticed the other one into hijinks that he otherwise ought to have outgrown.

Stina and Rooster had slipped away together.

Ann-Charlotte found that she and Klas were left over today, too. All the others had plenty to do.

She half lay in an outdoor reclining chair; he was sitting on the edge of the grass a little ways from her, and breaking a twig blown down from the hanging birch into small pieces.

Once in a while he gave a sidelong glance in her direction. She was good-looking, really shapely. He liked her mini skirt, liked that she showed so much. He had a good view from where he was sitting. He thought it would be funny to joke around a little with her. If only Hasse had been there.

He hoped that she would say something. But he was a little afraid of her, too. He felt insecure, outside, not at home here. Everything was so different. Everyone spoke to each other in such a friendly way, no one screamed and swore. He didn't know that people could be like this. It was difficult, he would really have preferred to take off from all of this.

She clearly had nothing special to do either. He couldn't actually talk to a girl, could he? What did one say if one didn't say anything fresh? And here it was best if he watched himself; her mom was still his probation guardian, until he went away. Dad had not been able to change that anyway.

She ought to try and be friendly at least, since Mama invited him here. She was alone with him now, the one who was responsible for hospitality. And besides, she should do something, too, not just sit and fret about Gösta.

What should she say, what could they find to do?

She asked him if he wanted to walk with her down to the beach. It wasn't even a hundred meters away, close enough for safety. And down there was always something to do; you could find something that had floated ashore.

He stood up quickly, eagerly. As if he had been expecting it. As they walked she regretted asking him. Was there anything the two of them could amuse themselves with together? And wasn't it still risky to be alone with him?

There was a small brook down there this time of year, snowmelt from the woods and bogs above ran out in the inlet. Actually, it was only a ditch, but just at the last part by the beach it looked like a brook anyway.

She stopped at the water furrow that had carved itself in the sand closest to the water, poked at it with her shoe.

"We can dam up the brook if we want to," she said. She had done that together with her father when she was little. She didn't have any great desire to do it but she couldn't come up with anything else.

Klas would go along with it. They talked about how they would do it, where the dam should be placed, if they should divert the water to one side while they built it. They agreed that they should first find the right stones and pieces of board that they could use.

While they talked, Klas loosened up, no longer had such a hard time getting his words out. He talked almost like he would have talked to a guy. He didn't think about the peculiarity of being able to talk to a girl like that.

They piled up a little supply of beach finds, planned, built, helped each other carry stones. And laughed when their embankment suddenly collapsed and Klasse ended up standing in water over his shoes.

Now they were two children playing who were having fun together. They weren't so old either; their childhood was almost around the corner. Not children anymore maybe—but not really adults either. They threw their shoes and socks in the bushes, he rolled up his pant legs and they stood and felt the cold water rushing around their feet.

That short skirt had bothered him the whole time, though he had almost completely forgotten it when they were building the dam. When she stood as she was standing now so that he could see all the way up to the edge of her panties, he couldn't resist. He thought then he had to have some fun with her, even though Hasse wasn't there. She was a girl in any case, made for it, as Hasse used to say.

He pulled up her skirt with a yank and tried to push his hand in.

She started to fall forward but didn't scream. She came upright, pushed him so hard that now it was he who fell over. She took a step away, stopped and looked at him.

"You will stop that now," she said.

He kept quiet. Stood there confused, didn't know what he wanted.

To try again—or run away from everything.

Suddenly she felt sorry for him, her anger cooled. He was so clumsy, did not understand girls at all. She felt like she had to help him somehow, help him become a little more sensible.

"Listen," she said. "Don't you want us to be friends?"

He swallowed, answered a little unwillingly with his: "ye-es…."

"You have to stop doing that kind of thing."

Luckily no one could hear them now. What would Hasse have thought. Friends with a girl…

It was impossible to continue making the dam now. Besides, there really wasn't much more they could do. They sat down on some pieces of lumber that lay across the tufts of lingonberry bushes by the sandy beach.

It was like a little bench. She poked with her toes in the sand, he found some pebbles that he threw in the water, saw how the rings they left quickly fanned out and disappeared.

She asked, he answered—a little unsure as yet. He thought he would like it out on the farm in the country, he liked animals and being outside. If only the people were good.

Without her asking more, he started to tell her about the reform school. He bragged at first about his exploits. But then it slipped out: terror of all the one who had been stronger than himself, fear of being locked up.

"You're away from it now," she said. "And you don't ever have to go back there. If you don't want to."

She wasn't afraid of him any longer, now she knew that he wasn't dangerous. She leaned back comfortably against the pine trunks behind her, stretching. The short skirt left a little more than her winter-white legs bare.

Carefully he placed his hand on her leg.

"Can I keep it like this?"

What should she answer? She felt sorry for him. For his seeming so insecure. For his having to go away from home, maybe forever.

"Yes, of course, you can," she said. "If you keep it still."

She placed her hand over his. Maybe so his hand would stay still, maybe to keep it there.

It was easy to talk with him; they only talked about things that mattered to oneself or about things that were almost meaningless. About what was nearby. She was maybe a little tired of discussing. Gösta always discussed, everything, he could discuss everything to pieces. Just sitting and making small talk was something he never wanted to do; he thought that was a waste of time.

After all that time with Gösta, it felt good to not be on tenterhooks, to be allowed to say stupid things sometimes. And not to have to feel inferior. Gösta could act pretty superior sometimes, show that he thought she was dumb.

But Klasse was insecure and inferior now. As if he had just gotten a smack on his fingers. It was a kind of too bad about him. And then everything he had told her. He had talked about his father, too.

She felt like she had to comfort him; he had surely not meant anything so bad, he didn't understand better. She patted him quickly on the cheek. Then she took his hand again.

"You're nice," she said. "You must promise to write and tell me how things are going. I think it will work out, I know it will."

He would have liked to answer. But he didn't dare; it sat like a dumb clump in his throat.

He had never been able to be with anyone else like this before. With Lotta he had been able to talk, about things that he didn't want to mention to anyone else. And with her he had been able to feel a gentleness, been able to stay with his hand there so long that he had been able to experience warmth and trust.

The girls he had met before had screamed and beaten him off. His contact with them had been a matter of seconds, and hostile; the thief's contact with the one who is robbed. This was something new and incomprehensible, almost frightening. He became helpless.

"I've never been friends with anyone besides my brother before," he said.

She said, which wasn't really true any longer, that she had a boyfriend she was together with. Klas would surely meet a girl to be together with soon, maybe out there in the country where he was going.

"You will have lots of friends," she said. "And all the girls will like you—if you only act sensibly around them."

Someone called from up at the cottage. Afternoon coffee was ready.

"Promise to write to me," said Lotta.

They walked hand in hand along the beach, over to the edge of the brook where they had placed their shoes and socks.

MAYBE A LITTLE BIT
OF EMELIE

It was only the end of April and still it felt like summer. The city lay and basked in the sunshine, an unusually large amount of people seemed to have time off, sat on park benches or strolled through the streets. A number of the bushes and trees had sent out light green leaves, like pale clouds of green.

Henning had been on an errand out in Vällingby. He had his car with him. He thought he would take the Essingeleden motorway home; he had only driven on it in the darkness before.

He drove down the steep, concrete ditch-like descent of Drottningholmsvägen, and turned onto the motorway, into the tunnel sparkling with lights beneath Fredhäll, out across the Essinge Islands. The city and the water spread out beneath him; the construction at Nybohov stood like a heavy square fortress on the hill. And then lots of enormous viaducts and concrete spirals, roads over and under each other, like a completely new city.

Of course, he took the wrong turn, came out on Södertäljevägen and had to drive to the next roundabout to be able to go back toward town.

He had promised Maj to go out to the cemetery and place flowers on the grave. It was Emelie's birthday today, she would have been ninety-eight. He remembered that Ann-Charlotte might be at home and maybe would feel like going with him. She was a little lonely now that it was apparently over with Gösta.

He drove toward town again, toward Hornstull. Emelie had once told him that her father had come to Stockholm walking on this road, over the old pontoon bridge. Nothing was left now of that old road that had been there. But somewhere along here was where he must have walked, the Henning he had gotten his name from. Fifteen was how old he had been, younger than Lars-Olov, but alone in the world, on his way to the city he would work and live in for the rest of his short life.

And he disappeared almost without a trace. The only tangible remembrance that was still left of him was that fragile embroidered handkerchief that Emelie had received on her eighth birthday, and Maj had since set under glass and in a frame. Eighth birthday ... that was exactly ninety years ago today.

When on one occasion he had told this story, about the boy who had come walking, someone had said: that's how my grandfather came here, too. And he had a cow with him as start-up capital for his new life; he drove it along before him.

The city belonged to the immigrants, if they hadn't been it would certainly have died out. They had come in every era, continued to come. From the provinces, from other cities, other countries. They and their descendents were there and built the city, were part of it.

Together they had created the city, immigrants and natives. Together they had shaped it once in the past and with that, also its present and its future. Most of them had, even so, barely left any traces behind. Their names might remain in church records and census registers, but there is nobody who remembers them, their graves have been obliterated, their bones have rotted.

The city of today is a result of previous generations' dreams and work, but also a child of the present, an expression of we who are living and working here now. The city will never be finished, complete. It is transformed ceaselessly, renewed and changed. At the same time, it is eternal, in some way all of the past still remains, stored away.

The old pontoon bridge had not floated where the new bridge stood. It had gone across to that part of Brännkyrkagatan that was now called Hornstullsgatan. The tall buildings along the shoreline had recessed corners, as if they were still leaving room for the old toll pavilion that had stood there once upon a time.

He turned down toward the shore: here he came, here they came, his family, walking to the city.

Ann-Charlotte was at home, sitting inside even though it was such beautiful weather. She always finished early on Fridays. Sometimes she went out with friends, of course, but lately she been mostly by herself, a little out of humor.

A letter had arrived from Klas, she told Henning, now. Klas wrote in such a funny way, he was not very good at spelling and grammar. But he seemed to be happy where he was.

The letter had cheered her up, it was clear.

She would gladly go along.

When they drew near the graves where Emelie and Jenny lay, they saw that someone was already there. It was Gunnar. Since he lived so close he usually went there often, he told them. And today he had had a special reason. Now Henning and Lotta might as well come home to Tistelvägen with him and drink a cup of coffee in the garden, it was so beautiful there now.

While they sat there together with Gunnar and Hjordis, Gunnar talked about Emelie. It would be ten years that summer since she died. He told about how much Emelie had meant to him, what she had done for him. How his stepfather had made life unbearable for him and how Emelie had brought him home to her.

"Sometimes," Gunnar said, "I feel like there has always been a struggle going on between Johan, my stepfather, and Emelie. It is going on now, too, though they both are dead. Like between evil and good. When Johan gets to dominate, people have failed and perished. Emelie has helped many but not been able to save everyone, not those who have avoided her.

"He was thinking of his half-sister, Tyra, who had married a good-for-nothing named David Berg. Of Per, who had been the one of Tyra's children that had never come into Emelie's sphere, of Per's sons. Somewhere he had read that it took three generations to create hopeless criminals. Per's sons were the fourth generation, definitely impossible cases."

Henning told him that things seemed to be going really well for Per's youngest son, at any rate he was liked at the farm where he had gone, apparently was behaving himself.

"Then somehow Emelie has reached him after all," said Gunnar.

Henning looked a little thoughtfully at Lotta. He wondered if she might have some part in it. Of course, he had watched a little uneasily as she and Klas had walked off out in the country, had wondered if the boy wasn't a little dangerous. But Lotta had apparently tamed him. He wondered how she had set about it.

"Klas is actually decent," she said. "I don't believe at all that he is a hopeless case."

Gunnar showed them his gooseberry bushes. They were clad in small newborn shoots now. When he saw those bushes he always thought of Emelie. They had had bushes like that at Fjällgatan when he was a child.

As long as Gunnar and his generation were still alive, much of Emelie would also be alive. When you came to Henning's generation, the memory would have paled some; they had only known Emelie when she was old. And Lotta and her generation had only a very faint memory of Emelie.

They drove back to town. Whether it was because of Gunnar's gooseberry bushes or not, Henning took a detour past Fjällgatan. Which number Emelie had lived in once he didn't remember, but the house was, of course, gone anyhow. Otherwise there were a whole lot of old houses on the street.

The little outdoor café had not opened, but an ice cream stand had been set out and they each bought an ice cream and sat down on a bench. A black police boat swept past down on the water, with white foam around the bow; moored beside the shore of Skeppsholmen, the broad stern of the af Chapman sailing ship gleamed. Down in the harbor beneath them, work was in full progress, huge lifting cranes sank their claws into the cargo holds of the vessels.

Like this, in the spring sun, the city seemed clean and bright, powdered by the first light green foliage. When you saw it lying in the sunshine, it was easy to believe that life, too, was bright and beautiful, that there were no difficult and dark problems.

Some tourist buses arrived and happy people streamed out; on the other side of the water stood the brightly colored candy castles freshly painted at Gröna Lund amusement park, the flags were fluttering on Kastellet's red towers, the sun gleamed on the windows of the buildings on Skeppsholmen, over at Gärdet and far out on Lidingö.

"Klas said hello in his letter," Lotta said. He thought he'd had fun at Easter. Otherwise he was happy where he was now. And it was probably lucky that he is away from the city, Lotta said, because his brother, Hans has run away from the institution he had been put in. And it was he who lured Klas into everything.

"Maybe Gunnar was right," Henning said. "Maybe there is a little bit of Emelie in you."

"I don't think so," answered Lotta. "He said that she only lived for others. I don't do that, I want to live myself."

Suddenly she said: "I don't know what I'm going to do tonight. Inger has invited me over this evening; there should to be a whole lot of people there. But I haven't hung out with that gang for so long. Gösta thought they were so childish and silly so never wanted us to see them."

"Of course, you should go," he said. "You need to meet people your own age, you have been sitting at home way too much for a while now. It could really be fun for you."

"I guess I should go then," she said. He saw that she was relieved at his supporting the idea, that she needed a little support, a little help to get out and go back to her old friends.

"Let's go home, then," he said. "We can surprise Barbro with dinner on the table when she comes in."

CITY
IN THE WORLD

The city waited. Beyond Västerbron the sky was orange colored, above Strömmen and the Baltic lay a thin gray-blue veil. The streetlights had not been turned on yet, but the colored neon lights of the advertisements were beginning to glitter on the facades at Kornhamnstorg and Slussplan.

A few small Djurgården ferries darted across the surface of the water, a Finland ferry was backing out from Skeppsbron. The shiny metallic windows of Kaknästornet, the Stockholm TV tower, glistened as they reflected the setting sun.

A city in the world, on a calm outer fringe. A little outside the big thoroughfares and the big complexes. But still a part, jointly implicated, jointly responsible.

The girl was on her way to meet her friends. She walked briskly, assuredly, felt at home in the city and wasn't especially afraid of the many alcoholics and professional beggars that always hung around Slussen.

This evening, the last Friday in April 1968, she was going to meet up with friends that she had not seen for a long time, and she was full of anticipation, thought it felt like being part of a community again. This summer she was going to travel abroad in Europe. She had been abroad before with her family, but what awaited her was something new: to get to discover it with her own eyes, to be in charge of herself.

When she reached a point where she could see water on both sides of her, she stopped for a moment. The sky was still flaming behind Västerbron and the shades of blue were growing denser above the waters of Strömmen. A subway train and a railroad train came rolling along at the same time on their bridges across the water at Kornhamn, disappearing into the tunnels under Söder. The traffic was still grinding along; lines of cars moved, tightly congested, around Slussen's cloverleaf; the bright eyes of the headlights shone, the red taillights glowed when the cars stopped and clustered together at a traffic light.

Before her, the windows and roofs of the city glowed and glittered, black towers rose above the jumble of buildings. The city lay as if on a shining silver tray of water, extended to her like a gift.

Now she saw the promises glimmering in front of her. Only one year left in school. Soon an adult, soon trying things out for real. Young—and thus the world was still young, it wasn't too late, there was a tomorrow.

She felt like the city lay in the world, that the world concerned her, that she had to dare to wander out into it. That one had to dare to be at home in it.

The girl dreamed. The world waited.

MAIN CHARACTERS AND FAMILIES IN THE *STOCKHOLM SERIES*

NILSSON

Henning (b. 1845, d. 1879) and *Lotten* (b. 1848, d. 1889) have the following children: *August* (b. 1868, see Bodin), *Emelie* (b. 1870), *Gertrud* (b. 1871, see Lindgren), *Olof* (b. 1879, d. 1902). Olof marries *Jenny* Fält (b. 1881); their daughter is *Maj* (b. 1900), has a child with Erik Karlsson, *Henning* Nilsson (b. 1923). Later on Maj marries John Sjöberg (b. 1891, d. 1956). With the singer Julius Törnberg Jenny has a daughter, *Elisabet* Törnberg (b. 1910) who marries *Lennart* Eriksson (b.1909), their daughter is *Monika* (b. 1945). Henning Nilsson marries *Barbro* (b. 1928). They have two children, *Ann-Charlotte* (b. 1950) and *Lars-Olov* (b.1952).

LINDGREN

Thumbs (Ture, b. 1845, d. 1924) and *Matilda* (b. 1845, d.1910) have three sons: *Rudolf* (b. 1868, d. 1924) marries Gertrud Nilsson, *Knut* (b. 1870, d. 1946), who settled in Göteborg with his family, and Mikael (b. 1875, d. 1948). Rudolf and Gertrud emigrate to America with their children. One of their daughters is *Greta* (b. 1892), by the married name of Greer, who has a daughter, *Jean* (b. 1923), by the married name of Wardner.

BODIN

Fredrik (b. 1835, d. 1898) and *Annika* (b. 1846) adopt August Nilsson as their son; he receives the name Bodin.
August marries *Ida* Wide (b. 1868); their children are: *Karl Henrik* (b. 1895), *Charlotta,* (b. 1897), *Anna* (b. 1898), *Fredrik* (b. 1900, d. 1918), and *Elisabet* (b. 1904).
All their children, except for Fredrik, who died young, are married and have children. Karl Henrik's oldest son is *Claes* (b. 1922).

With Bärta (see Karlsson) August has a son, Gunnar Karlsson.

KARLSSON

Johan (b. 1870, d. 1905) and *Bärta* (b. 1868, d. 1917) have the following children: *Tyra* (b. 1895, see Berg), *Beda* (b. 1897), *Erik* (b.
1899) and *Bengt* (b. 1900). With August Bodin, Bärta has a son,
Gunnar Karlsson (b. 1889). *Erik* Karlsson, later Karge, has a son
with Maj Nilsson (see Nilsson). Erik marries *Irene* (b. 1903). They
have two daughters, *Lena* (b. 1933) and *Berit* (b. 1936).
Lena marries *Joseph* Schönlank (b. 1918). Their children are *Peder*
(b. 1959) and *Greta* (b. 1961). Berit marries *Lars-Erik* Göransson
(b. 1930). Their son is *Johan* (b. 1966). Bengt is married to *Britta*
(b. 1907). They have several children. Gunnar is married to *Hjördis*
(b, 1892). Their children *Mary* (b. 1922) and *Torsten* (b. 1927) are
married and have their own children.

BERG

David ("Yellow David," b. 1879, d. 1955) and Tyra Karlsson have
the following children: *Allan,* (b. 1918), *Stig* (b. 1920, d. 1944),
Per (b. 1921), and *Gun* (b. 1923). Allan is married to *Dagny*
("Daggan," b. 1919). Their children are *Stina* (b. 1943) and *Tage*
(b. 1946). Per is married to *Lilian* (b. 1915). Their sons are *Hans*
(b. 1948) and *Klas* (b. 1950). Gun is married to *Olle* Holm (b.
1916). Their children are *Bertil* (b. 1946), *Eva* (b. 1950) and *Inger*
(b. 1953). David's sister, *Dora* Berg (b. 1883, 1945), has a daughter, *Rut* (b. 1912, d. 1967).

The "Stockholm Series" was begun in 1958 and
completed in the spring of 1968.

TIME FRAMES
FOR
CHAPTERS IN THE *STOCKHOLM SERIES*

City of My Dreams 1860–1880

I

1860 City of My Dreams
Bridge to Reality
Into the New
Close to the Wilderness
In the Darkness
1861 The Real Stockholmer
Farewells and Arrivals
Summer in Your Hand
Long, Heavy Workdays
1862 Just Desserts
The Beautiful Spring
Boat Rocker Summer

II

1862–1865 The Promise
1866 Doorways to the East
Quartet and Solo
August Washing
1867 Refugees
The Frost-blighted Spring
The Blue Hill
So Near Yet So Far
Someone's Knocking

at the Door
1868 The Flames
Drought and Thirst
The Big Day

III

1872 The Children
Games and Shadows
Saturday Brothers
A Longshoreman Becomes
 a Baker
Storm and Darkness
1873 The Ringing of Bells
Freedom or Security
Summer's Victories
The Newcomers
The Trouble Spot
1874 An Island in the Sea
Sunday in the Greenery

IV

1876 Desert and Wasteland
1878 A Gift for Emelie
The Threshold
An Unknown Shore
Autumn's Burdens